*Man, the State
and War*

Man, the State and War

A THEORETICAL ANALYSIS

Kenneth N. Waltz

COLUMBIA UNIVERSITY PRESS

New York

Columbia University Press
Publishers Since 1893
New York   Chichester, West Sussex

Library of Congress Cataloging-in-Publication Data
Waltz, Kenneth Neal, 1924–
   Man, the state, and war : a theoretical analysis / Kenneth N. Waltz.
     New York : Columbia University Press, 2001.
        p. cm.
     Originally published: 1959. With new pref.
     Includes bibliographical references and index.
     ISBN: 978-0-231-12537-6
     1. International relations–Philosophy.   2. State, The.   3. War.

                                            2001042082

♾

Columbia University Press books are printed on permanent
and durable acid-free paper.
Printed in the United States of America
20 19 18 17 16 15 14 13 12 11

CONTENTS

PREFACE TO THE 2001 EDITION

ALMOST five decades have passed since I wrote a doctoral dissertation called "Man, the State, and the State System in Theories of the Causes of War." After all these years, it is pleasant to recall the origins and evolution of the manuscript.

In 1950, when my wife and I were graduate students at Columbia, I devoted the academic year to two demanding tasks—preparing for the two-hour oral examination that determined one's academic fate and securing a long enough delay in my recall by the army to enable me to be around for the birth of our first child. By April of 1951, I had finished preparing for my minor field, international relations, and planned to spend the few remaining weeks on a final review of my major field, political theory. At that moment I learned that Professor Nathaniel Peffer, who was to be my principal examiner in international relations, was in poor health and would not serve on committees for students minoring in the field. I thereupon asked Professor William T. R. Fox to replace Peffer and explained that, as was Professor Peffer's custom, we had agreed that I would concentrate on certain topics, such as imperialism and European diplomatic history, and leave largely aside such other topics as international law and organization. After phoning the all-knowing departmental secretary, Edith Black, and finding that such arrangements were indeed often made, Professor Fox turned to me and in a kindly voice said, in effect: Nevertheless when you offer international relations as a field for examination, you cover the field rather than breaking it into bits and concentrating on a few topics.

Under other circumstances, I might have postponed the examination till fall—a sensible plan since word was around that two-thirds of graduate students flunked their orals. By fall, however, I would be in the army again. Graduate students called Professor Fox

"Superpower Fox" after the title of his book *The Superpowers*, which gave the name to an era. My wife and I therefore gathered all of the books we could find dealing with the ever-elusive concept of power in international relations.

Attempting to ingest a wide-ranging literature in one gulp, I became puzzled by the contrasting views of authors who, while ostensibly dealing with the same subject matter, arrived at different and often contradictory conclusions. How could I make sense of the literature? While sitting in Columbia's Butler library, a light flashed in my mind. On a now very yellowed piece of paper, I hastily wrote what I thought of as three levels of analysis employed in the study of international politics. I had found the clue that enabled me to organize the recalcitrant materials of the subject matter and lodge them securely in my mind.

Whiling away four months at Fort Lee, Virginia, I wrote an outline of the proposed dissertation. About fifteen pages long, it covered everything from utopias to geopolitics to the prospective population explosion, all of which were fitted into the tripartite format. I sent the outline to Professor Fox and went to see him when I was in northern New Jersey while on leave from the army. His comment on the outline was that it might be useful for a course I would someday teach. He suggested that meanwhile I spend a day writing a three- or four-page outline of the dissertation. I did so. Many weeks later, a letter reached me in Korea saying that the tenured members of the department did not understand what I proposed to do but agreed that I should be allowed to go ahead and do it.

In the fall of 1952, I returned to New York City, too late to begin teaching even had a job been available. Professor Fox, newly head of the Institute of War and Peace Studies, fortunately had offered me a research assistant's position in the Institute. I was to spend half of my time on the dissertation and half on the revision of a manuscript by the historian Alfred Vagts. The manuscript, piled on a desk at the Institute, was fully nine inches high. In the spring of 1954, I completed the dissertation and the teaching of a year's course on international politics; by the end of the summer, I had reduced the Vagts manuscript to publishable proportions.[1] Five years later, my dissertation was published as *Man, the State, and War: A Theoretical Analysis.*

That is the story of the genesis of this book. The following pages reflect on its substance. At the outset, I used the term "levels of analysis" to fix the location of the presumed principal cause of international political outcomes. My wife persuaded me to use the more accurate and elegant term "image"—more accurate because one who thinks in terms of levels easily slips into thinking that choosing a level is merely a question of what seems to fit the subject matter and suits one's fancy. "Image" is also the better term because, although analytic thinking is appropriate to some problems of international politics, a wider understanding of international politics requires a systemic approach, which at once draws attention to third-image effects and enables one to comprehend all three "levels."

The word "image" suggests that one forms a picture in the mind; it suggests that one views the world in a certain way. "Image" is an apt term both because one cannot "see" international politics directly, no matter how hard one looks, and because developing a theory requires one to depict a pertinent realm of activity. To say "image" also suggests that in order to explain international outcomes one has to filter some elements out of one's view in order to concentrate on the presumably fundamental ones. In relating the first and second images to the third, I viewed the third image as "the framework of state action" and "as a theory of the conditioning effects of the state system itself."[2] Explaining international outcomes requires one to examine the situations of states, as well as their individual characteristics.[3]

What I then called "the state system," I later defined more precisely as the structure of the international political system. Strictly speaking, *Man, the State, and War* did not present a theory of international politics. It did, however, lay the foundation for one. It developed concepts and identified problems that continue to be major concerns for students and policy makers. Chapter four, the longest one in the book, examines the basis for, and questions the validity of, what is wrongly called "the democratic peace theory." (It is a thesis, or a purported fact, but not a theory.) I drew a distinction between interventionist and noninterventionist liberals and warned of the dangers lurking in the inclinations of the former, a warning now often unheeded by the makers of American foreign policy. Peace, after all, is the noblest cause of war, and if democracies are the one peaceful form of the state, then all means used to cause other states to become democratic are justified. The means that may be used to achieve the Clinton administration's goal of "enhancing democracy" make noninterventionist liberals shudder. I questioned the validity of the democratic peace thesis by posing the third image against the second and by invoking the authority of Jean-Jacques Rousseau. To expect states of any sort to rest reliably at peace in a condition of anarchy would require the uniform and enduring perfection of all of them.

Americans have long believed that their country promotes universal values abroad. The belief has two consequences. First, when the country acts to maintain a balance, as in entering World War I and in countering the Soviet Union during the Cold War, justification of the policy is expressed not in power-political terms but in terms of strengthening the forces of freedom in the world and advancing the cause of democracy. Second, Americans find it hard to believe that other countries may resent and fear America's extending its influence and increasing its control internationally. It is difficult for Americans to believe that their present preponderance of power, even when accompanied by good intentions, is a worry for states living in its shadow. *Man, the State, and War* explains how balances result not from the malevolence of men or of states but from the condition in which all states exist.[4]

The tendency of states to balance is rooted in the anarchy of states. So are other practices and concerns of states. War may break out in the present for fear that a satisfactory balance will turn into an imbalance against one's own country in the future. What is now aptly called "the shadow of the future," and often thought to further cooperation among states, is shown to be an important cause of war, with World War I used as an extended example.[5] Moreover, conflict is shown to lie less in the nature of men or of states and more in the nature of social activity.[6] Conflict is a by-product of competition and of efforts to cooperate. In a self-help system, with conflict to be expected, states have to be concerned with the means required to sustain and protect themselves. The closer the competition, the more strongly states seek relative gains rather than absolute ones.[7]

The durability of *Man, the State, and War* attests to the continuity of international politics. The many important events of recent decades have left the anarchic structure of international politics intact, and thus, the relevance of the book remains. Questions of major concern—the prevalence of balance-of-power politics, the causal weight of forces identified by one or another of the three images, the effects of the shadow of the future, the importance of relative versus absolute gains—are questions that continue to concern students of international politics.

NOTES

1. *Defense and Diplomacy* (New York: King's Cross Press, 1956).
2. See p. 231.
3. See p. 170.
4. See especially pp. 198–223.
5. See chapter 5, especially pp. 130 ff.
6. See p. 168.
7. See pp. 198, 224.

FOREWORD (1959)

MAN, THE STATE, AND WAR is the second of the Topical Studies in International Relations to be published. The series was planned to demonstrate some of the contributions which existing bodies of knowledge are capable of making to the understanding of modern international relations. Even in a relatively new field of academic specialization, it is not necessary for the scholar to make an absolutely fresh start. Indeed, it is incumbent upon him not to fail to draw on existing storehouses of knowledge. One of those storehouses least systematically inventoried for its usefulness for international relations is classical Western political thought. Each volume in the Topical Studies series was meant to be such an inventory. It is particularly appropriate that *Man, the State, and War* be included in the series.

Professor Waltz has chosen to investigate the particular contribution which classical political theory makes to understanding the causes of war and to defining the conditions under which war can be controlled or eliminated as the final arbiter of disputes between groups of men in the absence of central authority. There are other fundamental questions of interest to the student of international relations to which classical political theorists have sought to provide answers, but none is so central as the question with which Professor Waltz is concerned.

His method has been to describe the answers which certain representative theorists have given and then in alternate chapters to discuss some of the implications and applications of classical insights to contemporary social science research and choices in the field of public policy. Thus, his work is far more than a work of exegesis. He is concerned not only with what certain towering figures in the history of Western political thought have really meant, but even more with what difference it makes that they thought and wrote as they did.

His concern is not an antiquarian one, and his is not purely an "art for art's sake" point of view.

The Topical Studies series, in major part, was organized in 1947 by Dr. Grayson Kirk, now president of Columbia University, but then professor of international relations in that university. His administrative burdens made it necessary for someone else to assume direct editorial responsibility for the series; and he requested me to assume such responsibilities in 1951. The studies in the series have been made possible by a grant from the Carnegie Corporation to Columbia University. Neither the foundation nor the university thereby assumed responsibility for the findings of the various contributors to the Topical Studies series. As I observed in the foreword to the earlier volume in the series, Alfred Vagts's *Defense and Diplomacy* (New York: King's Crown Press, 1956), the opinions expressed are those of the authors alone and to them properly belongs the credit as well as the responsibility.

WILLIAM T. R. FOX

Institute of War and Peace Studies
Columbia University
New York City
April 6, 1959

PREFACE (1959)

THE pages that follow reflect a direct concern with international relations and a long-standing interest in political theory. The latter dates from my years at Oberlin College where John and Ewart Lewis led me to feel the fascination of theory and to understand its importance in the study of politics. Later, at Columbia University, I was fortunate enough to be one of the students of the late Franz Neumann, whose brilliance and excellence as a teacher can never be forgotten by those who knew him.

My most immediate and my deepest debts are to William T. R. Fox. From the first vague outline of the manuscript to the final version here presented, he willingly gave his advice and perceptive criticisms. Moreover, as Director of Columbia University's Institute of War and Peace Studies, he made it possible for me to devote summers and parts of the academic year as well to research and writing. It is insufficient to say that because of him this is a better book, for without his encouragement and counsel it is difficult to see how there would be any book at all.

I have been unusually fortunate in my other critics as well: Herbert A. Deane and John B. Stewart, both of Columbia University, and Kenneth W. Thompson of the Rockefeller Foundation. Each was kind enough to read the entire manuscript at some stage of its preparation, and Professor Stewart patient enough to read it at two different stages. Each made suggestions that saved me from many errors and, more important, that caused me to reconsider and often to recast substantial parts of the manuscript, though I did not always come to conclusions they would accept.

My wife has done more than keep the children quiet and move commas around, more than criticize and read proof; she did most of the research for one chapter and contributed ideas and information to all of them. I should also like to thank the Columbia University

Press for its understanding of the problems an inexperienced author must face and its generous assistance to him in overcoming them.

Excerpts from the works of others often conveyed the ideas I had in mind with more felicity than I could hope to achieve. I have therefore quoted freely and wish to thank the following publishers for their kind permission to quote from copyrighted works: George Allen and Unwin, Ltd., for John Hobson's *Imperialism;* Constable and Company, Ltd., for Jean Jacques Rousseau's *A Lasting Peace through the Federation of Europe,* translated by C. E. Vaughan; E. P. Dutton and Company, Inc., for Jean Jacques Rousseau's *The Social Contract,* translated by G. D. H. Cole (Everyman's Library edition); William Morrow and Company, Inc., for Margaret Mead's *Coming of Age in Samoa* (copyright 1928 by William Morrow and Company) and *And Keep Your Powder Dry* (copyright 1942 by Margaret Mead); the Philosophical Library for *Psychological Factors of Peace and War,* edited by T. H. Pear; and the Social Science Research Council for Otto Klineberg's *Tensions Affecting International Understanding.*

KENNETH N. WALTZ

Swarthmore College
April, 1959

Man, the State
and War

CHAPTER I. INTRODUCTION

ASKING who won a given war, someone has said, is like asking who won the San Francisco earthquake. That in wars there is no victory but only varying degrees of defeat is a proposition that has gained increasing acceptance in the twentieth century. But are wars also akin to earthquakes in being natural occurrences whose control or elimination is beyond the wit of man? Few would admit that they are, yet attempts to eliminate war, however nobly inspired and assiduously pursued, have brought little more than fleeting moments of peace among states. There is an apparent disproportion between effort and product, between desire and result. The peace wish, we are told, runs strong and deep among the Russian people; and we are convinced that the same can be said of Americans. From these statements there is some comfort to be derived, but in the light of history and of current events as well it is difficult to believe that the wish will father the condition desired.

Social scientists, realizing from their studies how firmly the present is tied to the past and how intimately the parts of a system depend upon each other, are inclined to be conservative in estimating the possibilities of achieving a radically better world. If one asks whether we can now have peace where in the past there has been war, the answers are most often pessimistic. Perhaps this is the wrong question. And indeed the answers will be somewhat less discouraging if instead the following questions are put: Are there ways of decreasing the incidence of war, of increasing the chances of peace? Can we have peace more often in the future than in the past?

Peace is one among a number of ends simultaneously entertained. The means by which peace can be sought are many. The end is pursued and the means are applied under varying conditions. Even though one may find it hard to believe that there are ways to peace not yet tried by statesmen or advocated by publicists, the very complexity of the problem suggests the possibility of combining activities in different ways in the hope that some combination will lead us closer to the goal. Is one then led to conclude that the wisdom of the statesman lies in trying first one policy and then another, in doing what the moment seems to require? An affirmative reply would suggest that the hope for improvement lies in policy divorced from analysis, in action removed from thought. Yet each attempt to alleviate a condition implies some idea of its causes: to explain how peace can be more readily achieved requires an understanding of the causes of war. It is such an understanding that we shall seek in the following pages. To borrow the title of a book by Mortimer Adler, our subject is "How to Think about War and Peace." The chapters that follow are, in a sense, essays in political theory. This description is justified partly by the mode of inquiry—we proceed by examining assumptions and asking repeatedly what differences they make—and partly by the fact that we consider a number of political philosophers directly, sometimes in circumscribed fashion, as with St. Augustine, Machiavelli, Spinoza, and Kant, and sometimes at length, as with Rousseau. In other places we shall concentrate on a type of thought, as in the chapters on behavioral scientists, liberals, and socialists. But what is the relevance of the thoughts of others, many of them living far in the past, to the pressing and awful problems of the present? The rest of the book is an answer to this question, but it is well at the outset to indicate the lines along which we shall proceed.

Why does God, if he is all-knowing and all-powerful, permit the existence of evil? So asks the simple Huron in Voltaire's tale, and thereby confounds the learned men of the church. The theodicy problem in its secular version —man's explanation to himself of the existence of evil— is as intriguing and as perplexing. Disease and pestilence, bigotry and rape, theft and murder, pillage and war, appear as constants in world history. Why is this so? Can one explain war and malevolence in the same way? Is war simply mass malevolence, and thus an explanation of malevolence an explanation of the evils to which men in society are prey? Many have thought so.

For though it were granted us by divine indulgence to be exempt from all that can be harmful to us from without [writes John Milton], yet the perverseness of our folly is so bent, that we should never cease hammering out of our own hearts, as it were out of a flint, the seeds and sparkles of new misery to ourselves, till all were in a blaze again.[1]

Our miseries are ineluctably the product of our natures. The root of all evil is man, and thus he is himself the root of the specific evil, war. This estimate of cause, widespread and firmly held by many as an article of faith, has been immensely influential. It is the conviction of St. Augustine and Luther, of Malthus and Jonathan Swift, of Dean Inge and Reinhold Niebuhr. In secular terms, with men defined as beings of intermixed reason and passion in whom passion repeatedly triumphs, the belief has informed the philosophy, including the political philosophy, of Spinoza. One might argue that it was as influential in the activities of Bismarck, with his low opinion of his fellow man, as it was in the rigorous and austere writings of Spinoza. If one's beliefs condition his expectations and his expectations condition his acts, acceptance or rejection of Milton's statement becomes important in

[1] Milton, "The Doctrine and Discipline of Divorce," in *Works*, III, 180.

the affairs of men. And, of course, Milton might be right even if no one believed him. If so, attempts to explain the recurrence of war in terms of, let us say, economic factors, might still be interesting games, but they would be games of little consequence. If it is true, as Dean Swift once said, that "the very same principle that influences a bully to break the windows of a whore who has jilted him, naturally stirs up a great prince to raise mighty armies, and dream of nothing but sieges, battles, and victories," [2] then the reasons given by princes for the wars they have waged are mere rationalizations covering a motivation they may not themselves have perceived and could not afford to state openly if they had. It would follow as well that the schemes of the statesman Sully, if seriously intended to produce a greater peace in the world, were as idle as the dreams of the French monk Crucé— idle, that is, unless one can strike at the roots, the pride and petulance that have produced the wars as they have the other ills that plague mankind.

There are many who have agreed with Milton that men must look to man in order to understand social and political events, but who differ on what man's nature is, or can become. There are many others who, in effect, quarrel with the major premise. Does man make society in his image or does his society make him? It was to be expected, in a time when philosophy was little more than a branch of theology, that the theologian-philosophers would attribute to human agency what many philosophers before and since have described as the effects of the polity itself. Rousseau, among many who could be mentioned, makes a clean break with the view that, man being a social animal, one can explain his behavior in society by pointing to his animal passion and/or his human reason. Man is born and in his natural condition remains neither good nor

2 Swift, *A Tale of a Tub.*

bad. It is society that is the degrading force in men's lives, but it is the moralizing agency as well. And this latter effect Rousseau was unwilling to surrender even had he thought it possible for men to retreat to the state of nature. This is his position, consistently reflected in his various works, though the myth persists that he believed the savage noble and lamented the advent of society.[3] Man's behavior, his very nature, which some have taken as cause, is, according to Rousseau, in great part a product of the society in which he lives. And society, he avers, is inseparable from political organization. In the absence of an organized power, which as a minimum must serve as the adjudicating authority, it is impossible for men to live together with even a modicum of peace. The study of society cannot be separated from the study of government, or the study of man from either. Rousseau, like Plato, believes that a bad polity makes men bad, and a good polity makes them good. This is not to say that the state is the potter and man a lump of clay posing no resistance to the shape the artist would impart. There are, as Rousseau recognized, similarities among men wherever they may live. There are also differences, and the search for causes is an attempt to explain these differences. The explanation of consequence—whether one is worried about the recurrence of theft or of war—is to be found in studying the varying social relations of men, and this in turn requires the study of politics.

Can man in society best be understood by studying man or by studying society? The most satisfactory reply would seem to be given by striking the word "or" and answering "both." But where one begins his explanation of events makes a difference. The Reverend Thomas Malthus once wrote that, "though human institutions appear to be the obvious and obtrusive causes of much mischief

[3] For further discussion of Rousseau, see ch. vi, below.

to mankind; yet, in reality, they are light and superficial, they are mere feathers that float on the surface, in comparison with those deeper seated causes of impurity that corrupt the springs, and render turbid the whole stream of human life."[4] Rousseau looked at the same world, the same range of events, but found the locus of major causes in a different ambit.

Following Rousseau's lead in turn raises questions. As men live in states, so states exist in a world of states. If we now confine our attention to the question of why wars occur, shall we emphasize the role of the state, with its social and economic content as well as its political form, or shall we concentrate primarily on what is sometimes called the society of states? Again one may say strike the word "or" and worry about both, but many have emphasized either the first or the second, which helps to explain the discrepant conclusions reached. Those who emphasize the first in a sense run parallel to Milton. He explains the ills of the world by the evil in man; they explain the great ill of war by the evil qualities of some or of all states. The statement is then often reversed: If bad states make wars, good states would live at peace with one another. With varying degrees of justification this view can be attributed to Plato and Kant, to nineteenth-century liberals and revisionist socialists. They agree on the principle involved, though they differ in their descriptions of good states as well as on the problem of bringing about their existence.

Where Marxists throw the liberals' picture of the world into partial eclipse, others blot it out entirely. Rousseau himself finds the major causes of war neither in men nor in states but in the state system itself. Of men in a state of nature, he had pointed out that one man cannot begin

---

[4] Malthus, *An Essay on the Principle of Population,* pp. 47–48 (ch. x of the 1798 ed.).

to behave decently unless he has some assurance that others will not be able to ruin him. This thought Rousseau develops and applies to states existing in a condition of anarchy in his fragmentary essay on "The State of War" and in his commentaries on the works of the Abbé de Saint-Pierre. Though a state may want to remain at peace, it may have to consider undertaking a preventive war; for if it does not strike when the moment is favorable it may be struck later when the advantage has shifted to the other side. This view forms the analytic basis for many balance-of-power approaches to international relations and for the world-federalist program as well. Implicit in Thucydides and Alexander Hamilton, made explicit by Machiavelli, Hobbes, and Rousseau, it is at once a generalized explanation of states' behavior and a critical *point d'appui* against those who look to the internal structure of states to explain their external behavior. While some believe that peace will follow from the improvement of states, others assert that what the state will be like depends on its relation to others. The latter thesis Leopold Ranke derived from, or applied to, the history of the states of modern Europe. It has been used to explain the internal ordering of other states as well.[5]

Statesmen, as well as philosophers and historians, have attempted to account for the behavior of states in peace and in war. Woodrow Wilson, in the draft of a note written in November of 1916, remarked that the causes of the war then being fought were obscure, that neutral nations did not know why it had begun and, if drawn in, would not know for what ends they would be fighting.[6] But often to act we must convince ourselves that we do know

---

[5] Ranke, "The Great Powers," tr. H. H. Von Laue, in Theodore H. Von Laue, *Leopold Ranke.* And see, e.g., Homo, *Roman Political Institutions,* tr. Dobie, especially pp. 146, 364–69.

[6] Link, *Woodrow Wilson and the Progressive Era,* p. 257n.

the answers to such questions. Wilson, to his own satisfaction, soon did. He appears in history as one of the
many who, drawing a sharp distinction between peaceful
and aggressive states, have assigned to democracies all the
attributes of the first, to authoritarian states all the attributes of the second. To an extent that varies with the
author considered, the incidence of war is then thought to
depend upon the type of national government. Thus
Cobden in a speech at Leeds in December of 1849:

Where do we look for the black gathering cloud of war? Where do
we see it rising? Why, from the despotism of the north, where one
man wields the destinies of 40,000,000 of serfs. If we want to know
where is the second danger of war and disturbance, it is in that
province of Russia—that miserable and degraded country, Austria—
next in the stage of despotism and barbarism, and there you see
again the greatest danger of war; but in proportion as you find the
population governing themselves—as in England, in France, or in
America—there you will find that war is not the disposition of the
people, and that if Government desire it, the people would put a
check upon it.[7]

The constant interest of the people is in peace; no government controlled by the people will fight unless set
upon. But only a few years later, England, though not
set upon, did fight against Russia; and Cobden lost his
seat in 1857 as a result of his opposition to the war. The
experience is shattering, but not fatal to the belief; for it
relives in the words of Wilson, for example, and again in
those of the late Senator Robert Taft. In the manner of
Cobden but in the year 1951, Taft writes: "History shows
that when the people have the opportunity to speak they
as a rule decide for peace if possible. It shows that arbitrary rulers are more inclined to favor war than are the
people at any time." [8] Is it true, one wonders, that there
is a uniquely peaceful form of the state? If it were true,

[7] Cobden, *Speeches*, ed. Bright and Rogers, I, 432–33.
[8] Robert A. Taft, *A Foreign Policy for Americans*, p. 23.

how much would it matter? Would it enable some states to know which other states they could trust? Should the states that are already good seek ways of making other states better, and thus make it possible for all men to enjoy the pleasures of peace? Wilson believed it morally imperative to aid in the political regeneration of others; Cobden thought it not even justifiable. Agreeing on where the causes are to be found, they differ in their policy conclusions.

But what of those who incline to a different estimate of major causes? "Now people," President Dwight Eisenhower has said, "don't want conflict—people in general. It is only, I think, mistaken leaders that grow too belligerent and believe that people really want to fight." [9] Though apparently not all people want peace badly enough, for, on a different occasion, he had this to say: "If the mothers in every land could teach their children to understand the homes and hopes of children in every other land—in America, in Europe, in the Near East, in Asia— the cause of peace in the world would indeed be nobly served." [10] Here the President seems to agree with Milton on where cause is to be found, but without Milton's pessimism—or realism, depending on one's preconceptions. Aggressive tendencies may be inherent, but is their misdirection inevitable? War begins in the minds and emotions of men, as all acts do; but can minds and emotions be changed? And, if one agrees that they can be, how much and how fast can whose minds and feelings be changed? And, if other factors are relevant as well, how much difference would the changes make? The answers to these questions and to those of the preceding paragraph

[9] Quoted by Robert J. Donovan, "Eisenhower Will Cable Secret Geneva Reports," in New York *Herald Tribune*, July 13, 1955, p. 1.

[10] Eisenhower, address to a meeting of the National Council of Catholic Women. Text in New York *Times*, November 9, 1954, p. 14.

are not obvious, but they are important.   How can they best be sought?

Some would suggest taking possible answers as hypotheses to be investigated and tested empirically.   This is difficult.   Most English liberals at the time of the First World War argued, as did Wilson, that the militarist and authoritarian character of the German state prompted Germany to seek the war that soon spread to most of the world.   At the same time some liberals, most notably G. Lowes Dickinson, argued that no single state could be held guilty.   Only by understanding the international system, or lack of system, by which the leaders of states were often forced to act with slight regard for conventional morality, could one understand and justly assess the processes by which the war was produced.[11]   Dickinson was blasted by liberals and socialists alike for reversing the dominant inside-out explanation.   Acceptance or rejection of explanatory theses in matters such as this most often depends on the skill of the pleaders and the mood of the audience. These are obviously not fit criteria, yet it would be foolish to argue that simply by taking a more intensive look at the data a compelling case could be built for one or the other explanatory theory.   Staring at the same set of data, the parties to the debate came to sharply different conclusions, for the images they entertained led them to select and interpret the data in different ways.   In order to make sense of the liberals' hypothesis we need somehow to acquire an idea of the interrelation of many possibly relevant factors, and these interrelations are not given in the data we study.   We establish or, rather, assert them ourselves.   To say "establish" would be dangerous; for, whether or not we label them as such, we cannot escape from philosophic assumptions.   The idea we entertain becomes a filter through which we pass our data.   If the

[11] Dickinson, *The European Anarchy, passim.*

data are selected carefully, they will pass like milk through cheesecloth. The recalcitrance of the data may cause us to change one filter for another, to modify or scrap the theory we hold—or it may produce ever more ingenious selection and interpretation of data, as has happened with many Marxists trying to salvage the thesis that with the development of capitalism the masses become increasingly impoverished.

If empirical investigations vary in incidence and in result with the ideas the empiricists entertain, it is worth asking ourselves if the ideas themselves can be subjected to scrutiny. Obviously they can be. The study of politics is distinguished from other social studies by concentration upon the institutions and processes of government. This focuses the political scientists' concern without constituting a self-denying ordinance against the use of materials and techniques of other social scientists.[12] On the latter point there is no difficulty for the student of international relations; there is considerable difficulty on the former, for international relations are characterized by the absence of truly governmental institutions, which in turn gives a radically different twist to the relevant processes. Yet there is a large and important sense in which traditional political philosophy, concentrating as it does upon domestic politics, is relevant for the student of international relations. Peace, it is often said, is the problem of the twentieth century. It is also one of the continuing concerns of political philosophers. In times of relative quiescence the question men put is likely to be: What good is life without justice and freedom? Better to die than live a slave. In times of domestic troubles, of hunger and civil war, of pressing insecurity, however, many will

[12] Cf. David B. Truman, "The Impact on Political Science of the Revolution in the Behavioral Sciences," in Bailey *et al., Research Frontiers in Politics and Government,* pp. 202–31.

ask: Of what use is freedom without a power sufficient to establish and maintain conditions of security? That life takes priority over justice and freedom is taken to be a self-evident truth by St. Augustine and Luther, by Machiavelli, Bodin, and Hobbes. If the alternative to tyranny is chaos and if chaos means a war of all against all, then the willingness to endure tyranny becomes understandable. In the absence of order there can be no enjoyment of liberty. The problem of identifying and achieving the conditions of peace, a problem that plagues man and bedevils the student of international relations, has, especially in periods of crisis, bedeviled political philosophers as well.

R. G. Collingwood once suggested that the best way to understand the writings of philosophers is to seek out the questions they were attempting to answer. It is here suggested that the best way to examine the problems of international political theory is to pose a central question and identify the answers that can be given to it. One may seek in political philosophy answers to the question: Where are the major causes of war to be found? The answers are bewildering in their variety and in their contradictory qualities. To make this variety manageable, the answers can be ordered under the following three headings: within man, within the structure of the separate states, within the state system. The basis of this ordering, as well as its relevance in the world of affairs, is suggested in the preceding pages. These three estimates of cause will subsequently be referred to as images of international relations, numbered in the order given, with each image defined according to where one locates the nexus of important causes.

Previous comments indicate that the views comprised by any one image may in some senses be as contradictory as are the different images *inter se*. The argument that war is inevitable because men are irrevocably bad, and the argument that wars can be ended because men can be changed, are contradictory; but since in each of them individuals are taken to be the locus of cause, both are included in the first image. Similarly, acceptance of a third-image analysis may lead to the false optimism of the world federalists or to the often falsely defined pessimism of a *Realpolitik* position. Since in all respects but one there may be variety of opinion within images and since prescription is related to goal as well as to analysis, there is no one prescription for each image. There are, however, in relation to each image-goal pairing, logical and illogical prescriptions.

One can say that a prescription is wrong if he can show that following it does not bring about the predicted result. But can one ever show that a prescription was actually followed? One often hears statements like this: "The League of Nations didn't fail; it was never tried." And such statements are irrefutable. But even if empirical disproof were possible, the problem of proving a prescription valid would remain to be solved. A patient who in one period of illness tries ten different medications may wonder just which pill produced the cure. The apportioning of credit is often more difficult than the assigning of blame. If a historical study were to show that in country A increases in national prosperity always followed increases in tariffs, to some observers this might seem to prove that high tariffs are a cause of prosperity; to others, that both of these factors are dependent on a third; and to still others, nothing at all. The empirical approach, though necessary, is not sufficient. The correlation of events means nothing, or at least should not be taken to mean anything, apart from the analysis that accompanies it.

If there is no empirical solution to the problem of prescription verification, what solution is there? Prescription is logically impossible apart from analysis. Every prescription for greater peace in the world is then related to one of our three images of international relations, or to some combination of them. An understanding of the analytical terms of each of the images will open up two additional possibilities for accepting or rejecting prescriptions. (1) A prescription based on a faulty analysis would be unlikely to produce the desired consequences. The assumption that to improve men in a prescribed way will serve to promote peace rests on the further assumption that in some form the first image of international relations is valid. The latter assumption should be examined before the former is made. (2) A prescription would be unacceptable if it were not logically related to its analysis. One who suffers from infected tonsils profits little from a skillfully performed appendectomy. If violence among states is caused by the evilness of man, to aim at the internal reform of states will not do much good. And if violence among states is the product of international anarchy, to aim at the conversion of individuals can accomplish little. One man's prognosis confounds the other man's prescription. If the validity of the images themselves can be ascertained, the critical relating of prescription to image becomes a check on the validity of prescriptions. There is, however, an additional complicating factor. Some combination of our three images, rather than any one of them, may be required for an accurate understanding of international relations. We may not be in a situation where one can consider just the patient's tonsils or his appendix. Both may be infected but removing either may kill the patient. In other words, understanding the likely consequences of any one cause may depend on understanding its relation to other causes. The possible interrelation of causes makes the problem of estimating the merit of various prescriptions more difficult still.

What are the criteria of merit? Suppose we consider again the person who argues that "bad" states produce war, that "good" states would live peacefully together, that therefore we must bring states into accord with a prescribed pattern. To estimate the merit of such a series of propositions requires asking the following questions: (1) Can the final proposition be implemented, and if so, how? (2) Is there a logical relation between prescription and image? In other words, does the prescription attack the assigned causes? (3) Is the image adequate, or has the analyst simply seized upon the most spectacular cause or the one he thinks most susceptible to manipulation and ignored other causes of equal or greater importance? (4) How will attempts to fill the prescription affect other goals? This last question is necessary since peace is not the only goal of even the most peacefully inclined men or states. One may, for example, believe that world government and perpetual peace are synonymous, but one may also be convinced that a world state would be a world tyranny and therefore prefer a system of nation-states with a perpetual danger of war to a world state with a promise of perpetual peace.

We shall try to facilitate the answering of the questions just raised, first by a critical consideration of each image and then by a consideration of the interrelation of images. Of what follows, Chapters II, IV, and VI give a basic explication of the first, second, and third images, respectively, largely in terms of traditional political philosophy. Chapters III, V, and VII further illustrate and exemplify each of the images in turn. Chapter VIII serves both as a brief essay on the interrelation of images and as a conclusion.

CHAPTER II. THE FIRST IMAGE

International Conflict and Human Behavior

There is deceit and cunning and from these wars arise.

CONFUCIUS

ACCORDING to the first image of international relations, the locus of the important causes of war is found in the nature and behavior of man. Wars result from selfishness, from misdirected aggressive impulses, from stupidity. Other causes are secondary and have to be interpreted in the light of these factors. If these are the primary causes of war, then the elimination of war must come through uplifting and enlightening men or securing their psychic-social readjustment. This estimate of causes and cures has been dominant in the writings of many serious students of human affairs from Confucius to present-day pacifists. It is the leitmotif of many modern behavioral scientists as well.[1]

Prescriptions associated with first-image analyses need not be identical in content, as a few examples will indicate. Henry Wadsworth Longfellow, moved to poetic expression by a visit to the arsenal at Springfield, set down the following thoughts:

> Were half the power that fills the world with terror,
> Were half the wealth bestowed on camps and courts,
> Given to redeem the human mind from error,
> There were no need of arsenals or forts.

[1] They are discussed at length in ch. iii, below.

Implicit in these lines is the idea that the people will insist that the right policies be adopted if only they know what the right policies are. Their instincts are good, though their present gullibility may prompt them to follow false leaders. By attributing present difficulties to a defect in knowledge, education becomes the remedy for war. The idea is widespread. Beverly Nichols, a pacifist writing in the 1930s, thought that if Norman Angell "could be made educational dictator of the world, war would vanish like the morning mist, in a single generation."[2] In 1920, a conference of Friends, unwilling to rely upon intellectual development alone, called upon the people of the world to replace self-seeking with the spirit of sacrifice, cooperation, and trust.[3] Bertrand Russell, at about the same time and in much the same vein, saw a decline in the possessive instincts as a prerequisite to peace.[4] By others, increasing the chances of peace has been said to require not so much a change in "instincts" as a channeling of energies that are presently expended in the destructive folly of war. If there were something that men would rather do than fight, they would cease to fight altogether. Aristophanes saw the point. If the women of Athens would deny themselves to husbands and lovers, their men would have to choose between the pleasures of the couch and the exhilarating experiences of the battlefield. Aristophanes thought he knew the men, and women, of Athens well enough to make the outcome a foregone conclusion. William James was in the same tradition. War, in his view, is rooted in man's bellicose nature, which is the product of centuries-old tradition.

---

2 Nichols, *Cry Havoc!* p. 164.
3 Hirst, *The Quakers in Peace and War*, pp. 521–25.
4 Russell, *Political Ideals*, p. 42. In one way or another the thought recurs in Lord Russell's many writings on international relations.

His nature cannot be changed or his drives suppressed, but they can be diverted. As alternatives to military service, James suggests drafting the youth of the world to mine coal and man ships, to build skyscrapers and roads, to wash dishes and clothes. While his estimate of what diversions would be sufficient is at once less realistic and more seriously intended than that of Aristophanes, his remedy is clearly the same in type.[5]

The prescriptions vary, but common to them all is the thought that in order to achieve a more peaceful world men must be changed, whether in their moral-intellectual outlook or in their psychic-social behavior. One may, however, agree with the first-image analysis of causes without admitting the possibility of practicable prescriptions for their removal. Among those who accept a first-image explanation of war there are both optimists and pessimists, those who think the possibilities of progress so great that wars will end before the next generation is dead and those who think that wars will continue to occur though by them we may all die. "Optimist" and "pessimist" are tricky words, yet it is difficult to find better ones. If they are defined simply according to expectations, which accords with popular usage, it is difficult if not impossible to place a given person in one or the other category. There are degrees of optimism and pessimism, and the same person may be optimistic about some things, pessimistic about others. The philosophic meanings of the terms are clearer and more useful. Pessimism in philosophy is the belief that reality is flawed, a thought expressed by Milton and Malthus in the statements cited in the previous chapter. Momentarily, more or less adequate restraints upon the forces of evil may be contrived, but the expectation of

[5] James, "The Moral Equivalent of War," in *Memories and Studies*, pp. 262–72, 290.

a generally and permanently good result is prevented by constant awareness of the vitiating effects of an essential defect.[6] The optimist, on the other hand, believes that reality is good, society basically harmonious. The difficulties that have plagued man are superficial and momentary. The difficulties continue, for history is a succession of moments; but the quality of history can be changed, and the most optimistic believe that this can be done once and for all and rather easily. One comes back to expectations, but the expectations are rooted in different conceptions of the world. It needs to be pointed out that pessimism about the chances of ultimate success, in eliminating war for example, is not identical with a statement that nothing can be done about our present plight. The pessimist may be more hopeful than the optimist about postponing the war that threatens tomorrow; the optimist may believe that nothing is worth doing that falls short of applying the remedy that will supposedly bring final and complete success. The pessimist deserves the epithet because he believes final success impossible, but the epithet need not then be taken as one of opprobrium.

Within each image there are optimists and pessimists agreeing on definitions of causes and differing on what, if anything, can be done about them. Critical consideration of a given image may, moreover, be an insufficient basis for forming a general set of expectations, for the image itself may be faulty. This will become apparent as we seek to understand successive images. In the present chapter, we consider primarily those who assent to the proposition that to understand the recurrence of war one must look first to the nature and behavior of man and who, doing so, find ineradicable defects by which the evils of the world, including war, can be explained. In the next

6 Cf. Morgenthau, *Politics among Nations*, pp. 7–8.

chapter, we shall consider some of the many who, looking
to the same causes, are confident that they can be manipulated or controlled in order to produce if not a final condition of peace at least a notable decrease in the incidence
of war.

When Jonathan Dymond, an early nineteenth-century
pacifist, wrote that "whatever can be said in favour of a
balance of power, can be said only because we are wicked,"
he penned a statement to which both optimists and
pessimists subscribe.[7] The optimists see a possibility of
turning the wicked into the good and ending the wars that
result from present balance-of-power politics. The pessimists, while accepting the derivation of the balance of
power and war from human nature, see little if any possibility of man righting himself. Instead the balance of
power is accorded an honorable position by them, for, to
use Dymond's figure, it may truly prevent "tigers" from
tearing each other apart. And if occasionally it does not,
still faulty prophylaxis is better than none at all.

Optimists and pessimists agree in their analysis of cause
but, differing on the possibility of altering that cause, become each other's bitterest critics. Reinhold Niebuhr, a
theologian who in the last twenty-five years has written as
many words of wisdom on problems of international
politics as have any of the academic specialists in that subject, has criticized utopians, Liberal and Marxist alike,
with frequency and telling effect. Political realism, he
argues, is impossible without a true insight into man's
nature.[8] Everyone, of course, thinks his own theories
realistic. The optimists do, and they too think that they

[7] Dymond, *The Accordancy of War with the Principles of Christianity,*
p. 20.
[8] Niebuhr, *Christian Realism and Political Problems,* p. 101.

have based them on a correct view of man. Niebuhr's dissent is based on the thought that they have overlooked the potentiality of evil in all human acts. They have assumed that progress moves in a straight line, ever upward, whereas in fact each advance in knowledge, each innovation in technique, contains within itself the potentiality of evil as well as of good. Man widens his control over nature, but the very instruments that promise security from cold and hunger, a lessening of labor and an increase of leisure, enable some men to enslave or destroy others. Man, a self-conscious being, senses his limits. They are inherent. Equally inherent is his desire to overcome them. Man is a finite being with infinite aspirations, a pigmy who thinks himself a giant. Out of his self-interest, he develops economic and political theories and attempts to pass them off as universal systems; he is born and reared in insecurity and seeks to make himself absolutely secure; he is a man but thinks himself a god. The seat of evil is the self, and the quality of evil can be defined in terms of pride.[9]

This view is, of course, much older than Niebuhr. Within the Christian tradition, it is stated in classic terms by St. Augustine. Outside that tradition, it is elaborated in the philosophy of Spinoza. In the political writing of the twentieth century, it is reflected most clearly and consistently in the works of Hans Morgenthau. These four writers, despite their numerous differences, unite in basing their political conclusions upon an assumed nature of

[9] Niebuhr and Eddy, *Doom and Dawn*, p. 16: "It is the human effort to make our partial values absolute which is always the final sin in human life; and it always results in the most bloody of human conflicts." (I have used, here and elsewhere, only the part of the book that is written by Niebuhr.) Cf. Niebuhr, *The Nature and Destiny of Man*, I, 137, 150, 177, 181; and "Is Social Conflict Inevitable?" *Scribner's Magazine*, XCVIII (1935), 167.

man. St. Augustine and Spinoza can be used to illustrate the process of reasoning by which this is done.

St. Augustine had observed the importance of self-preservation in the hierarchy of human motivations. When we see that even the most wretched "fear to die, and will rather live in such misfortune than end it by death, is it not obvious enough," he asks, "how nature shrinks from annihilation?" [10] The desire for self-preservation is, with Augustine, an observed fact. It is not a principle sufficient to explain the whole of man's behavior. For Spinoza, however, the end of *every* act is the self-preservation of the actor. The laws of nature are simply statements of what this single end requires; natural right, a statement of what it logically permits.[11] The man who lives according to reason will demonstrate both courage and high-mindedness. That is, he will strive to preserve himself in accordance with the dictates of reason, and he will strive to aid other men and unite them to him in friendship. This is not a description of actual behavior; it is a description of behavior that is ideally rational. It is not because they are duties that the man who follows the dictates of reason behaves with courage and high-mindedness. Instead these characteristics are the necessary result of following reason. His endeavor to aid others is not unselfish behavior. Exactly the opposite: regard for others and the desire to cooperate with them result from the realization that

[10] Augustine, *City of God*, tr. Dods, Book XI, ch. xxvii.

[11] Spinoza, *Ethics*, Part IV, prop. xxxvii, note ii: "By sovereign natural right every man judges what is good and what is bad, takes care of his own advantage according to his own disposition, avenges the wrongs done to him, and endeavours to preserve that which he loves and to destroy that which he hates." References are to *The Chief Works of Benedict de Spinoza*, tr. Elwes, which contains *A Theologico-Political Treatise, A Political Treatise*, and *The Ethics*. Volume and page references will be given in parentheses only where a standard system of reference alone does not make easy location of a passage possible.

mutual assistance, the division of labor, is necessary to his own sustenance and preservation.[12] Logically, as with first-image optimists, this leads to anarchism: "that all should so in all points agree, that the minds and bodies of all should form, as it were, one single mind and one single body, and that all should, with one consent, as far as they are able, endeavour to preserve their being, and all with one consent seek what is useful to them all." [13] Reason accurately interpreting the true interest of each would lead all people to live harmoniously in society with no need for a political authority to control and direct them.[14]

Rather than being the end of Spinoza's political thought, this is only its beginning. Each man does seek his own interest, but, unfortunately, not according to the dictates of reason. This St. Augustine had explained by original sin, the act that accounts for the fact that human reason and will are both defective.[15] In Spinoza's philosophy this religious explanation becomes a proposition in logic and psychology. He constructs a model of rational behavior: Those acts are rational that lead spontaneously to harmony in cooperative endeavors to perpetuate life. This is not the condition in which we find the world. That men are defective then becomes an empirical datum requiring no explanation from outside; indeed there can be no explanation from outside, for God has become

---

12 Although according to Spinoza every self acts for its own preservation, self-preservation and self-realization tend to coincide in proportion as man's life is suffused with reason. Cf. *Ethics*, Part IV, prop. viii and apps. iv–v; Part V, props. xxxviii–xlii.

13 *Ethics*, Part IV, prop. xviii, note. For the preceding analysis see especially Part III, prop. lix, note; Part IV, props. xxix–xl; and *Theologico-Political Treatise*, chs. v, xvi (I, 73, 202–203).

14 Cf. Augustine, *City of God*, tr. Dods, Book XV, ch. v: "But with the good, good men, or at least perfectly good men, cannot war."

15 *Ibid.*, Book XI, ch. vii; Book XII, ch. i.

nature.[16]   Men are led not by the precepts of pure reason but by their passions.   Men, led by passion, are drawn into conflict.   Instead of being mutually helpful, they behave in a manner that is mutually destructive.   Each seeks to be first among men and takes more pride in the harm he has done others than in the good he has done himself. Reason can moderate the passions, but this is so difficult that those who think that men "can ever be induced to live according to the bare dictate of reason, must be dreaming of the poetic golden age, or of a stage-play." [17]

Spinoza's explanation of political and social ills is based on the conflict he detects between reason and passion.   St. Augustine, Niebuhr, and Morgenthau reject the dualism explicit in Spinoza's thought: the whole man, his mind and his body, are, according to them, defective.   Despite this difference, the substratum of agreement remains; for each of them deduces political ills from human defects. Niebuhr, for example, rejects Marx's assertion that exploitation of man by man is caused by the division of society into classes, with the comment that both class divisions and exploitation result from a "tendency in the human heart." [18]   And Morgenthau sees "the ubiquity of evil in human action" arising from man's ineradicable lust for power and transforming "churches into political organizations . . . revolutions into dictatorships . . . love for country into imperialism." [19]

As the statement by Morgenthau suggests, the explana-

[16] *Ethics*, Part I, props. xxvi, xxix: Individuals, their minds and bodies, are nothing but modes of God; and God is nothing but the totality of nature.

[17] *Political Treatise*, ch. i, sec. 5.

[18] Niebuhr, *Christianity and Power Politics*, pp. 145–46.   Cf. Gregg, *The Power of Non-Violence*, pp. 131–32: "Fear and greed are roots of war as well as of capitalism."   Comparing this statement with the statements of Niebuhr and Morgenthau makes clear a similarity in the analyses of the optimists and their critics.

[19] Morgenthau, *Scientific Man*, pp. 194–95.

tion that suffices for domestic ills serves as well to explain frictions and wars among states. Augustine attributes to man's "love of so many vain and hurtful things" a long list of human tribulations, ranging from quarrels and robberies to murders and wars.[20] Spinoza, though he proclaims peace as the end of the state, finds that states are natural enemies and as such must constantly be on guard, one against the other: not because states are never honorable and peaceful, but because they may at any moment become dishonorable and belligerent; not because cooperation is against their best interests, but because passion often obscures the true interests of states as of men. And Niebuhr writes simply that war has its origin in "dark, unconscious sources in the human psyche." [21]

Further reflecting the resemblance between them, pessimists, like optimists, often appear to believe that war could be eliminated if only men could be changed. The thought is indirectly expressed by St. Augustine when out of his world-weary wisdom he writes: "For though there have never been wanting . . . hostile nations beyond the empire, against whom wars have been and are waged, yet, supposing there were no such nations, the very extent of the empire itself has produced wars of a more obnoxious description." [22] The idea that political form is but a secondary causal factor is put more directly by Niebuhr. "The ideal possibility of any historic community," he writes, "is a brotherly relation of life with life, individually within the community and collectively between it and others." But even the "internal peace of a community is always partly coercive [and] . . . the external peace between communities is marred by competitive strife." In-

[20] Augustine, *City of God*, tr. Dods, Book XXII, ch. xxi; cf. Book XIV, ch. ii.
[21] Niebuhr, *Beyond Tragedy*, p. 158.
[22] Augustine, *City of God*, tr. Dods, Book XIX, ch. vii.

ternally an oligarchy is needed to overcome the perils of anarchy; externally power is required to ward off the foreign foe. Both necessities arise from sin and remain as necessities "because men are not good enough to do what should be done for the commonweal on a purely voluntary basis." [23] Where Spinoza juxtaposes reason and the human passions that becloud it, Niebuhr poses love against the sin that overwhelms it. Sin is cause, and love, if it could overcome sin, would be cure. "Only a forgiving love, grounded in repentance, is adequate to heal the animosities between nations." [24]

CRITICAL EVALUATION

First-image pessimists accept the relevance of the optimists' ideal while rejecting the possibility of achieving it. Thus Spinoza contemplates the pleasures of the state of peaceful anarchy that would be possible were men truly rational, and Niebuhr accepts the Christian myth of the Garden of Eden or the Stoic myth of the Golden Age as portraying standards of action that remain at once an impossibility in history and a source of inspiration to mortal men.[25] But what is the relevance of an impossible ideal? Clearly if men could agree upon their goals and were perfectly rational in seeking them, they would always figure out and follow the best practicable solution for any given problem. If they were truly loving, they would always be willing to "turn the other cheek" but would in fact find no occasion for doing so. Neither of these con-

---

[23] Niebuhr, *Faith and History*, pp. 219–20; cf. *Moral Man and Immoral Society*, p. 93: "The man in the street, with his lust for power and prestige thwarted by his own limitations and the necessities of social life, projects his ego upon his nation and indulges his anarchic lusts vicariously."

[24] Niebuhr, *An Interpretation of Christian Ethics*, p. 128; cf. *Christian Realism and Political Problems*, pp. 116–17.

[25] For example, Niebuhr, *An Interpretation of Christian Ethics*, p. 148; *Faith and History*, pp. 143–44.

ditional statements describes the actual behavior of men—
they are neither perfectly rational nor truly loving, nor,
the pessimist adds, will they ever become so. Thus Morgenthau rejects the assumption of "the essential goodness and
infinite malleability of human nature," and explains political behavior by the sometimes merely blind, sometimes
too cleverly egotistic behavior of men, a behavior that is
the undeniable and inevitable product of a human nature
that "has not changed since the classical philosophies of
China, India, and Greece endeavored to discover" the
laws of politics.[26]

The attribution of political ills to a fixed nature of man,
defined in terms of an inherent potentiality for evil as well
as for good, is a theme that constantly recurs in the
thought of Augustine, Spinoza, Niebuhr, and Morgenthau.
There is an important sense in which the attribution is
justified. To say that man acts in ways contrary to his
nature is *prima facie* absurd. The events of world history
cannot be divorced from the men who made them. But
the importance of human nature as a factor in causal
analysis of social events is reduced by the fact that the
same nature, however defined, has to explain an infinite
variety of social events. Anyone can "prove" that man is
bad simply by pointing to evidence of his viciousness and
stupidity. To relate unwanted events, such as crime and
war, to this viciousness and stupidity is then a simple task.
Although this is insufficient to establish the validity of the
first image, it is nevertheless difficult, if not impossible, to
counter such a particular interpretation of an image by
trying to check it against events. To try to do so is to bog
down in a welter of facts and value judgments. Do such
evidences of man's behavior as rapes, murders, and thefts
prove that he is bad? What about the counterevidence

[26] Morgenthau, *Politics among Nations*, pp. 3–4. Cf. Niebuhr, *Beyond Tragedy*, p. 30.

provided by acts of charity, love, and self-sacrifice? Is the amount of crime in a given society proof that the men in it are bad? Or is it amazing that under the circumstances there is not more crime? Maybe we have so *little* crime and so *few* wars because men, being good, adjust so amazingly well to circumstances that are inherently difficult! To say, then, that certain things happen because men are stupid or bad is a hypothesis that is accepted or rejected according to the mood of the writer. It is a statement that evidence cannot prove or disprove, for what we make of the evidence depends on the theory we hold. As Emile Durkheim has pointed out, "the psychological factor is too general to predetermine the course of social phenomena. Since it does not call for one social form rather than another, it cannot explain any of them." [27] To attempt to explain social forms on the basis of psychological data is to commit the error of psychologism: the analysis of individual behavior used uncritically to explain group phenomena.

Without an understanding of man's nature, one is often told, there can be no theory of politics. Applying the dictum, Niebuhr writes that "political strategies," invariably involving "the balancing of power with power," are made necessary by "the sinful character of man." [28] Leaving aside the problem of whether or not one agrees with this statement, we may ask what difference agreement or disagreement would make. Human nature may in some sense have been the cause of war in 1914, but by the same token it was the cause of peace in 1910. In the intervening years many things changed, but human nature did not. Human nature is a cause then only in the sense that if men were somehow entirely different, they would not

[27] Durkheim, *The Rules of Sociological Method,* tr. Solovay and Mueller, p. 108.
[28] Niebuhr, *Christianity and Power Politics,* p. 4.

need political control at all. This calls to mind the runner who, when asked why he lost the race, replied: "I ran too slowly." The answer, though correct, is not very helpful. A more helpful answer may or may not be possible. One might ask the runner how he trained, what kind of shoes he wore, how well he slept the night before, and whether or not he paced himself properly. Answers to such questions, while not affecting the innate capabilities of the athlete, may provide clues to more impressive performances in the future. It would be foolish to prescribe a regimen for the athlete without considering his physical characteristics, but dwelling obsessively upon the invariant factors that affect his performance may divert attention from the factors that can be manipulated. Similarly one may label human nature the basic or primary cause of war, but it is, according to those whom we here consider, a cause that human contrivance cannot affect.

Spinoza claimed to explain human behavior by reference to psychological factors.[29] But the search for causes is an attempt to account for differences. If men were always at war, or always at peace, the question of why there is war, or why there is peace, would never arise. What does account for the alternation of periods of war and peace? While human nature no doubt plays a role in bringing about war, it cannot by itself explain both war and peace, except by the simple statement that man's nature is such that sometimes he fights and sometimes he does not. And this statement leads inescapably to the attempt to explain why he fights sometimes and not others. If human nature is *the* cause of war and if, as in the sys-

---

[29] "I would have it known," he writes, "that all this demonstration of mine proceeds from the necessity of human nature . . . —I mean, from the universal effort of all men after self-preservation." His effort in politics has been "to deduce from the very condition of human nature . . . such things as agree best with practice." *Political Treatise*, ch. iii, sec. 18; ch. i, sec. 4.

tems of the first-image pessimists, human nature is fixed, then we can never hope for peace. If human nature is but one of the causes of war, then, even on the assumption that human nature is fixed, we can properly carry on a search for the conditions of peace.

How damaging are these criticisms to the systems erected by first-image pessimists? Very damaging indeed where the pessimists have in fact attempted to derive specific political conclusions directly from an assumed nature of man. This cannot be done, but with their method other and very important things can be. Where Durkheim points out that the psychological factor, since it does not call for specific social forms, cannot explain any of them, one can well imagine Augustine or Niebuhr replying that, on the contrary, the psychological factor explains all of them. "Caesars and saints," Niebuhr has written, "are made possible by the same structure of human character." Or again, "Human nature is so complex that it justifies almost every assumption and prejudice with which either a scientific investigation or an ordinary human contact is initiated." [30] This admits one part, while denying another part, of Durkheim's critical intention.   Human nature may not explain why in one state man is enslaved and in another comparatively free, why in one year there is war, in another comparative peace.   It can, however, explain the necessary imperfections of all social and political forms. Thus Niebuhr admires Marx for exposing the contradictions of bourgeois democracy and at the same time criticizes the Marxist illusion that a change in forms will give birth to an earthly utopia.[31]   And St. Augustine, far from implying that because wars occur within a world state, political organization is irrelevant, intends instead to

[30] Niebuhr, *Christianity and Power Politics*, p. 157; *Does Civilization Need Religion?* p. 41.
[31] Niebuhr, *Christianity and Power Politics*, ch. 11.

convey the thought that though political solutions will be imperfect they are nevertheless necessary. The basic assumptions of Augustine and Niebuhr, Spinoza and Morgenthau, are useful in descrying the limits of possible political accomplishment.

What is valid in Durkheim's criticism is, however, indicated by a set of tendencies displayed by the pessimists: on the one side, to develop a politics and economics without content; on the other, to introduce realms of causation that go beyond the psychology of man in order to get content. The first is illustrated by Niebuhr's criticism of Augustine. While Augustine argues that the consequences of original sin make government necessary, he fails to distinguish relative orders of merit among social and political institutions. His keen perception of the consequences of anarchy makes him willing to abide tyranny. On this point, Niebuhr's criticism is forthright and convincing. Augustinians, he writes, "saw the dangers of anarchy in the egotism of the citizens but failed to perceive the dangers of tyranny in the selfishness of the ruler. Therefore they obscured the consequent necessity of placing checks upon the ruler's self-will." [32] But Niebuhr himself sometimes betrays a similar habit. For example, his comments on freedom and control in economics and on the relation between economics and politics derive more from his theological position than from a close analysis of economic and political problems and forms. While his general comments are often sound, his specific statements are as often arbitrary—whether one agrees or disagrees, it is difficult to see the basis for them. Niebuhr's concentration on the finitude of man has led to some brilliant insights, as close and constant attention to a single factor often does, but it has also led to judgments that could as

[32] Niebuhr, *Christian Realism and Political Problems*, p. 127; cf. *Christianity and Power Politics*, pp. 50 ff.

easily be reversed.[33]   And this could be done on the basis
of a similar definition of human nature, quite in the way
that Niebuhr disagrees politically with St. Augustine while
accepting his view of man.

For understanding the significance of first-image analysis
in international relations, the second tendency of the pessimists is more important. Though Spinoza thinks he has
been able to explain political phenomena by reference to
qualities inherent in man, he also clearly makes the point
that under different conditions men behave differently.
When not united, men must constantly be on guard one
against the other; when they live within a commonwealth
they often enjoy at least a modicum of peace and security.
Without the restraints of government, Augustine points
out, men would slaughter each other until man is extinct.
Orderly government may make all the difference between
death and the possibility of living to an old age with
relative safety and happiness. Augustine and Spinoza
recognize the point implicitly, without making explicit
admissions. Niebuhr and Morgenthau tackle more
directly the problem of relating causes to each other.
Niebuhr explicitly distinguishes primary from secondary
causes. "All purely political or economic solutions of the
problem of justice and peace deal with the specific and
secondary causes of conflict and injustice," he declares.
"All purely religious solutions deal with the ultimate and
primary causes." Although proponents of one kind of

[33] Cf. Niebuhr, *The Irony of American History*, ch. v; *The Children of
Light and the Children of Darkness*, ch. iii; *Reflections on the End of an
Era, passim*. In different terms, Thompson makes a similar point. See
"Beyond National Interest: A Critical Evaluation of Reinhold Niebuhr's
Theory of International Politics," *Review of Politics*, XVII (1955), 185–86;
and "The Political Philosophy of Reinhold Niebuhr," in Kegley and
Bretall, eds., *Reinhold Niebuhr, His Religious, Social, and Political
Thought*, pp. 169–73. Arthur Schlesinger, Jr., has given a number of
examples that highlight the accidental qualities of Niebuhr's judgments
on contemporary politicians and their policies. See "Reinhold Niebuhr's
Rôle in American Political Thought and Life," in *ibid.*, pp. 137–43.

solution often exclude the other, both kinds are necessary.[34] Niebuhr makes clear, for example in his criticism of Augustine, that a realistic understanding of Christian tenets requires that men concern themselves with degrees of merit in social and political institutions. None can be perfect, but the imperfections of democracy are infinitely preferable to the imperfections of totalitarianism. Perfect justice being impossible, men become concerned with weighing possible palliatives, with striving for those that promise a little more justice or freedom, security or welfare, and seeking to avoid those that may lead to a little less. For Niebuhr, the impossibility of earthly perfection does not justify the Augustinian unconcern, found in Luther, Hobbes, and Karl Barth, with the comparative qualities of alternate forms and policies.[35]

This intense and practical concern with questions of a little more or a little less has the interesting effect of moving the "secondary" causes to the center of the stage. One might say that from his basic cause Niebuhr derives one maxim: do not expect too much. From his identification of secondary causes he derives his other conclusions: just what to expect under different conditions, which conditions must be changed to minimize unwanted effects and achieve others, and, generally, what the rules of conduct must be for the conscientious citizen or politician.

Too much concern with the "primary" cause of conflict leads one away from a realistic analysis of world politics. The basic cause is the least manipulable of all causes. The causes that in fact explain differences in behavior must be sought somewhere other than in human nature itself. Niebuhr recognizes this when he writes that "the particu-

---

[34] Niebuhr and Eddy, *Doom and Dawn*, p. 6; cf. *Leaves from the Notebook of a Tamed Cynic*, pp. 88–91.

[35] Niebuhr, *The Nature and Destiny of Man*, I, 220–22; *The Self and the Dramas of History*, p. 119.

lar plight of modern civilization is in a sense not caused by the sinfulness of human nature or by human greed. The greed of collective man must be taken for granted in the political order." [36] But power can be organized under government and the pretensions of one group or state can be checked by the assertions of another.[37] From a correct understanding of secondary causes comes the real chance for peace. The same overbalancing of primary by secondary causes is evident in Morgenthau—war from man's lust for power, he says, peace from world government.[38] And, with world government presently impossible, Morgenthau, like Niebuhr, argues convincingly the inescapable necessity of balance-of-power politics.[39]

Perhaps some circumscribed comments on the persistent debate between the "realists" and their critics will make the practical meaning of the comments on first-image pessimists clearer. Since Morgenthau has been slighted somewhat in the previous discussion and since it is around him that the battle rages, we shall concentrate on him and his critics in the succeeding pages.

Morgenthau recognizes that given competition for scarce goods with no one to serve as arbiter a struggle for power will ensue among the competitors, and that consequently the struggle for power can be explained without reference to the evil born in men. The struggle for power arises simply because men want things, not because there is some evil in their desires. This he labels one of the two roots of conflict, but even while discussing it he seems to pull unconsciously toward the "other root of conflict and concomitant evil"—"the *animus dominandi*, the desire for

---

[36] Niebuhr and Eddy, *Doom and Dawn*, p. 8.

[37] Niebuhr, *Discerning the Signs of the Times*, pp. 71, 104; *Moral Man and Immoral Society*, p. 272.

[38] Morgenthau, *Scientific Man*, pp. 187–203; *Politics among Nations*, pp. 477, 481.

[39] Morgenthau, *Politics among Nations*, Part IV.

power." This is illustrated by a statement such as the following: "The test of political success is the degree to which one is able to maintain, to increase, or to demonstrate one's power over others." [40] Power appears as an end-in-itself, whereas a greater emphasis on the first root of political discord would credit power as an instrument necessary for success in competitive struggles. Morgenthau, however, often considers the drive for power that inheres in men as a datum more basic than the chance conditions under which struggles for power occur. This is indicated by his statement that "in a world where power counts, no nation pursuing a rational policy has a choice between renouncing and wanting power; *and, if it could,* the lust for power for the individual's sake would still confront us with its less spectacular yet no less pressing moral defects." [41]

We have here two ideas: first, that struggles for preference arise in competitive situations and force is introduced in the absence of an authority that can limit the means used by the competitors; second, that struggles for power arise because men are born seekers of power. What are the implications for international politics of this dual explanation? One who accepts the second idea will define national interest in terms of power, because men naturally seek power. One who accepts the first idea will also define national interest in terms of power, but this time because under certain conditions power is the means necessary to secure the ends of states. In the one instance, power is an end; in the other, an instrument. The lines of analysis are obscured, for if it turns out that power is a *necessary* means, then power inevitably takes on some of the qualities of an end. Whether one adopts the first or the second explanation, or mixes the two, may then make little differ-

---

[40] Morgenthau, *Scientific Man*, pp. 192, 196.
[41] *Ibid.*, p. 200. Italics added.

ence in the policy conclusions reached. It may, however, confuse the analyst and flummox his critics.

Realists have tended to accept the idea of a neat dichotomy between two schools of thought. This is implicit in Niebuhr's statement, previously cited, that the basis of all political realism is a sophisticated view of man, and in Kennan's definition of the conduct of government as a "sorry chore . . . devolving upon civilized society, most unfortunately, as a result of man's irrational nature, his selfishness, his obstinacy, his tendency to violence." [42] It is explicit in Morgenthau's assertion that modern political thought divides into two schools—the utopians with their optimistic philosophies of man and politics and the realists who see that the world "is the result of forces which are inherent in human nature." It is evident as well in the distinction of Gerald Stourzh between those who think that the progress of reason and science makes government increasingly unnecessary and "those who hold that there is an ineradicable element of selfishness, pride, and corruption in human nature" and who therefore "refuse to concede to reason and to 'scientific principles' such a paramount role in political things." [43]

Governments, political manipulations, and balances of power may be necessary in part because of man's passion and irrationality, but they are necessary for other reasons as well. The division of political approaches into two categories is misleading because it is based on an incomplete statement of the causes of conflict and the consequent necessities of politics. The dichotomy is often accepted by the critics of the realists as well. In a review of John Herz's *Political Realism and Political Idealism*, Quincy

[42] Kennan, *Realities of American Foreign Policy*, p. 48.
[43] Morgenthau, "Another 'Great Debate': The National Interest of the United States," *American Political Science Review*, XLVI (1952), 961–62; Stourzh, *Benjamin Franklin and American Foreign Policy*, pp. 1–2.

Wright comments on the self-styled realists as follows: "Thus when it is said that states pursue power as their supreme value, the philosophical question is at once raised: Ought power to be the supreme value of states? The 'realist' answers affirmatively, asserting that states should pursue their national interests and the supreme national interest is the augmentation of the state's power position. They are, however, then asserting not a self-evident axiom but an ethical norm, and an ethical norm which is by no means uncontroversial." [44] As a criticism of Morgenthau this can be accepted, but not as a criticism of Herz; and even as a criticism of Morgenthau it commits the error of acquiescing in the confusions he has himself introduced. If one becomes intrigued with statements such as those previously cited in which a power drive rooted in man is asserted to be the primary cause of worldly ills, then it may be fair to say that Morgenthau has made a normative statement that one may accept or reject according to his inclination. According to Herz's analysis, however, states look to their comparative power positions because of the "security dilemma," born of a condition of anarchy, that confronts them.[45] Power appears as a possibly useful instrument rather than as a supreme value that men by their very natures are led to seek. Whether or not power should be "the supreme value of states" is then not the question. Rather one must ask when, if ever, it will be a supreme value and when merely a means.

The attempt to derive a philosophy of politics from an assumed nature of man leads one to a concern with the role of ethics in statecraft without providing criteria for distinguishing ethical from unethical behavior. This diffi-

[44] Wright, "Realism and Idealism in International Politics," *World Politics*, V (1952), 122.
[45] Herz, *Political Realism and Political Idealism*, ch. ii, sec. ii.

culty is reflected in the comments of a critic who is worried
by the problem of giving content to Morgenthau's proposed guide for foreign policy, "the national interest."
Grayson Kirk suggests that "one source of this difficulty
[with content] lies in an unwillingness to admit that many
of our policy-makers, during this so-called Utopian period
[in the history of American foreign policy], have undertaken to express the national interests of the United States
in terms of moral principles, not because they were con-
fused theorists, but because they honestly believed that
our best national interests lay in the widest possible acceptance of certain moral and legal principles as guides of
international conduct." [46] Whether or not certain statesmen "honestly believed" that they were expressing our
national interests when they sought "the widest possible
acceptance of certain moral and legal principles as guides
of international conduct" is a matter of personal concern
only.   It is more important to ask whether or not the
conditions of international politics permit statesmen to
think and act in terms of the moral and legal principles
that may be both serviceable and acceptable in domestic
politics.   Everyone is for "the national interest."   No
policy is advanced with the plea that, although this will
hurt my country, it will help others. The problems are
the evaluative one of deciding which interests are legitimate and the pragmatic one of deciding what policies will
best serve them. To solve these problems one needs as
much an understanding of politics as an understanding of
man—and the one cannot be derived from the other.

On numerous occasions Morgenthau has displayed admirable sophistication and discernment in his political
commentary.   He has analyzed skillfully the implications
of international anarchy and distinguished action possible

[46] Kirk, "In Search of the National Interest," *World Politics*, V (1952),
113.

internally from action possible externally, but it is not all the fault of his critics that they have had difficulty in conceiving the relation intended by him between his views of man and his theories of politics.

CONCLUSION

The evilness of men, or their improper behavior, leads to war; individual goodness, if it could be universalized, would mean peace: this is a summary statement of the first image. For the pessimists peace is at once a goal and a utopian dream, but others have taken seriously the presumption that a reform of individuals sufficient to bring lasting peace to the world is possible. Men are good; therefore no social or political problems—is this a true statement? Would the reform of individuals, if realized, cure social and political ills? The difficulty obviously lies in the word "good." How is "good" to be defined? "Those people are good who spontaneously act in perfect harmony with one another." This is a tautological definition, but nevertheless a revealing one. What first-image analysts, optimists and pessimists alike, have done is: (1) to notice conflict, (2) to ask themselves why conflict occurs, and (3) to pin the blame on one or a small number of behavior traits.

First-image optimists betray a naïveté in politics that vitiates their efforts to construct a new and better world. Their lack of success is directly related to a view of man that is simple and pleasing, but wrong. First-image pessimists have expertly dismantled the air castles of the optimists but have had less success in their endeavors to build the serviceable but necessarily uninspiring dwellings that must take their place. They have countered a theory of politics built on an optimistic definition of man's capabilities by pointing out that men are not what most pacifists and many liberals think them. Niebuhr and

Morgenthau say to the optimists: You have misunderstood
politics because you have misestimated human nature.
This is, according to them, the real error of the liberals.[47]
Instead it should be called *an* error of many liberals. A
more important error, into which some but by no means
all liberals have fallen, is to exaggerate the causal importance of human nature; for, as Niebuhr himself points out
in a statement cited earlier, human nature is so complex
that it can justify every hypothesis we may entertain. At
a minimum, nevertheless, first-image pessimists provide a
valuable warning, all too frequently ignored in modern
history, against expecting too much from the application
of reason to social and political problems. And this is an
example of a possibly useful result of first-image analysis.

While demonstrating the usefulness of the first-image,
Augustine and Spinoza, Niebuhr and Morgenthau also
help to make clear the limits of its serviceability. To take
either the position that men can be made good and then
wars will cease to occur or the position that because men
are bad wars and similar evils never will end may lead one
to a consideration of social and political structure. If
changing human nature will solve the problem, then one
has to discover how to bring about the change. If man's
evil qualities lead to wars, then one has to worry about
ways to repress his evilness or to compensate for it. Often
with those who expect an improvement in human behavior
to bring peace to the world, the influence of social-political
institutions is buried under the conviction that individual
behavior is determined more by religious-spiritual inspiration than by material circumstance. With those who link
war to defects inherent in man, the impetus is more clearly
in the opposite direction. To control rapacious men re-

---

[47] Niebuhr, *Reflections on the End of an Era*, p. 48; Morgenthau,
Scientific Man, passim. For extended analysis of liberal thought in
domestic and international politics, see below, ch. iv.

quires more force than exhortation. Social-political institutions, especially if the writer in question is this-world oriented, tend to move to the center of the stage. The assumption of a fixed human nature, in terms of which all else must be understood, itself helps to shift attention *away* from human nature—because human nature, by the terms of the assumption, cannot be changed, whereas social-political institutions can be.

CHAPTER III. SOME IMPLICATIONS

OF THE FIRST IMAGE

The Behavioral Sciences and

the Reduction of Interstate Violence

If to do were as easy as to know what were good to do, chapels had
been churches, and poor men's cottages princes' palaces.
PORTIA, IN *The Merchant of Venice*, I, ii

THE most important causes of political arrangements and
acts are found in the nature and behavior of man. This
statement represents the minimum of agreement found
among those whom we have classified as first-image analysts. They hold in common the conviction that what is
important for politics is found beneath the political surface. Optimists and pessimists agree on where to look,
but, having looked, describe differently what they see and
thus arrive at contradictory conclusions. Giving up on
men, pessimists turn in their prescriptions to political remedies. The unity of the first image is more perfectly preserved by those who, seeing the cause of war in men, seek
to change them. This is obviously the line of attack of
those who, assenting, perhaps without realizing it, to a
major assumption of pacifism, assert that wars will not end
until men in one way or another become better. The extent to which many modern behavioral scientists approxi-
mate this way of thinking is not often appreciated. This
is understandable. Those whom we have called optimists
have in the past most often placed their faith in religious-
moral appeals and improved but nevertheless traditional

systems of education. The modern behavioral scientist places his faith in a number of more complicated devices. His assumptions about the nature of man are usually less rigid, his solutions less individualistic. Where the optimists of the past were inclined to rely on emotional appeals, the modern social scientist investigates; where the pessimists gave up on man, the social scientist attempts to turn his findings into a prescription for social action.

The literature we shall consider in the present chapter is intentionally not representative of behavioral scientists as a group, although it is broadly representative of what has been written by them on the subject of war and peace. Relatively few of the total number of psychologists, for example, have turned their hands to the problem of war. Those who have are often those least likely to take a modest view of the contributions of their own discipline. And many of the articles that are published are occasional pieces written by men who momentarily take their eyes off the white mouse laboriously finding his way through an artificial maze only to plunge into a maze that, though not by design, is quite as baffling to the psychologist as the mouse's is to him. If asked to say what psychology can contribute to the solution of one of man's most pressing problems, it is understandable that one who has dedicated his life to the study of psychology should not shrug his shoulders and say that psychology has only a limited contribution to make. A few do say this. Edward Tolman, for example, in his *Drives toward War,* and Herbert Goldhamer, in his article "The Psychological Analysis of War," show that they fully appreciate the limitations of a psychological approach to war and peace and themselves put forth some of the criticisms made in this chapter. But most of the statements that see the light of day are less modest and more naïve. As an attempt to go further in estimating the applicability of first-image analysis, the pres-

ent chapter takes seriously the claims of some modern
social scientists that science applied to man in society can
solve social problems, among them war.

There has never been a shortage of plans for world peace.
Those who are strongly enough motivated to develop one
are often convinced that the only reason wars continue is
that statesmen refuse to listen to them. The behavioral
scientists are no different in respect to confidence. They
are different in another respect. What they have is not a
plan but a method, and the method, they are convinced,
generates answers to social problems. The conviction is
not new. "The duty of the statesman," wrote Emile
Durkheim in 1895, "is no longer to push society toward an
ideal that seems attractive to him, but his role is that of
the physician: he prevents the outbreak of illnesses by good
hygiene, and he seeks to cure them when they have appeared." [1] John Dewey supplied a philosopher's support.
The new role of philosophy, he predicted, will be to project "an idea or ideal which . . . would be used as a method
of understanding and rectifying specific social ills." Its
obligation is to contribute "in however humble a way to
methods that will assist us in discovering the causes of
humanity's ills." [2] Many political scientists have adopted
the same attitude. In 1930, for example, Harold Lasswell
wrote: "The political methods of coercion, exhortation,
and discussion assume that the role of politics is to solve
conflicts when they have happened. The ideal of a politics of prevention [and the politics of prevention is itself
the ideal] is to obviate conflict by the definite reduction
of the tension level of society by effective methods." The
point, according to Lasswell, is no longer so much to make

[1] Durkheim, *The Rules of Sociological Method,* tr. Solovay and Mueller,
p. 75.
[2] Dewey, *Reconstruction in Philosophy,* pp. 107, 142.

changes in the organization of government but to reorient minds, especially the minds of those most influential in society. The preventive politics of the future will be allied to medicine and psychopathology, to physiological psychology and to related disciplines.[3] Political science gives way to the behavioral sciences, and this is the case in the international as in the domestic sphere. "The political psychiatrist," writes Lasswell, "assuming the desirability of enabling human activities to evolve at a minimum of human cost, approaches the problem of war and revolution as one detail of the whole task of mastering the sources and mitigating the consequences of human insecurity in our unstable world." [4]

Lasswell sums up admirably the aspirations of the behavioral scientists. Society is the patient, in the phrase of Lawrence Frank. According to some the patient can be cured by doctoring the individuals who compose it, according to others by improving the social arrangements presently producing the tensions that so often find their imperfect dissolution in war. The English psychologist J. T. MacCurdy noted in the heat of one world war that "preventive psychiatry is beginning to show its fruits" and urged that "it is therefore not illogical to entertain a hope that similar efforts may ultimately prevent war." [5] In the same fashion but from a different academic perspective, the American anthropologist Clyde Kluckhohn, in the midst of another such war, identified "the central problem of world peace" as one of minimizing and controlling "aggressive impulses." [6]

In surveying behavioral-science literature on the subject

[3] Lasswell, *Psychopathology and Politics*, pp. 198–202.
[4] Lasswell, *World Politics and Personal Insecurity*, p. 26.
[5] MacCurdy, *The Psychology of War*, p. 11.
[6] Kluckhohn, *Mirror for Man*, p. 277. The same thought expressed in identical words appeared in his "Anthropological Research and World Peace," in *Approaches to World Peace*, p. 149.

of war, however, one finds not only a bewildering, if understandable, variety of estimated causes and supposed remedies but also a discouraging vagueness or unrealism both in the analyzing of causes and in the prescribing of remedies.   L. L. Bernard, a sociologist and social psychologist long concerned with problems of war and peace, urges that "we need to know what dangerous social conditions actually to correct in order to prevent wars."   But what these conditions are and what can be done about them is, despite his rather lengthy book on the subject, largely left for future research to determine.[7]   Where Bernard is vague, others in being specific reveal more clearly their lack of realism.   Thus James Miller, formerly professor of psychology and psychiatry at the University of Chicago and now on the staff of the Mental Health Research Institute, thinks the cause of peace might be greatly advanced if we could plant one thousand trained social scientists in the Soviet Union, disguised as Russians, who would use the latest techniques of public opinion sampling to find out what the Russians are thinking.   Gordon Allport advocates arranging the entrance to the General Assembly of the United Nations, the Security Council, and Unesco so that the delegates will have to pass through the playground of a nursery school on the way to their meetings.   And J. Cohen, another psychologist, believes that the cause of peace might be promoted if women were substituted for men in the governing of nations.[8]

[7] Bernard, *War and Its Causes*, p. 222.   And see especially his concluding chapter, "What Can Be Done about War?"

[8] James G. Miller, "Psychological Approaches to the Prevention of War," in Dennis *et al.*, *Current Trends in Social Psychology*, pp. 284–85; Gordon W. Allport, "Guide Lines for Research in International Cooperation," in Pear, ed., *Psychological Factors of Peace and War*, pp. 148–49; J. Cohen, "Women in Peace and War," in *ibid.*, pp. 91–110. Allport's proposal brings to mind a suggestion once made by the pacifist Beverly Nichols: namely, that a model of a hideously wounded soldier be placed in the center of the table at every disarmament conference. *Cry Havoc!* p. 5.

These examples are cited to illustrate a type of recommendation that occurs over and over again in the literature we are considering. They are of no significance until the systematic analyses from which they derive are considered. Obviously Miller, Allport, and Cohen are proposing the use of specific devices, which they hope will help to accomplish some of their more general objectives. What are these more general objectives? The nature of behavioral-science literature on the subject of war and peace makes it difficult to say. There are many tracts urging that the behavioral sciences do have a tremendous contribution to make to world peace. There are a few longer works that, after making the same assertion, add a good many details of what we know about the effects of infant care, everybody's psyche, the variations of custom in different tribes, and the relation between culture or society and individual behavior. But there is a shortage of systematic attempts to relate the behavioral sciences to the problems of international politics, past, present, or future.

Nevertheless one can distinguish several different approaches within the behavioral sciences. It is widely held that increased understanding among peoples means increased peace. It is almost as widely held that the improved social adjustment of individuals would, by decreasing feelings of frustration and insecurity, lessen the incidence of war. A considerable number, relying more exclusively on the decisive influence of political leaders, urge that our governors be more adequately trained and more carefully selected. Others argue that wars occur because men expect war; to abolish war, the expectations of men must be changed. And finally, some confine the contribution of the behavioral sciences to helping present governments define their goals and select their methods more scientifically. A look at the idea that promoting international understanding will promote peace can serve conveniently as an introduction to the behavioral-science approach to international relations.

"We cannot know everything, but the more we know the better."[9]   This statement is as true when applied to the problem of controlling war as it is when applied to controlling crime or disease.   When applied to the problem of eliminating war it often has a special meaning. The meaning is made clear in the following statement of James Miller: "Ignorance of the desires, aims, and characteristics of other peoples leads to fear and is consequently one of the primary causes for aggression."[10]   How is such a general proposition to be related to actual conditions of war and peace?   It is true, for example, that the tendency of a Japanese person to smile as he is being reprimanded is interpreted by Americans unfamiliar with the habit as sheer impertinence.   But how do such misunderstandings bring about wars among states?   And if the processes can be described, can it be maintained that they account for all, or even most, wars?   Conversely, does understanding always promote peace, or do nations sometimes remain at peace precisely because they do not understand each other very well?   Are we in a cold war with the Soviet Union because we do not understand Communist societies well enough, or because the more clearly we come to understand them the less we like them—or for still other reasons entirely outside the purview of the anthropologist and the social psychologist?

Evidently the correlation between peace and knowledge operates in less obvious ways.   Lawrence Frank, who has attempted to bring the data and insights of the behavioral sciences to bear on a variety of problems ranging from

[9] Klineberg, *Tensions Affecting International Understanding*, p. 92.
[10] Miller, "Psychological Approaches to the Prevention of War," in Dennis *et al.*, *Current Trends in Social Psychology*, p. 284.

child care to world peace, makes this clear.[11] The traditional routes to world order—via religious brotherhood, or
conquest, or world federalism—have, he points out, one
defect in common. They all propose that one creed, or
one state, or one philosophy come to dominate the world.
Frank, speaking as a cultural anthropologist, emphasizes
instead the positive value of diversity. Every culture has
its weaknesses; every culture has its special merits. Variety makes the world a better, and a more exciting, place
in which to live. Instead of seeking to reduce the variety,
we should seek to understand the reasons for it and the
value of it. And if we can come to understand the essential similarities, that we all face the same "life tasks" even
though we may meet them in somewhat different ways,
then we will have developed the basis if not for mutual
admiration at last for mutual forbearance.[12]

Competition for the same ends has, however, accounted
for more wars than the illusion that Lawrence Frank is
trying to combat, the illusion that people and cultures are
so very much different. Close cultural affinity has not
slowed the flow of blood, as is amply illustrated in the history of Western Europe. Nor has increased knowledge
always been a dependable road to more sympathetic understanding. Quite the opposite. Friedrich von Schlegel by
traveling abroad increased his knowledge of other peoples.
The result, as with many later Romantics, was not to increase his tolerance of diverse values but to increase his
nationalist fervor.[13] Alfred Milner, shortly after arriving

[11] See the collection of his articles, dating from 1916 to 1946, in *Society
as the Patient*. Reference here is to "World Order and Cultural Diversity," in *ibid.*, pp. 389–95.

[12] Cf. Kluckhohn, *Mirror for Man*, p. 273: "The anthropologist's solution is unity in diversity: agreement on a set of principles for world
morality but respect and toleration for all activities that do not threaten
world peace."

[13] Hayes, *The Historical Evolution of Modern Nationalism*, pp. 103–4.

in Egypt to serve under Sir Evelyn Baring, expressed his hope that international hatred and suspicion could be reduced by getting the nations "to understand one another better." Sir Evelyn, imparting the wisdom of experience, replied: "I'm afraid, my dear Milner, that the better they understand one another, the more they will hate one another."[14] The political scientist Karl Deutsch, summing up the evidence, concludes that "many emotionally, culturally, and politically sensitive individuals react to a sojourn abroad . . . with a far stronger assertion of nationalism and of allegiance to their own language, culture, and people."[15]

Frank urges increased knowledge of other cultures. He hopes that increased knowledge will produce a humility and forbearance that will serve as the firm basis of a productive, peaceful cooperation among all people as they face their common "life tasks."[16] But increased knowledge, while it makes some people humble, makes others more arrogant. On balance, will increased knowledge lead to a big enough increase in tolerance?[17] Since we cannot assume that it will, we can only say that it should. Frank's plea is that people ought to be more tolerant, and his argument is that the plea for tolerance is scientifically based. That, unfortunately, is not enough to establish its practical relevance.

14 Oliver, *The Endless Adventure*, III, 177n.

15 Deutsch, "The Growth of Nations: Some Recurrent Patterns of Political and Social Integration," *World Politics*, V (1953), 185.

16 Cf. Kluckhohn again: "But the world with all its variousness can still be one in its allegiance to the elementary common purposes shared by all peoples." *Mirror for Man*, p. 289.

17 And how big is big enough? This question will be considered in ch. vi, below. The difficulties and the possibilities of promoting international cooperation through increased understanding are well illustrated in *Diversity of Worlds*, a report on a conference of Frenchmen and Americans by two politically sophisticated *rapporteurs*, Raymond Aron and August Heckscher. See especially their concluding remarks.

We have not exhausted the meaning of the phrase "from knowledge, peace." In Frank's article, knowledge was to be the road to greater tolerance. In other formulations the knowledge gained by studying different cultures is to be put to use to improve the various societies (or to make one great society) so that war will no longer be an accepted social institution. The reasoning goes something like this: War is simply a social institution, not a necessary product of man's nature. This is proved by the fact that in some societies war is unknown. Since institutions are social inventions, if we want to get rid of one institution, we must invent another to take its place.[18] People engage in duels only so long as the custom of dueling exists in their society. Trial by combat gives way to trial by jury when people perceive the bad effects of the old system and invent a better one. Warfare, like the duel and trial by combat, "is just an invention known to the majority of human societies by which they permit their young men either to accumulate prestige or avenge their honor."[19] But how can we devise the social invention that will make war as obsolete as the duel? Margaret Mead gives the answer: "If we wish to build a world which will use all men's diverse gifts, we must go to school to other cultures, analyze them and rationalize our findings. We must find models and patterns which, orchestrated together on a world scale, will make a world as different from the old as the machine world was from the craft industries of the Middle Ages." We must learn whatever we can from wherever we can. We must study the rapidly disappearing primitive tribes in order to tap their wisdom before the chance to do so is irrevocably lost. We must train "a legion of men and women who will understand

18 Mead, *And Keep Your Powder Dry*, pp. 182–83, 211–14, 242.
19 Mead, "Warfare Is Only an Invention—Not a Biological Necessity," *Asia*, XL (1940), 402–5.

the highly technical job of analyzing civilizations, of using institutions and sets of habits to build with, as well-trained engineers use torques and stresses and tensions." We "must know what the Chinese mothers say to their babies and how they hold them, to develop their special virtues; and what the Russian mothers say to their babies and how they hold them, to develop theirs." We must ask: "What have the English and the Australians, the French and the Greeks and the Abyssinians and the Chinese, the Russians and the Brazilians, AND the Germans, the Japanese, the Italians and the Hungarians to contribute."[20]

We had better pause to ask what all of this is for. It is for peace, or, more accurately, for the preservation of our values as peacefully as possible. But just how do we get from that Chinese mother whispering baby talk, to peace in the world? Just how do we use what we have learned about Hungarians and Brazilians, or Samoans, to decrease the incidence of violent conflict? Mead wants us to use all the information we can get to engineer a new society in which the opportunities open to every individual are maximized and aggressive tendencies are effectively discouraged.[21] If for the moment we grant her utopian assumption that cultural anthropology, if we have enough of it, will tell us how to engineer a society for peace, what needs to be said of her second assumption—that the knowledge could be put to work effectively? How can the changes she calls for be brought about? One way she mentions is education. But, as Kurt Lewin remarks, "It seems to be easier for society to change education than for education to change society." Moses led Israel forty years in the wilderness so that the slave generation might die and a new generation learn to live in

---

[20] Mead, *And Keep Your Powder Dry*, pp. 9, 235, 249, 256, 259. And cf. the second of President Eisenhower's statements quoted on p. 9 of ch. i.
[21] *Ibid.*, pp. 139–40, 187, 240, 256.

freedom. There may, Lewin says, be no faster method for the permanent cultural reeducation of a whole country.[22] Ruth Benedict expresses the same estimate still more positively. "Even given the freest scope by their institutions," she writes, "men are never inventive enough to make more than minute changes. From the point of view of an outsider the most radical innovations in any culture amount to no more than a minor revision."[23] And, strangely enough, the conclusion was anticipated by Mead herself. The great and far-reaching changes in culture, she wrote in a book first published in 1928, "are the work of time, a work in which each individual plays an unconscious and inconsiderable part."[24] The point is not to accuse her of inconsistency because over a period of fourteen years she changed her mind. The point is simply that her earlier attitude seems the more realistic and is the one that other social scientists, at least when writing about almost any problem other than war, have most often adopted. The anthropologists are, of all the behavioral scientists, most likely to have the "big picture" in view. They are also the ones who most often discourage the expectation that orderly social change can be produced rapidly.

The duel analogy is as misleading to the modern anthropologist as it was to the nineteenth-century pacifist. If the work of the anthropologist contains any promise for world peace, it is the promise that by listening to him, and to many others as well, we may be able to inch forward now and then. Lewin, Benedict, and Mead in her more conservative youth cautioned against the expectation that scientifically gathered data can be used to produce major social change. The specific terms of the caution issued by

[22] Lewin, *Resolving Social Conflicts*, pp. 4, 55.
[23] Benedict, *Patterns of Culture*, p. 76; cf. pp. 226, 229, 251.
[24] Mead, *Coming of Age in Samoa*, p. 154.

Mead are instructive.   Comparative study of cultures convinced her that adolescence need not be a period of vexation.   In Samoan society it is not so.   Culture pattern,
not human nature, accounts for adolescent frustration.
Why then can American parents not apply Samoan techniques to help the adjustments of at least their own children?   The answer is best given in Mead's words: "The
individual American parents, who believe in a practice
like the Samoan, and permit their children to see adult
human bodies and gain a wider experience of the functioning of the human body than is commonly permitted
in our civilisation, are building upon sand.   For the child,
as soon as it leaves the protecting circle of its home, is
blasted by an attitude which regards such experience in
children as ugly and unnatural."[25]   The parents who perform the experiment will likely do more harm than good.
If all, or substantially all, American families followed the
enlightened practice, our adolescents would presumably be
happier.   But Mead is too good an anthropologist to expect anything like that to happen.[26]   Because most families will not consciously and voluntarily adopt a practice
that violates mores built up over centuries, it does no
good, in fact it does harm to the children involved, for a
few to do so.[27]

The solution that is rational if substantially everyone
follows it may be worse than useless if adopted by a minority.   If this is true as applied within a society to the ways

[25] *Ibid.*, p. 145.

[26] *Ibid.*, p. 154: "But, unfortunately, the conditions which vex our
adolescents are the flesh and bone of our society, no more subject to
straightforward manipulation upon our part than is the language which
we speak."

[27] What can parents do?   Mead says they must teach their children
how to think, rather than what to think.   They must teach them to
accept the burden of choice and to be tolerant. (*Ibid.*, p. 161.) This
would seem to require as much innovation as would the teaching of
new sex habits!

parents rear their children, may it not also be true of attempts to "restructure" societies for peace? War, like adolescent vexation, is not inherent in human nature. Comparative anthropology proves this. But is it any easier to root war out of a world society than it is to root adolescent frustration out of ours? Is it enough to say, with Benedict and Lewin, that the process will be unconscionably slow? Must we not introduce the problem of timing—the difficulty of obtaining simultaneous action among independent units, like families or states—as an additional complicating factor? If one or a small number of states were to catapult some behavioral scientists into positions where they would pass upon policy, how would that increase the chances for world peace? In such a circumstance, advice on how to "keep your powder dry" might be more important than concern for the nostrums that would mean peace among states if adopted by all of them.[28]

Raising the question of practicability has led to the identification of two constant and pervasive difficulties: the time required for change and the timing of the changes. There is an intermediate difficulty equally as crucial: How does a policy scientist begin to change even a single society? When Lasswell says that the point is no longer to reorganize governments but to reorient minds, is this because the organization of government is the less important task, or because it is already, in some states at least, pretty well taken care of? Would Lasswell, if he could have his wish, rather change the Soviet system of education or the Soviet system of government? The question makes no sense. But the reason it makes no sense is interesting:

[28] Behavioral scientists might, of course, be able to give advice on how to do this, as is implied in Mead's title and mentioned occasionally by her. See *And Keep Your Powder Dry*, p. 214, and her "The Study of National Character," in Lerner and Lasswell, eds., *The Policy Sciences*.

one cannot conceive of a change in Soviet education without a prior change in Soviet government.[29]   If we could
give Soviet children the kind of education the behavioral
scientists would prescribe, then we might entertain some
hope for a change in the Soviet government, say, twenty
years from now.   But the "if" is not operational, and the
disciplines comprised by the behavioral sciences cannot
suggest ways of making it so.

We have raised three problems.   First, the problem of
pace: How much time will it take to remodel people and
societies for peace even assuming that we have determined
scientifically just what changes are needed?   And then
what we might call the political problem on two levels:
How does one institute change within a society, and how
does one deal with the added complications that arise when
two or more societies must be dealt with?   These difficulties are widely reflected in the literature of the behavioral
sciences, as will be illustrated in the following discussion.
The discussion will fall into three pieces, roughly reflecting the three preceding critical considerations.

1.   Isaiah Berlin has characterized the new outlook in
political philosophy as the "notion that answers to problems exist not in rational solutions, but in the removal of
the problems themselves."[30]   The view is nowhere better
exemplified than in the literature of the behavioral sciences.   Can we not stop this concentration on trapping
rats, asks the psychiatrist-anthropologist Alexander Leigh-

[29] Cf. Lewin, above, p. 52. Difficulties like this account for Lasswell's
stipulation that world government must precede world order.   At least
that seems to be the implication of the following sentence: "The prerequisite of a stable order in the world is a body of symbols and practices
sustaining an elite which propagates itself by peaceful methods and
wields a monopoly of coercion which it is rarely necessary to apply to the
uttermost." *World Politics and Personal Insecurity*, p. 237.   Cf. below,
pp. 68–72.

[30] Berlin, "Political Ideas in the Twentieth Century," *Foreign Affairs*,
XXVIII (1950), 356–57.

ton, and concentrate on the conditions that breed them? What we need, he says, is the "physician's obsession with getting at causes and not tinkering with symptoms only."[31] But sometimes doctors do deal with symptoms rather than causes. They prescribe spectacles, for example, and some people go through most of their lives in this unhappy state, with the cause still there, resigned to compensating for, rather than removing, the problem. The practice is not an unusual one. Frank Lloyd Wright, when confronted with the problem of designing a hotel to be built in an area where earthquakes occur frequently, did not say: "See here, your buildings have been falling down because of the earthquakes. Remove the cause—earthquakes—and I'll design a very nice hotel for you." In the political sphere as well this kind of adaptation to circumstances is often used. The American and British governments might be taken as examples of mechanical schemes that have worked rather well.[32] A police force is another such mechanical device that has its positive virtues, although Leighton's logic, if strictly applied, would force us to condemn policemen for diverting community resources into the "trapping of rats" when society should be busy educating them to behave as tame white mice.

Certainly, rather than use a mechanical device, it would be preferable to have one's eyes *cured*. Admittedly Wright's problem would have been greatly simplified, and he could have built a nicer hotel for less money, if some physical scientist had first *solved* the earthquake problem.

[31] Leighton, *Human Relations*, p. 161.

[32] Productive cooperation of large numbers of men over extended periods of time has traditionally depended on two things: the existence of a community of interest and feeling and the use of mechanical devices to preserve order within it. The behavioral sciences, with their penchant for basic causes, often overlook the indispensable role and the positive contributions of the mechanical devices, which, in their eyes, deal more with symptoms than with causes.

And it might be infinitely preferable to have the behavioral scientists improve men and conditions so that governments and police forces could be dispensed with. But if we could imagine this possible, we would still have to ask how long it would take. James Miller speaks as though fifteen years, dating from 1948, would be just about enough time to bring the millennium.[33] T. H. Pear betrays the same naïveté. The war-minded attitude can be identified, he says, and, because attitudes arise through social learning, it can be changed. To accomplish this, little time would be required, for "culture-patterns can be changed quickly," as is proved, he says, by the Maoris, the Japanese, and the Russians.[34] So long as one fails to consult the historical evidence in any detail, this statement may be convincing. In every social change, however, there is a relation between time and force. Generally speaking, the greater the force the more rapidly social change will occur. The Maoris and the Japanese were both suddenly subject to the impact of a powerful civilization almost entirely new to them. Under the impact they changed many of their past customs—and kept many others. In the case of the Maoris and the Japanese, physical force supplemented the force constituted by cultural impact. In the case of the Russians, it was more nearly physical force alone. In any event, it would be difficult, in view of both the time and the force factors, to predict just what changes would be produced by just what means.[35]

The error into which Miller and Pear, and Mead at her

[33] Miller, "Psychological Approaches to the Prevention of War," in Dennis *et al., Current Trends in Social Psychology.*
[34] Pear, "Peace, War and Culture-Patterns," in Pear, ed., *Psychological Factors of Peace and War,* p. 21.
[35] The keenest and most sobering comments on the problems of planning and prediction that I have seen are made by Chester I. Barnard, "On Planning for World Government," in *Approaches to World Peace,* pp. 825–58.

worst, have fallen is the old rationalist fallacy, the identification of control with knowledge. They are assuming that once we know how to end war, we have solved the problem—that the problem is all one of knowing and not at all one of doing.[36] If wars are caused by immaturities and anxieties[37] or by neuroses and maladjustments[38] or by frustrations encountered in the process of socialization,[39] or by some combination of such causes, and if the behavioral scientists can tell us what should be done to remove these causes, we still have a good bit more than half the battle to fight.

For world peace we must start on the community level to develop "people with greater understanding and capacity to act in international affairs." So urges Alexander Leighton.[40] "The removal of tensions which lead to war is a thing which has never yet been done, but people are slow to try new means to avert it." So writes John Rickman, noted British psychiatrist.[41] "No peace without mental health." These words Otto Klineberg quotes with

[36] Cf. H. V. Dicks, "Some Psychological Studies of the German Character," in Pear, ed., *Psychological Factors of Peace and War*, p. 217: "We are literally threatened with extinction unless we learn to understand, and so control, the people who have the possibility of setting the enormous destructive forces in motion." And notice how difficult it is to conceive a possible relation between the activities of the Unesco Tensions Project (see Klineberg, *Tensions Affecting International Understanding*, pp. 215–17, for a summary list of activities in progress) and any effective action to prevent war. The same must be said of Allport's list of proposed research topics. "Guide Lines for Research in International Co-operation," in Pear, ed., *Psychological Factors of Peace and War*, pp. 155–56.

[37] Cf. Harry Stack Sullivan, "Tensions Interpersonal and International: A Psychiatrist's View," in Cantril, ed., *Tensions That Cause Wars*, ch. iii.

[38] Cf. John Rickman, "Psychodynamic Notes," in *ibid.*, ch. v.

[39] Cf. Dollard *et al.*, *Frustration and Aggression*, especially pp. 88–90: and John Dollard, "Hostility and Fear in Social Life," in Newcomb and Hartley, eds., *Readings in Social Psychology*.

[40] Leighton, "Dynamic Forces in International Relations," *Mental Hygiene*, XXXIII (1949), 23.

[41] Rickman, "Psychodynamic Notes," in Cantril, ed., *Tensions That Cause Wars*, p. 203.

approval.[42]   If we could rebuild people and rebuild societies we could have peace: this is the promise contained in
the examples just cited.   The nature of the promise is
such that he who bases his hope for peace on it becomes
thereby a utopian.   There is, however, another possibility.
One may accept the premises and reject the note of optimism.   George Kisker, for example, starts out in much
the same way as Miller and Pear.   For peace, he writes, we
must seek to "understand the minds" of men; only when
we deal with their "motives" do we approach the "fundamental levels of the problem."   For world peace we must
first put our own homes and minds in order.[43]   But as a
psychologist Kisker has to admit that a solution having
clear thinking as its first requirement is no solution at all.
He concludes:

> It has been pointed out that since intelligence and good sense have
> never held sway for more than brief periods in human affairs, there
> is little reason to believe that such intelligence and good sense are
> likely to predominate in the near future.   Considering the psycho-
> logical and social immaturity of mankind, it is naïve to hope that
> men in our time can learn to live at peace with themselves or with
> others.[44]

The easy identification of knowledge and control results
either in a roseate, but sterile, optimism or in the blackest
pessimism.   Either way what originally seemed like the
promise of the policy sciences quickly withers away.

2.   Mead, in her prescriptions for building a peaceful
world, continually uses the personal pronoun "we": "If
we wish to build a world . . ."; "If we set ourselves the
task . . ."; "We must find models and patterns. . . ."[45]
Who are the "we" and how do they bring about the

[42] Otto Klineberg, "The United Nations," in Kisker, ed., *World Tension*,
p. 281.
[43] Kisker, "Conclusions," in Kisker, ed., *World Tension*, pp. 303–5, 313.
[44] *Ibid.*, p. 316.
[45] See above, pp. 51–52.

changes required for a world at peace? Klineberg has pointed out that agreement with Unesco's emphasis on the minds of men leaves unanswered the question: Whose minds are important? "Do the tensions related to international conflict arise in the minds of the mass of the people, or are they significant only when they influence those leaders responsible for the international policy of their respective countries?"[46] Klineberg answers, properly, that both are important in different ways. While remembering that the elites are recruited from the public at large and share in its opinions and prejudices, one may, with Gabriel Almond, "speak of the policy and opinion elites, the articulate policy-bearing stratum of the population which gives structure to the public, and which provides the effective means of access to the various groupings. One might almost say 'who mobilize elites, mobilizes the public.'"[47] The role of the elites would seem to offer the behavioral scientist an opportunity to apply his techniques. And so some of them have thought.

The thought is clearly justified if it is argued simply that a wider familiarity with some of the findings and conclusions of the behavioral sciences could help many political and social leaders in the performance of their daily tasks. More than this is often meant. William Borberg, formerly permanent representative of Denmark at the United Nations, clearly and succinctly presents the fairly widespread view that the way to get world peace is to apply what the behavioral scientists (here primarily the psychologists and psychiatrists) know to the training and selection of those who run governments.[48] Men *want* peace, he says, yet they have wars. This must mean that

46 Klineberg, *Tensions Affecting International Understanding*, p. 4.
47 Almond, *The American People and Foreign Policy*, p. 138.
48 Borberg, "On Active Service for Peace," *Bulletin of the World Federation for Mental Health*, II (1950), 6–9.

there are somewhere some mistakes in organization. Discarding the hypothesis that there may be something wrong in organization at the international level, he concludes that the fault has been in the leadership of the Great Powers. Twice in our lifetime men mentally unfit have been brought to positions of such power that they were able to plunge the greater part of the world into horrible wars. "Must we," asks Borberg, "necessarily have a shooting war for domination or for ideologies, in the middle of the twentieth century, when science might solve almost all our problems?" Borberg thinks not. He finds his hope in the increased competence of the mental health experts. They will, he says, recognize the leader who says " 'my ideology or your death' " as "an obsessed, domineering, unintegrated personality, who . . . is in reality fighting his own childish egotism. In other words he is a patient—but he is armed." But what to do about it? "Your human duty and your duty as scientists," he says to the mental health experts, "is by all the scientific means at your disposal to prevent him from remaining in power." George Kisker goes further. We should prevent psychological incompetents from getting into positions of power in the first place; we should recognize that political leaders must be selected on bases other than emotion, political manipulation, or historical accident.[49]

If this were done, we might very well be able to screen out the Hitlers, the Mussolinis, the Francos, and maybe

[49] Kisker, "Conclusions," in Kisker, ed., *World Tension*, p. 310. Kisker's statement is reminiscent of Plato and of many "scientific" approaches through the ages. Behavioral-science literature provides a fairly large number of examples of this kind of thinking, some of which appear in the present chapter. A striking example is the following statement by Ralph Linton: "The really successful society is the one which trains its members to be content with harmless symbols and to strive toward goals which it can award them without inconvenience." "Present World Conditions in Cultural Perspective," in Linton, ed., *The Science of Man in the World Crisis*, p. 206.

even some United States congressmen. This would no doubt improve governments and might thereby increase the prospects for peace. But is it conceivable that we, whoever the "we" may be, will be able to persuade the governments of the world to adopt the scheme? Is it, for example, likely that we could establish the psychological screening system in the United States? And what would we do if some wily fellow, a new Hitler, should slip through the meshes of some other country's screen? To say that we should get rid of him by "all the scientific means" of the mental health experts, if it means anything at all, must mean that tyrannicide is to be numbered among their scientific methods. Or perhaps the exactitude of the tests applied by the experts would enable one country to proceed with enough certainty to justify its undertaking a preventive war against the newly enslaved country? In the 1860s, psychologists might have agreed that in the interests of peace and stability both Bismarck and Napoleon III would have to go. And some might have advocated getting rid of Palmerston and Lord John Russell as well. But to act on the psychologist's advice would have caused more wars than it could ever have prevented.

This is obviously not what Borberg intends. His recommendations are, on the contrary, innocuous. He advocates peace through the rewriting of the Preamble to Unesco's Charter. "Since war begins in the minds of men," he would have it read, "it is *in the minds of those men who are most influential in decisions for or against war* that the defenses of peace must be constructed." We should seek to explain to the leaders what the social sciences, and especially the psychological sciences, might do; for if we can just change their outlook we might well have peace.

Such an approach to world peace rests on the simple assumption that since we know the answer, fully or in large part, to the question of why wars occur, all that remains is to get some policy makers to listen to it.   Adherents of this approach are legion.   We shall cite two.[50]   Hadley Cantril, introducing the separate and joint products of a Unesco conference, writes:

> If those responsible for high policy could and would act on the combined advice of these eight social scientists as contained in their common statement, there is little doubt in my mind that the tensions now being experienced by people all over the world would be decreased with considerably more speed and surety than seems now to be the case.[51]

Gordon Allport, at the conclusion of one of his contributions to world peace, warns:

> Should any "hard-headed" statesman scorn the guide lines here offered as an expression of futile idealism, he himself would stand revealed as the most impractical of men.   For scientific facts in the social field, as in any field, can be disregarded only with peril.   The Einsteinian equation, $E = MC^2$, was once dismissed as pedantry.   The formula led to the release of atomic energy.   The "pedantry" of social science might even now contribute enormously to the establishment of peace and international co-operation were its applications understood and employed by policy makers.[52]

I am afraid that if I were a statesman, hardheaded or not, I should have great difficulty knowing which guide lines to follow.   This is not only because much of the advice given by one behavioral scientist is contradicted by other behavioral scientists, but also because most of the advice given by one man, or as the consensus of one group, is

[50] It is only fair to point out that examples can easily be found among the more politically oriented as well, of whom world-goverrment advocates are merely the most obvious.

[51] Cantril, ed., *Tensions That Cause Wars,* p. 14.

[52] Allport, "Guide Lines for Research in International Cooperation," in Pear, ed., *Psychological Factors of Peace and War,* p. 154; cf. p. 143: "Policy makers . . . can and should open their minds continually to the documented advice of social scientists. When it is good, they should follow it."

either hopelessly vague or downright impossible to follow. Take the "common statement" of Cantril's eight as an example. They are for educational systems that oppose national self-righteousness; they believe that nations should see themselves as others do; and they are for more international research in the field of the social sciences. These fairly specific suggestions are preceded by two more general in scope. We ought to maximize social justice, and, because peace requires keeping national tensions and aggressions within manageable proportions and directing them to constructive ends, "fundamental changes in social organization and in our ways of thinking are essential."[53] Of the suggestions here given, it is hard to see how the ones that a government might follow could bring world peace in the near or in the far-distant future. And the ones that might bring peace provide no practical guidance at all.

In summary, we can say that with a working-through-the-leaders approach, two problems arise: What advice shall we give them, and how shall we ensure that the leaders of all the important countries follow it? In the examples so far considered, the behavioral scientists have written as though the first problem were all-important. Actually, the second is the more important, as will presently be argued.

3. There is a marked tendency among behavioral scientists to require some kind of willingness on the part of the nations to cooperate before their solutions can take effect. This is reflected in Cantril's words, "if those responsible for high policy could and would act on the combined advice. . . ." It is made more explicit by John Swanton. "If, without any further world organization," he writes, "the nations of the earth could agree to settle their diffi-

[53] Cantril, ed., *Tensions That Cause War*, pp. 17–21.

culties in peaceful ways and cooperate to enforce such set-
tlements on all nations which persist in resorting to violence, and if they gave sufficient evidence of their genuine
determination to do so, the master nerve of war would be
severed."[54]   Cantril overlooks the fact that it is somewhat
harder to get the policy makers of the various states to take
the combined advice of any group than it is to figure out
what the content of that advice should be.   Swanton simply puts all the difficulties into the "if" clauses.   If, as
they seem to assume, a unanimous and constant agreement among states, or their governors, is the first necessity,
can they tell us how to get such agreement, or only how
to operate after we have it?   Too often what the behavioral scientists have said is: If only men (or societies) were
all well adjusted and rational, then we would have peace.[55]
They have then gone on to write—and this is where one
must become critical—as though the behavioral sciences
are useful because they can help us once we reach this
state of near, if not utter, perfection.   In other words,
their effectiveness begins immediately after the problem is
solved.

There is a complementary and perhaps even more widespread illusion, the illusion that the behavioral scientists
are advancing the cause of world peace when they propose solutions that depend for their efficacy upon the prior
existence of world government.[56]   This is often done by

54 Swanton, *Are Wars Inevitable?* p. 33.

55 Cf. K. T. Behanan, "Cultural Diversity and World Peace," in Dennis
et al., Current Trends in Social Psychology, p. 69: "The peace of the
world must be founded, if it is not to fail, upon the intellectual and moral
solidarity of mankind, upon a common view of values, which common
view can be created only by the universal development in the minds of
all peoples of a rational, scientific outlook on life and its problems."

56 A variant here is to offer advice with the promise that we shall find
it useful only after the national governments have improved somewhat.
Cf. Abram Kardiner: "The triumph of empirically derived directives for

implication. The French sociologist Georges Gurvitch, regarding international tensions as primarily artificial, would compel nations to abandon their ignorance of each other and to eliminate "distortions of the truth, false rumors, false representation of national characters, etc. . . . from the radio, movies, press, and textbooks of all nations." This would be done by "some international action possibly concerted by Unesco."[57]   A good bit of concerting would quite obviously be required.   Is it imaginable that this could be done by any international organization lacking the principal attributes of government?   It is not, yet Gurvitch apparently considers this part of his proposed program as sociological as the rest.[58]   Gordon Allport's reasoning is similar.   "The indispensable condition of war," he writes, "is that people must *expect* war and must prepare for war, before, under war-minded leadership, they make war."   The way to end war is then to end the expectation of war: "Only by changing the expectation in both leaders and followers, in parents and in children, shall we eliminate war."   This is a little baffling until we find out how he hopes that the change in expectation will be brought about. The UN is, he says, "dedicated . . . to altering expectancies.   It provides a means for making peaceful solutions of conflicts possible. . . . the success of

---

social action can only follow in the wake of a triumph for greater democracy and of an increased desire to gain insight into the psychological fabric of the forces that can either hold society together or tear it apart and destroy it." "The Concept of Basic Personality Structure as an Operational Tool in the Social Sciences," in Linton, ed., *The Science of Man in the World Crisis*, p. 122.

[57] Georges Gurvitch, " A Sociological Analysis of International Tensions," in Cantril, ed., *Tensions That Cause Wars*, p. 252.

[58] One wonders, for example, if Gurvitch could have remained optimistic had he recalled the long history of political controversy in France over questions of educational policy, a controversy that in the interwar years was often rooted in official doubts about the national and military orientation of teachers.

UN will be guaranteed as soon as the people and their leaders really *expect* it to succeed." And he concludes that *"when men are fully confident that international organizations can eradicate war, they will then at last succeed in doing so."*[59] Nothing that Allport has written reveals how the expectation can become real unless the nations somehow achieve a magically complete and enduring agreement never to fight no matter what their other disagreements, or unless the UN achieves the powers traditionally associated with government.

While some of the behavioral scientists rely implicitly on a future world government to make real the psychological or sociological solutions they have advanced, others of them have made this dependence explicit. The behavioral scientist may be driven to the conclusion that world government is necessary by an awareness of the immense complications and contradictions in the causal factors leading to any act of war. "Only in a very loose and general sense," Mark May points out, "can it be said that fear favors war and a sense of security promotes peace, that war is motivated by hate and peace by love, or that war is favored by habits of competition and aggression while peace is promoted by habits of cooperation. Love for country is clearly a prominent motive in war and both fear and hatred may be used to motivate peace." This is borne out by May's observation that where states have a peaceful history with one another all of the following factors, many of which rest on contradictory psychological attitudes, may be found: dread of war, fear of defeat and the consequences of war, friendship based on fear of a common enemy, pacifism promoted by religious or educational forces, and friendship based on common ties of culture.

[59] Gordon W. Allport, "The Role of Expectancy," in Cantril, ed., *Tensions That Cause Wars*, pp. 48, 75, 77.

Peace, then, is made up of a compound of contradictory feelings and motives.[60]

May's thesis is that "the conditions which determine social attitudes and opinions, particularly those that are involved in war or peace, are in large part products of social conditioning." But what kind of social conditioning could produce for nation after nation the peculiar combinations of forces and feelings that have in point of historical fact produced periods of peace? There is for May only one solution transcending the difficulty: If we are to have peace, we must learn loyalty to a larger group. And before we can learn loyalty, the thing to which we are to be loyal must be created. Social psychology offers little hope for peace among independent sovereign states; a strong centralized authority, i.e., world government, becomes the "psychological" foundation for peace.[61] Except for the peculiar use of the word "psychological" in the last sentence, May is saying quite clearly that psychology and social psychology must depend on the political framework within which they operate. Lazarsfeld and Knupfer make the same point for the same reasons. "As for the hatred of war," they write, "the last few years have shown us that unwillingness to go to war on the part of some nations may operate merely to encourage aggression on the part of others. The social and psychological forces impelling rivalry between nations are too strong to be controlled by a vague allegiance to 'all men everywhere,' or to

[60] May, *A Social Psychology of War and Peace*, pp. 220, 225. Cf. Freud, *Civilization, War and Death*, ed. Rickman, p. 90.

[61] May, *A Social Psychology of War and Peace*, pp. 21, 30, 228–34. This is like calling world government the economic foundation of peace. May uses the word "psychological" in an all-inclusive sense. Thus the "psychological" foundation of peace is, in his mind, whatever foundation, political or otherwise, is required. This has the merit of bringing within his purview as a psychologist more of the relevant factors than many psychologists have considered, although the usage robs the word "psychological" of precise meaning.

the ideal of 'international cooperation.' It seems that a concrete international authority is needed around which people can build up new identifications and supranational loyalties." Once such a development has taken place, they add, other techniques, such as the use of mass communications, can profitably be used.[62]

A closely allied reason for the same conclusion is the fact, emphasized earlier, that the methods of the policy sciences are so very slow. The case is argued most clearly and cogently by E. F. M. Durbin.[63] It is his thesis that "war is due to the expression in and through group life of the transformed aggressiveness of individuals." Since personal character derives from environment as well as from inherited nature, it may be possible to "change the character of adult behaviour by changing the environment in which our unchanged hereditary element develops." We might be able to rear "a generation of men and women who will defend their rights and yet willingly concede equal rights to others, who will accept the judgment of third parties in the resolution of disputes, who will neither bully nor eat humble pie, who will fight, but only in defense of law, who are willing and friendly members of a positive and just society."[64] This we might be able to do, but at best it would take generations before our efforts would affect the course of international relations. "In the meantime, if this is all the hope there is we shall have per-

[62] P. F. Lazarsfeld and Genevieve Knupfer, "Communications Research and International Cooperation," in Linton, ed., *The Science of Man in the World Crisis,* p. 466.

[63] Durbin and Bowlby, *Personal Aggressiveness and War.* The following discussion is based on pp. 40–48.

[64] Cf. the conclusion of a political scientist who has attempted to apply the findings of anthropologists and psychologists to problems of international relations: "Instead of merely seeking to deprive men of the will to resist those whose aim is to enslave them, the goal of the minds-of-men theory might even be to strengthen their resistance in the face of threats of violence." Dunn, *War and the Minds of Men,* p. 11.

ished by half a dozen wars."[65]   But this is not all the hope, for the theory here developed "implies among many other important things for the study of society, a theory of the value of government."[66]   The fundamental aggressiveness of human beings is, according to Durbin, the cause of war.   If we could remove the cause by changing human beings we could end war, but we cannot change them quickly and in any case we cannot hope to eliminate all elements of aggressiveness.   Therefore, we must in the first instance rely on an approach that deals not with "causes" but with "symptoms," the forceful restraint of the aggressive minority.   The summary is worth giving in Durbin's own words:

Thus, as we see it, there are two ways and only two in which war can be reduced in its frequency and violence—one slow, curative, and peaceful, aimed at the removal of the ultimate causes of war in human character by a new type of emotional education—the other immediate, coercive, and aimed at symptoms, the restraint of the aggressor by force.[67]

But at this point can it any longer be said what is "cause" and what is "symptom"?   If, for example, one political structure may bring peace and another does bring war, the latter can appropriately be called the "cause" of war.   The reasoning is just that used by the psychologists who distinguish between men who are "spoiling for a

[65] Cf. Freud, *Civilization, War and Death*, ed. Rickman, p. 95: Those who would have peace await changes in men "conjure up an ugly picture of mills which grind so slowly that, before the flour is ready, men are dead of hunger."

[66] Cf. Tolman, *Drives toward War*, p. 92: Politics and psychology should combine to teach us the necessity of federating for our own preservation.

[67] Cf. Freud again, *Civilization, War and Death*, ed. Rickman, p. 88: "There is but one sure way of ending war and that is the establishment, by common consent, of a central control which shall have the last word in every conflict of interests.   For this, two things are needed: first, the creation of such a supreme court of judicature; secondly, its investment with adequate executive force."

fight" and those who are so well adjusted that they fight only for good reason (à la Durbin), and then go on to say that the existence of the former type is the "cause" (or, in other formulations, the "basic cause") of war.   If some men were not willing to fight, we would have no wars. From this point of view, the manipulating of men in order to make all of them nonfighters attacks the "basic cause" of war.   In the same way we can say: Within France men do not wage war, between France and Germany they do; the different political organization on the national and international levels must then account for this.   To manipulate political structure is consequently to attack the "basic cause" of war.

CONCLUSION

That he had established the possibility of science becoming a cumulative study, Galileo considered to be one of his most important contributions.   Thus after referring in one of his works to the "facts . . . I have succeeded in proving," he adds: "and what I consider more important, there have been opened up to this vast and most excellent science . . . ways and means by which other minds . . . will explore its remote corners."[68]   Natural scientists have been able to reach higher by standing on the shoulders of their predecessors.   Behavioral scientists often express the hope, and sometimes the conviction, that they can proceed in the same fashion.[69]   To date they have not.   Many of them, admitting this to be true, attribute it to the tender age of their disciplines, compared, for example, with phys-

[68] Galilei, *Dialogues concerning Two New Sciences,* tr. Crew and De Salvio, pp. 153–54.
[69] As an example of hope with some conviction, see Leiserson, "Problems of Methodology in Political Research," *Political Science Quarterly,* LXVIII (1953), 567.

ics or biology. As well as a becoming humility, this explanation contains implicit within it the promise that, given more time for basic research and the sharpening of tools, the behavioral sciences can, by applying increasingly large bodies of organized data to social problems, achieve a transformation of society that will compare favorably with the accomplishments of natural science.

While the scientists of society aim at cumulation, they display more noticeably a tendency to repeat past patterns. Thus some of the examples cited in the body of this chapter bring to mind the methods of the philosophers of the Enlightenment, others the optimism of nineteenth-century liberals; some the once seemingly easy assumption of the Marxists that institutions thwarting men can be rapidly sloughed off and replaced by more serviceable ones, others the touching faith of modern-day pacifists. To cite, in the order indicated, a few examples of the recurrence of thought patterns may help to suggest the limitations of social science that others have laid bare in more methodological and metaphysical critiques.

Helvétius thought that morality, *"the science of the means invented by men to live together in the most happy manner possible,"* would "advance in proportion as the people acquire more knowledge." And Diderot, sharing the conviction, designed his Encyclopedia at once to further and to diffuse such knowledge.[70] The equating of doing with knowing, identified above, finds here its closest parallel, and the two lines, distant in time, meet in content where we find Gordon Allport urging that for peace we must have "an *encyclopedia of the uniformities and*

[70] Helvétius, *A Treatise on Man,* tr. Hooper, p. 12n. Cf. Diderot's article "Encyclopédie," in *Oeuvres complètes de Diderot,* ed. Assézat, XIV, 415, where he describes the purpose of an encyclopedia as being, among others, "que nos neveux, devenant plus instruits, deviennent en même temps plus vertueux et plus heureux."

similarities in respect to aspirations, beliefs and practices of all peoples." [71]   The success of seventeenth-century science produced the scientific politics of the eighteenth century.   That body of thought found its critic in Hume; more recently the work has had to be done afresh by such critics as Niebuhr and Casserley.[72]

The parallel with nineteenth-century liberalism is often as impressive.   Norman Angell has served in the present as publicist for the classical economists' conviction that war is an uneconomic venture.   Angell believes, as many of them had believed, that with the lesson driven home wars would no longer be fought.   The broadening of terms does not disguise the fact that the sociologist W. Fred Cottrell has fallen prey to the same illusion.   After distinguishing five model situations in which peace is possible, he declares most promising the one in which it is clear to the elite that war is an unrewarding mode of behavior. His final paragraph drives home both his point and mine. "Among the present prerequisites for peace," he concludes, "the only one the present existence of which seems in doubt is a clear understanding on the part of all elites that war is inferior to peace in pursuit of their values." [73] Behavioral scientists often appear as nineteenth-century liberals with a less powerful method.   Allowing Cottrell to continue the paragraph makes clear his relation to Marx as well, and the indebtedness of both of them to the

71 Allport's comments on Arne Naess's "The Function of Ideological Convictions," in Cantril, ed., *Tensions That Cause Wars*, p. 289.   In Mann's *Magic Mountain*, Settembrini, a shrewd characterization of a nineteenth-century liberal, subspecies Mazzini, has spent the better part of a lifetime on a similar project, his labors fed by the illusion common to those just mentioned.

72 From among the many others who could be cited, I mention Casserley because his criticisms are fundamental and his work is not well known among American social scientists.   See his *Morals and Man in the Social Sciences.*

73 Cottrell, "Research to Establish the Conditions for Peace," *Journal of Social Issues*, XI (1955), 14, 20.

scientific politics of the Enlightenment. "But," he writes, "even if this estimate should prove to be false and it becomes clear that war will be sought under present conditions, then research can show how structure or other conditions must be altered to deprive presently powerful elites of their ability to choose war, or how some presently existing condition must be altered so that these elites will then choose not to go to war. Presumably, elites now make their decisions on the basis of some kind of calculation about the outcome of war." Knowledge leads to control, and control is possible because institutions, and thus men (or is it the other way around?), are infinitely manipulable. Marx, more realistic on one point at least, saw the relation between force and change. Big changes come with difficulty: a revolution is necessary to rid men of the "muck of ages." [74] But he was less safe, for he overlooked the fact that major force once set in motion is impossible to predict or to control. Ultimately both Cottrell and Marx are rationalists in politics, Marx overestimating the efficacy of reason following the socialist revolution, Cottrell overestimating as well the efficacy of reason in bringing about his proposed revolution in the ways of men.

Finally, considering a quality shared by pacifists and many behavioral scientists suggests the more general point that in the absence of an elaborated theory of international politics the causes one finds and the remedies one proposes are often more closely related to temper and training than to the objects and events of the world about us. The pacifist's appeal, like that of Alexander Leighton, is for treatment of the deep-seated causes of war. The one approaches this from the realm of spirit, the other with the techniques of psychiatry. The pacifist waits and quietly hopes that men will behave as God intended they should,

[74] Marx and Engels, *The German Ideology*, tr. Pascal, p. 69.

or goes out to convert others to the faith that is said to have moved mountains before and presumably can move them again. Faith, courage, and character are needed. The behavioral scientist has at times asked as much, and demonstrated as poorly how they might be sufficient. Thus Helmut Callis, seeking to identify the means to peace, writes: "As soon as we then have the courage and character to apply scientific knowledge to our social relations, man, the creator of culture, should also be able to find cultural means to attain for humanity the maximum rewards in living." [75]

The point of all this is not that every contribution the behavioral scientist can make has been made before and found wanting, but rather that the proffered contributions of many of them have been rendered ineffective by a failure to comprehend the significance of the political framework of international action. In such a circumstance, their prescriptions for the construction of a more peaceful world can only be accidentally relevant.

If all men were perfectly wise and self-controlled, we would have no more wars. If communities could be constructed, universally, that satisfied all of the desires and provided outlets for all of the potentially destructive drives of men, we would have no more wars. But the implied analysis of cause is inadequate, and the prescriptions based on it are those of idle dreamers. When idle dreamers awake they either become pessimists, like George Kisker, or they enlarge their analyses to include more of the relevant causal factors. The relevance of political structure is appreciated by those who, like May and Durbin, add to their social-psychological proposals for peace a stipulation that world government first be established. What is not

[75] Callis, "The Sociology of International Relations," *American Sociological Review*, XII (1947), 328.

realized by some of them is that their solutions have then become more political than social-psychological, and that unless they devise a way by which men of affairs can establish the kind of world government needed, they have proposed no solution at all. Social-psychological realism has here produced political utopianism. At the other extreme are those who simply ignore the role of politics and propose apolitical solutions as though they were to operate in a vacuum. They say in effect: "These proposals are solutions to the war problem—if only someone will accept them." Neither procedure gets us anywhere.

The failure to distinguish between fixed and manipulable causes is itself at least partly a product of ignoring the political context of social action. In the present chapter it was pointed out that the "preventive politics" of Lasswell assumes the existence of a particular political system. Perhaps because the assumption has not often been made explicit, its relevance is lost to the view of many behavioral scientists as they transfer their talents from the domestic to the international scene.[76] One cannot fail to be struck by this fact in any general examination of behavioral-science literature on the subject of war and peace. For example, Klineberg, in his survey of those past activities of the behavioral scientists that might contribute to understanding war and preventing it, nowhere finds occasion to mention politics. Allport considers psychology and psychiatry sufficient for understanding international relations in the immediate present. He adds that "for 'long-run' causation, social, historical, and eco-

[76] Cf. Almond's remark, in reviewing Kluckhohn's *Mirror for Man* and Leighton's *Human Relations:* "In making applications of their hypotheses to the international relations of modern nations . . . the anthropologists simply lack professional knowledge of modern politics." "Anthropology, Political Behavior, and International Relations," *World Politics,* II (1950), 281.

nomic influences are often decisive"—but not political influences.[77] "There is every reason to believe," writes Donald Young in his foreword to Klineberg's survey, "that what has been learned about interpersonal and intergroup relations within the borders of a single country, with suitable reorientation, can be applied to the understanding of people's behavior even when the complicating effects of a national boundary are involved."[78] But what reorientation is "suitable" is seldom considered. Without such "suitable reorientation," the insights of the behavioral scientists are like a number of pearls, or glass beads, lying around loose. Their value may be great but their use is slight unless they can either be placed in a setting or put on a string.

The relation between mathematics and economics provides a suggestive parallel. Most economists admit that mathematics has made important contributions to economic theory as well as having increased the ability of economists to handle their multifarious data. The contributions are possible where economists become mathematicians or where mathematicians are willing to acquire a sufficient knowledge of economic problems and theory. Alfred Marshall, a pioneer in mathematical economics and a distinguished student of mathematics before becoming an economist, steeped himself in economic theory before attempting mathematical formulations and even then continued to depreciate, perhaps unduly, the role of mathematical analysis.[79] Mathematics has contributed to economics; it has not replaced economics. The first is valuable, the second impossible. At the extreme, however, one finds behavioral scientists asserting that war and

[77] Allport criticizing Sullivan's "Tensions Interpersonal and International," in Cantril, ed., *Tensions That Cause Wars*, p. 136.
[78] Klineberg, *Tensions Affecting International Understanding*, p. viii.
[79] Hutchison, *A Review of Economic Doctrines*, pp. 63–74.

peace are not political problems but problems of individual and social adjustment. And those less extreme often betray an unwillingness to study the political problems and theories of international relations before offering to contribute their insights. The fault, of course, is not all theirs. One can easily identify and, if he chooses, study the main bodies of economic theory. Political theory, especially in the field of international relations, is more difficult to find. This may not mean that theory is here less important but that it is more difficult, or, more plausibly, not that it is more difficult but that for those seeking a theory that leads easily to the application of neat solutions it is less impressive.

Some of the behavioral scientists, one must admit, have made it clear that what they can do for a final solution of the war problem depends on the establishment of proper political conditions, and that what they can do in the meantime is to help their own governments maintain peace—or win wars—in an uneasy world. The limits of possible accomplishment are made narrower to the extent that the significance of the structure of international politics is more completely understood. Behavioral scientists facing a concrete problem—such as how to work harmoniously with allies—have proved less likely to make the kinds of errors we have been considering. This is simply another illustration of the present point: The more fully behavioral scientists take account of politics, the more sensible and the more modest their efforts to contribute to peace become.

International Conflict and the
Internal Structure of States

> However conceived in an image of the world, foreign policy is a phase of domestic policy, an inescapable phase.
>
> CHARLES BEARD, *A Foreign Policy for America*

THE first image did not exclude the influence of the state, but the role of the state was introduced as a consideration less important than, and to be explained in terms of, human behavior. According to the first image, to say that the state acts is to speak metonymically. We say that the state acts when we mean that the people in it act, just as we say that the pot boils when we mean that the water in it boils. The preceding chapters concentrated on the contents rather than the container; the present chapter alters the balance of emphasis in favor of the latter. To continue the figure: Water running out of a faucet is chemically the same as water in a container, but once the water is in a container, it can be made to "behave" in different ways. It can be turned into steam and used to power an engine, or, if the water is sealed in and heated to extreme temperatures, it can become the instrument of a destructive explosion. Wars would not exist were human nature not what it is, but neither would Sunday schools and brothels, philanthropic organizations and criminal gangs. Since everything is related to human nature, to explain anything one must consider more than human nature. The events to be explained are so many and so varied that human nature cannot possibly be the single determinant.

The attempt to explain everything by psychology meant, in the end, that psychology succeeded in explaining nothing. And adding sociology to the analysis simply substitutes the error of sociologism for the error of psychologism. Where Spinoza, for example, erred by leaving out of his personal estimate of cause all reference to the causal role of social structures, sociologists have, in approaching the problem of war and peace, often erred in omitting all reference to the political framework within which individual and social actions occur. The conclusion is obvious: To understand war and peace political analysis must be used to supplement and order the findings of psychology and sociology. What kind of political analysis is needed? For possible explanations of the occurrence or nonoccurrence of war, one can look to international politics (since war occurs among states), or one can look to the states themselves (since it is in the name of the state that the fighting is actually done). The former approach is postponed to Chapter VI; according to the second image, the internal organization of states is the key to understanding war and peace.

One explanation of the second-image type is illustrated as follows. War most often promotes the internal unity of each state involved. The state plagued by internal strife may then, instead of waiting for the accidental attack, seek the war that will bring internal peace. Bodin saw this clearly, for he concludes that "the best way of preserving a state, and guaranteeing it against sedition, rebellion, and civil war is to keep the subjects in amity one with another, and to this end, to find an enemy against whom they can make common cause." And he saw historical evidence that the principle had been applied, especially by the Romans, who "could find no better antidote to civil war, nor one more certain in its effects, than to oppose an enemy to the citizens."[1] Secretary of State William Henry Seward followed this reasoning when, in order to promote unity within the country, he urged upon Lincoln a vigorous foreign policy, which included the possibility of declaring war on Spain and France.[2] Mikhail Skobelev, an influential Russian military officer of the third quarter of the nineteenth century, varied the theme but slightly when he argued that the Russian monarchy was doomed unless it could produce major military successes abroad.[3]

The use of internal defects to explain those external acts of the state that bring war can take many forms. Such explanation may be related to a type of government that is thought to be generically bad. For example, it is often thought that the deprivations imposed by despots upon their subjects produce tensions that may find expression in foreign adventure. Or the explanation may be given in terms of defects in a government not itself considered bad. Thus it has been argued that the restrictions placed upon a government in order to protect the prescribed rights of its citizens act as impediments to the making and executing of foreign policy. These restrictions, laudable in original purpose, may have the unfortunate effect of making difficult or impossible the effective action of that government for the maintenance of peace in the world.[4] And, as a final example, explanation may be made in terms

[1] Bodin, *Six Books of the Commonwealth*, tr. Tooley, p. 168 (Book V, ch. v).

[2] "Some Thoughts for the President's Consideration," April 1, 1861, in Commager, ed., *Documents of American History*, p. 392.

[3] Herzfeld, "Bismarck und die Skobelewepisode," *Historische Zeitschrift*, CXLII (1930), 296n.

[4] Cf. Sherwood, *Roosevelt and Hopkins*, pp. 67–68, 102, 126, 133–36, 272, and especially 931; and Secretary of State Hay's statement in Adams, *The Education of Henry Adams*, p. 374. Note that in this case the fault is one that is thought to decrease the ability of a country to implement a peaceful policy. In the other examples, the defect is thought to increase the propensity of a country to go to war.

of geographic or economic deprivations or in terms of deprivations too vaguely defined to be labeled at all. Thus a nation may argue that it has not attained its "natural" frontiers, that such frontiers are necessary to its security, that war to extend the state to its deserved compass is justified or even necessary.[5] The possible variations on this theme have been made familiar by the "have-not" arguments so popular in this century. Such arguments have been used both to explain why "deprived" countries undertake war and to urge the satiated to make the compensatory adjustments thought necessary if peace is to be perpetuated.[6]

The examples just given illustrate in abundant variety one part of the second image, the idea that defects in states cause wars among them. It is possible, however, to think that wars can be explained by defects in some or in all states without believing that simply to remove the defects would establish the basis for perpetual peace. In this chapter, the image of international relations under consideration will be examined primarily in its positive form. The proposition to be considered is that through the reform of states wars can be reduced or forever eliminated. But in just what ways should the structure of states be changed? What definition of the "good" state is to serve as a standard? Among those who have taken this approach to international relations there is a great variety of definitions. Karl Marx defines "good" in terms of ownership of the means of production; Immanuel Kant in terms of abstract principles of right; Woodrow Wilson in terms of national self-determination and modern demo-

[5] Cf. Bertrand Russell, who in 1917 wrote: "There can be no good international system until the boundaries of states coincide as nearly as possible with the boundaries of nations." *Political Ideals*, p. 146.

[6] Cf. Simonds and Emeny, *The Great Powers in World Politics*, *passim;* Thompson, *Danger Spots in World Population*, especially Preface, chs. i, xiii.

cratic organization. Though each definition singles out different items as crucial, all are united in asserting that if, and only if, substantially all states reform will world peace result. That is, the reform prescribed is considered the sufficient basis for world peace. This, of course, does not exhaust the subject. Marx, for example, believed that states would disappear shortly after they became socialist. The problem of war, if war is defined as violent conflict among states, would then no longer exist.[7] Kant believed that republican states would voluntarily agree to be governed in their dealings by a code of law drawn up by the states themselves.[8] Wilson urged a variety of requisites to peace, such as improved international understanding, collective security and disarmament, a world confederation of states. But history proved to Wilson that one cannot expect the steadfast cooperation of undemocratic states in any such program for peace.[9]

For each of these men, the reform of states in the ways prescribed is taken to be the *sine qua non* of world peace. The examples given could be multiplied. Classical economists as well as socialists, aristocrats and monarchists as well as democrats, empiricists and realists as well as transcendental idealists—all can furnish examples of men who have believed that peace can be had only if a given pattern of internal organization becomes widespread. The prescriptions for forms of organization that will establish peace are reflections of the original analyses of the roles of some states in bringing about war. The different analyses could be compared in detail. Our purpose, however, is not so much to compare their content as it is to identify and criticize the assumptions that are commonly made, often unconsciously, in turning the analysis of cause into a

[7] See below, ch. v, pp. 125–28.
[8] See below, ch. vi, pp. 162–65.
[9] See below, pp. 117–19.

prescription for cure. For this purpose, we shall examine the political thought of nineteenth-century liberals. Because it is their thesis that internal conditions do determine external behavior, it is necessary first to consider their domestic political views. Doing so will also make it possible to draw some parallels between their strategies of political action internally and externally.

DOMESTIC POLITICS: LIBERAL VIEW

According to Hobbes, self-preservation is man's primary interest; but because enmity and distrust arise from competition, because some men are selfish, full of pride, and eager for revenge, everyone in a state of nature fears for his safety, and each is out to injure the other before he is injured himself. Finding life in a state of nature impossible, men turn to the state to find the security collectively that they are incapable of finding individually. The civil state is the remedy for the appalling condition of the state of nature, and, because for Hobbes there is no society, nothing but recalcitrant individuals on the one side and government on the other, the state must be a powerful one. Liberty Hobbes had defined as the absence of restraint, but men must sacrifice some liberties if they are to enjoy any of them and at the same time satisfy the impulse that looms larger, the impulse to stay alive.

There are three major variables in this analysis: the individual, his society, and the state. The first two variables determine the extent and type of functions the state must undertake. In individualistic theories, the state becomes the dependent variable. Members of the dominant schools of thought in late eighteenth- and nineteenth-century England were as individualistic as Hobbes, but they rejected usually Hobbes's view of human nature and always his opinion of the social results of selfishly motivated behavior. Most of them believed, on the one hand, that man is generally pretty good and, on the other, that even though individual behavior may be selfishly oriented, still there is a natural harmony that leads, not to a war of all against all, but to a stable, orderly, and progressive society with little need for governmental intervention.

The two most important questions that can be asked of any social-economic system are: What makes it run at all? What makes it run smoothly? To these questions, liberal political writers in nineteenth-century England answered almost unanimously that individual initiative is the motor of the system and competition in the free market its regulator. That the emphasis was on individual initiative is a point that scarcely need be labored. It is as evident in Adam Smith, who laid the formal foundations of English liberalism, as it is in John Stuart Mill, who marks its apex. Mill's conclusion that "the only unfailing and permanent source of improvement is liberty, since by it there are as many possible independent centres of improvement as there are individuals," is but an echo of the opinion expressed earlier by Smith when he wrote: "The uniform, constant, and uninterrupted effort of every man to better his condition, the principle from which public and national, as well as private, opulence is originally derived is frequently powerful enough to maintain the natural progress of things toward improvement, in spite both of the extravagance of government and of the greatest errors of administration." [10] Not only are individuals the source of progress in society, but they are themselves constantly improving. "The more men live in public," wrote Jeremy

[10] J. S. Mill, *On Liberty*, p. 87 (ch. iii); Smith, *The Wealth of Nations*, pp. 389–90 (Book II, ch. iii); cf. *The Theory of Moral Sentiments*, p. 218 (Part IV, ch. ii). Page references are to Schneider, ed., *Adam Smith's Moral and Political Philosophy*, which contains abridgments of *The Theory of Moral Sentiments*, *Lectures on Justice, Police, Revenue, and Arms*, and *An Inquiry into the Nature and Causes of the Wealth of Nations*.

Bentham, "the more amenable they are to the moral sanction." They become "every day more virtuous than on the former day . . . till, if ever, their nature shall have arrived at its perfection." Perfection may not be achieved, but progress toward perfection is as relentless as the downward course of rivers.[11] Restraints on individuals are then more than personally annoying denials of liberty, for they pollute the very wellsprings of social improvement.

"Leave us alone," a motto appearing on the title page of a Benthamite tract, is what the nineteenth-century liberal would have the citizen shout, and keep shouting, at his would-be governors.[12] But men, though they may be treading the path to perfection, have not yet reached its end; and government, though its laws restrain, does not constitute the only restraint exercised by men over men. Do not such considerations require, even in the minds of nineteenth-century liberals and utilitarians, a role for government larger than at first they seem to contemplate?

Liberals were inclined to limit government on principle, the principle following, as with Godwin, from an optimistic assessment of the moral qualities and intellectual capabilities of mankind. The utilitarians were inclined to limit government only by the test of efficiency. In what ways could government contribute most to the happiness of the greatest number? Could a given task be done better *by* the individual citizen or *for* him? That the answer given by Bentham and his followers was more often *by* than *for* is in large part attributable to the influence of Adam Smith. What is important here is not the old principle of the division of labor but the new argument that the results of labor divided in the production and distribution of goods can be brought together again and dis-

---

[11] Bentham, *Deontology*, ed. Bowring, I, 100–1.
[12] Bentham, "Observations on the Restrictive and Prohibitory Commercial System," in *Works*, ed. Bowring, III, 85.

tributed equitably without the supervision of government. In the past, the fact that each manufacturer, each tradesman, each farmer, seeks not the public welfare but his own private good had led to the conclusion that government regulation is necessary to prevent chaos. If the government does not superintend in the general interest, who will? Smith's answer is that, given certain conditions, the impersonal forces of the market will do it. Production will be efficiently managed and goods equitably distributed by the market mechanism alone.

By an exaggerated reliance on the free-market regulator, the liberal definition of the good state as the limited state could be maintained even by those who rejected the assumption frequently associated with liberalism—that man is infinitely perfectible. "So vice is beneficial found, when it's by justice lopp'd and bound": so reads a couplet from the famous *Fable of the Bees,* given by its author, Bernard Mandeville, the significant subtitle, "Private Vices, Public Benefits." The greed of each man, Mandeville is saying, prompts him to work hard to advance his own fortunes, and this is good for all of society. The very vices of *man* contribute, indeed are essential, to the progress of *society*.[13] This is the very epitome of the principle of harmony, the blind faith that Voltaire satirized in the person of Dr. Pangloss who, through endless adversity, continued to proclaim that all is for the best in this best of all possible worlds.[14] But if the greed of each man causes him to work hard, for his own good and incidentally for the good of

[13] Mandeville, *The Fable of the Bees,* p. 11. Cf. his preface: "I demonstrate that if mankind could be cured of the failings they are naturally guilty of, they would cease to be capable of being raised into such vast potent and polite societies."

[14] Mill's statement, in a letter written in 1868, that "since A's happiness is a good, B's a good, C's a good, &c., the sum of all these goods must be a good," is a summary statement of the harmony principle that is found in somewhat different words in all the utilitarian writers. *Letters,* ed. Elliot, II, 116.

society, it may also cause him to cheat, to lie, and to steal, for his own good only. Thus arises the function of government. As the Abbé Morellet, a contemporary of Adam Smith's, wrote in a letter to the liberal Lord Shelburne: "Since liberty is a natural state and constraints are on the contrary the unnatural state, by giving back liberty everything again takes its place and all is in peace, provided only that thieves and murderers continue to be hanged." [15] Criminals must be punished. At a minimum, government exists to provide security to persons and their property. To this proposition not only liberals and utilitarians but almost anyone who has thought seriously of the problems of man in society would agree, though with great differences in the definition of property.

Justice is the first concern of government, but is justice, defined in narrow legal terms, also the last concern? One can point to many statements of liberals and utilitarians to indicate that in their minds it is. Their belief in the strictly limited state can, however, be demonstrated more convincingly by pointing to their own reactions to social facts they find distressing. Adam Smith, for example, was disturbed by a tendency displayed by the employer class to take advantage of its economic position in order to maximize profits, by monopolistic measures, at the expense of the landed and laboring classes. Seldom, observes Smith, do people of the same trade meet together, "even for merriment and diversion, but the conversation ends in a conspiracy against the public, or in some contrivance to raise prices." The government's role? It should do nothing to encourage the members of a trade to come together.[16] So convinced was Smith that unnatural inequalities were the product of governmental interference, as no doubt to a

---

[15] *Lettres de l'abbé Morellet a Lord Shelburne*, p. 102.
[16] Smith, *The Wealth of Nations*, pp. 375–7 (ch. xi, conclusion); p. 368 (ch. x, part ii).

large extent they were in his day, that he denounced all
but the most narrowly defined police functions of government, going so far as to applaud the repeal of laws against
regrating, forestalling, and engrossing, though such laws
were instrumental in maintaining the free market that lay
at the foundation of his ideal system.[17]   A similar concern
is evident in Ricardo, though the problem is differently
defined.   Ricardo substituted landowners for Smith's employers as the class whose interests diverge from those of
the other two classes. The income of the landowners increases not so much because of their own efforts but because of the increased pressure of population on land.
They appear then as parasites feeding on the increased
product of labor and capital. The remedy?   Repeal the
Corn Laws, reduce governmental debt, and reveal to the
people the true principles of Malthus.   But it is in the
works of a publicist, Harriet Martineau, that the foolishness and danger of all governmental activity beyond the
catching of criminals is most forcefully argued.   In one of
her tales, written to reveal the principles of the new economics in ways that all who could read, or listen, could
understand, the surgeon, once he understands the facts of
political economy, not only discontinues his charitable
work in the dispensary and foundling hospital but also
persuades a misguided friend to stop the £20 he had been
giving to charity each year. These, Miss Martineau
demonstrates, are actions nobler, because more rational
and more courageous, than acts ordinarily termed philanthropic.   And government, were it not in fear of public
censure, would follow the example.   If the example is
difficult to follow, the reasoning is not.   Charity does not
cure poverty but increases it, not only by rewarding im-
providence but also by encouraging the improvident to

[17] Hutt, "Pressure Groups and *Laissez-Faire*," *South African Journal of Economics*, VI (1938), 17.

increase and multiply. To drive home the lessons of the tale, should anyone have missed them, Miss Martineau summarizes at the end:

The number of consumers must be proportioned to the subsistence-fund. To this end, all encouragements to the increase of population should be withdrawn, and every sanction given to the preventive check; *i.e.* charity must be directed to the enlightenment of the mind, instead of to the relief of bodily wants.[18]

This was good Malthus, but not good politics. Yet the Philosophic Radicals of the 1830s attempted to translate such principles into a political program. While the Chartists clamored for reforms that would bring tangible and immediate results—universal suffrage, factory legislation, a more liberal poor law—John Stuart Mill, spokesman for the Radicals, justified an upper- and middle-class suffrage, ridiculed the proposed law for an eight-hour workday, and argued that if wages were low and work unavailable it was not because competition was unregulated but rather because the poorer classes ignored the teachings of Malthus. The Radical program was largely negative—remove taxes on necessaries, forbid flogging in the army, repeal the Corn Laws—with one major positive policy added, the establishment of a system of national education.[19] Both the negative and positive aspects are faithful reflections of the two principles indentified earlier as the basis of utilitarian-liberalism. The effort was to proscribe state action in order to let the natural harmony of interests prevail.

But are the assigned functions of the state sufficient to maintain the conditions that a laissez-faire economy and a liberal society require? The necessary conditions are described frequently: approximately equal units competing

---

18 Martineau, *Cousin Marshall*, ch. viii and Summary of Principles, in her *Illustrations of Political Economy*, Vol. III.
19 Stephen, *The English Utilitarians*, Vol. III, ch. 1, sec. iii.

freely, and individuals morally responsible and mentally alert. So long as the competing units are approximately equal, their success will be decided by comparative efficiency in meeting consumer demand. It soon became apparent that Smith, in arguing that government interventions were the main source of unnatural inequalities, was guilty at least of historical overgeneralization. If, in the absence of governmental intervention, some units come to dwarf others, will not fair, or economic, competition be replaced by unfair, or power, competition? For those who recognized, and some liberals did, that property is potentially power, it follows that economic inequality must give some an advantage in power over others.[20] In a given field, the manufacturer who survives may then be, not the most efficient, but merely the one with enough resources to harry his competitors into bankruptcy. John Stuart Mill concerned himself with precisely such a circumstance. In fact he subscribed £10 to a Co-operative Plate-Lock Manufactory that, in his words, was struggling against "unfair competition on the part of the masters in the trade." It appeared that the masters would be financially able to carry on business at a loss for a long enough time to drive out their new competitors. This Mill believed might justly be termed "the tyranny of capital." [21] Though Mill continued to prefer private solutions, he recognized that they were not always sufficient. This is especially evident in his treatment of the land problem. In contrast to Ricardo's negative remedies, Mill urged that unearned increases in land values be taxed away and was even willing to contemplate the state as universal landlord.[22]

---

[20] For example, Godwin, *Political Justice*, I, 19; II, 465; J. S. Mill, *Letters*, ed. Elliot, II, 21.

[21] J. S. Mill, *Letters*, ed. Elliot, II, 21.

[22] J. S. Mill, "The Right of Property in Land," in *Dissertations and Discussions*, V, 279–94; *Political Economy*, ed. Ashley, Book II, ch. ii, secs. 5, 6.

In the person of John Stuart Mill, utilitarian-liberalism moved from proscribing state action to prescribing what kind of state action is desirable. And the desirability of state action increased once it was determined that an unfettered society does not automatically realize and maintain the conditions described as prerequisite to the effective functioning of the free-market regulator. Mill gave evidence of understanding this in his comments on the two matters of policy just cited. And he gave evidence of understanding that such specific problems point to an underlying theoretical problem when he wrote to Carlyle that the negative principle of laissez faire, once it has accomplished its necessary works of destruction, "must soon expire." [23] To be replaced by what? Mill attempted to base policy prescriptions on a distinction between two kinds of acts, those that affect only the actor and those that affect others.[24] But what act of an individual does not affect others? The criterion proposed is scarcely sufficient for judging the legitimacy of governmental activities. This is well illustrated by the fact that under it Mill could entertain the notion that proof of ability to support a family should be required before marriage, an invasion of the private sphere that causes many less liberal than he to shudder.[25] The difficulty is that Mill has proposed to test policy by a standard that derives from a concern for individual freedom, and this is only one of the twin pillars of a liberal society. Actually Mill's concern has shifted to the second. What concerns him more each year is the lack of justice with which the free-market regulator allocates rewards among those who participate in the processes of production. Laissez faire may increase production. Does

---

[23] J. S. Mill, *Letters*, ed. Elliot, I, 157.
[24] J. S. Mill, *On Liberty*, p. 115 (ch. v).
[25] J. S. Mill, *Letters*, ed. Elliot, II, 48; *Political Economy*, ed. Ashley, Book II, ch. xi, par. 4.

it fairly distribute the fruits? Mill thinks not. James Mill had thought that the protection of law over property would ensure to each the greatest possible quantity of the produce of his own labor. His son emphasizes that the reward of the individual is more often "almost in an inverse ratio" to his labor and abstinence.[26]

Liberals and utilitarians described conditions necessary for the fair and efficient functioning of a laissez-faire society. There was then latent in the very logic of liberalism the possibility that governmental action would be required to realize and to maintain those conditions. If liberals and utilitarians have correctly described the necessary conditions, they may have to do more than spread the laissez-faire gospel in order to create and maintain them. The state may have to intervene in ways not originally contemplated; for example, in order to prevent extreme economic inequalities from arising. The laws passed by governments are not the only restrictions on individual freedom. Property, become power, may require regulation *in the interest of free and effective competition!* The thought was at least dimly perceived by Adam Smith when he wrote that "in the race for wealth and honours and preferments, [each] may run as hard as he can, and strain every nerve and every muscle, in order to outstrip all his competitors. But if he should jostle, or throw down any of them, the indulgence of the spectators is entirely at an end. It is a violation of fair play, which they cannot admit of." [27] It was suggested in the self-proclaimed socialism of John Stuart Mill's later years, a socialism that was fundamentally a search for the conditions, which he thought were not realized in the England of his time, un-

[26] James Mill, "Government," in *Essays*, No. I, pp. 4–5; J. S. Mill, "Socialist Objections to the Present Order of Society," *Fortnightly Review*, February, 1879, reprinted in J. S. Mill, *Socialism*, ed. Bliss, p. 73.

[27] Smith, *The Theory of Moral Sentiments*, p. 121 (Part II, Sec. II, ch. ii).

der which a fruitful and fair competition could take place.[28] It was explicitly recognized at the time of the First World War by Thomas Nixon Carver when he urged that "if the state would do a few right things it would then be unnecessary to do the thousand and one wrong or ineffective things now being advocated."[29] It finds its most recent and one of its most direct expressions in the work of two American economists reflecting upon their frustrating periods of government service. Competition, they write, "is a social institution established and maintained by the community for the common good."[30] The tenor of their book makes it clear that for *is* one should read *ought to be*. Limited government remains the ideal of what Wilhelm Röpke terms "liberal revisionism," but, as he points out, government though limited must be strong in its sphere. While remaining outside the market it must be able to prevent the inequalities of wealth that may distort or dominate it.[31]

The liberals' insistence on economy, decentralization, and freedom from governmental regulation makes sense only if their assumption that society is self-regulating is valid. Because a self-regulating society is a necessary means, in effect it becomes part of the liberals' ideal end. If a laissez-faire policy is possible only on the basis of conditions described as necessary, the laissez-faire ideal may itself require state action.

INTERNATIONAL RELATIONS: LIBERAL VIEW

Treitschke defined the primary duty of the state as "the double one of maintaining power without, and law with-

[28] Thus he was attracted by Owen, Fourier, and Blanc but not by Marx.

[29] Carver, *Essays in Social Justice*, p. 349.

[30] Adams and Gray, *Monopoly in America*, p. 117.

[31] Röpke, *The Social Crisis of Our Time*, tr. A. and P. Jacobsohn, pp. 192–93. For one of the best summaries of his proposed positive policies, see his *Civitas Humana*, tr. Fox, pp. 27–32.

in." The state's first obligation, he thought, "must be the care of its Army and its Jurisprudence, in order to protect and to restrain the community of its citizens." [32]   Adam Smith had said the same thing. The state is concerned externally with defense and internally with justice.   But while the liberal Smith and the unliberal Treitschke agree on a definition of the state's duties, they differ widely on what actions are necessary to discharge them.   In contrast to Hobbes, the problem of internal order was made easy for the liberals by optimistic assumptions about man and society.   In contrast to Treitschke, the problem of external security was made easy for them by optimistic assumptions about the characteristics of states and of the international community.   In domestic matters the state need perform only a minimum of functions.   In international matters, the absence of an ultimate political authority need pose only a minimum of problems.   The problems posed are nevertheless important.   Just as, with Hobbes, the liberals accept the state as performing necessary functions, so, with Treitschke, they accept war as the ultimate means of settling disputes among states.   War in international relations is the analogue of the state in domestic politics.   Smith, for example, with one insignificant exception, recognizes "that everything that is the subject of a law suit may be a cause of war." [33]   Bentham recognizes the necessity of states on occasion resorting to war in order to right a wrong, for the same reasons that individuals must sometimes have recourse to courts of

[32] Treitschke, *Politics*, tr. Dugdale and de Bille, I, 63.

[33] Smith, *Lectures on Justice, Police, Revenue, and Arms*, p. 330 (Part V, sec. 1).   It should be mentioned that Smith's various comments on international relations are uniformly more perspicacious than those of most liberals of the period.   See selections from his works in Wolfers and Martin, eds., *The Anglo-American Tradition in Foreign Affairs*, which is an excellently chosen collection of readings comprising many of the writers dealt with in this chapter.

law.[34] Spencer puts the analogy simply: "Policemen are soldiers who act alone; soldiers are policemen who act in concert." [35] And Sir Edward Grey, reflecting the experience of a Liberal foreign minister in wartime, writes in his memoirs that among states as within states force must be available to uphold law.[36]

Liberals accept the necessity of the state, and then circumscribe it. They accept the role of war, and then minimize it—and on the basis of a similar analysis. To understand the liberals' view of the state, it was necessary to analyze their conceptions of man and society; to understand the liberals' view of international relations, it is necessary to analyze their conceptions of the state and of the community of states.

Early liberals and utilitarians assumed an objective harmony of interests in society. The same assumption is applied to international relations. "I believe," wrote John Stuart Mill, "that the good of no country can be obtained by any means but such as tend to that of all countries, nor ought to be sought otherwise, even if obtainable." [37] This is so much the burden of liberal arguments, and the arguments have been so often made and so often summarized, that here only two things are necessary, to indicate the recurrence of ideas now identified with liberalism and to emphasize those aspects that will become important later in the analysis.

In the seventeenth century, La Bruyère asked: "How does it serve the people and add to their happiness if their

---

34 Bentham, "Principles of International Law," in *Works,* ed. Bowring, II, 538–39, 544.

35 Spencer, *Social Statics,* p. 118.

36 Grey, *Twenty-five Years,* II, 286.

37 J. S. Mill, *Letters,* ed. Elliot, II, 47; cf. "A Few Words on Non-Intervention," in *Dissertations and Discussions,* III, 249: "Is a nation at liberty to adopt as a practical maxim, that what is good for the human race is bad for itself, and to withstand it accordingly? What is this but to declare that its interest and that of mankind are incompatible?"

ruler extend his empire by annexing the provinces of his
enemies; . . . how does it help me or my countrymen that
my sovereign be successful and covered with glory, that
my country be powerful and dreaded, if, sad and worried,
I live in oppression and poverty?" The transitory interests
of royal houses may be advanced in war; the real interests
of all peoples are furthered by peace. Most men suffer because some men are in positions that permit them to
indulge their kingly ambitions. Three centuries later,
James Shotwell wrote: "The political doctrine of international peace is a parallel to the economic doctrine of
Adam Smith, for it rests similarly upon a recognition of
common and reciprocal material interests, which extend
beyond national frontiers." [38]   If real interests were given
full play, national boundaries would cease to be barriers.
Cooperation, or constructive competition, is the way to
advance simultaneously the interests of all people. In a
shop or a town, the division of labor increases everyone's
material well-being. The same must be true on a national
and on a global scale.[39] There are no qualitative changes
to damage the validity of the principle as the scale increases. The liberals' free-trade argument, put in terms
currently and locally relevant, was as simple as this: Do
Michigan and Florida gain by trading freely the auto-
mobiles of the one for the oranges of the other? Or
would Michigan be richer growing its own oranges under
glass, instead of importing the produce of "foreign" labor?
The answer is obvious. And since the principle is clear,
it must be true that where natural conditions of produc-

[38] La Bruyère, "Du souverain ou de la république," in *Oeuvres
complètes*, ed. Benda, pp. 302–3; Shotwell, *War as an Instrument of
National Policy*, p. 30.
[39] Cf. Cobden, *Speeches*, ed. Bright and Rogers, II, 161: "The intercourse between communities is nothing more than the intercourse of
individuals in the aggregate."

tion are less spectacularly different, the gain from trade, though smaller, will nevertheless be real. Each side gains from trade, whether between individuals, corporations, localities, or nations. Otherwise no trade would take place.

There was a time when even relatively untutored publicists understood not only this simplified version of the classical free-trade argument but a good many of its more subtle ramifications as well. From the argument it follows not only that free trade is the correct policy but also that attempts to enlarge the territory of the state, whether by annexing neighbors or acquiring colonies, are foolish. The expenses of conquering and holding cannot be balanced by advantages in trade, for the same advantages can be had, without expense, under a policy of free trade.[40] In its most general form, the liberals' argument becomes a simple bit of common sense. Ultimately, they are saying, the well-being of the world's people can increase only to the extent that production increases. Production flourishes in peace, and distribution will be equitable if all nationals are free to seek their interests anywhere in the world. War is destruction and enrichment from war must therefore be an illusion.[41] The victor does not gain by war; he may pride himself only on losing less than the vanquished. This reasoning is the root of the traditional war-does-not-pay argument, an argument dating back at least to Emeric Crucé early in the seventeenth century,

[40] Bentham, "Emancipate Your Colonies," in *Works,* ed. Bowring, IV, 407–18. In this message addressed to the National Convention of France in 1793 are set forth the principal arguments used by liberal scholars and publicists.

[41] See, e.g., Bright, *Speeches,* ed. Rogers, p. 469: "Do not all statesmen know, as you [my constituents] know, that upon peace, and peace alone, can be based the successful industry of a nation, and that by successful industry alone can be created that wealth which . . . tends so powerfully to promote the comfort, happiness, and contentment of a nation?"

developed in detail by Bentham and both Mills, used by
William Graham Sumner to condemn the American war
against Spain, and brought to its apogee by Norman
Angell who summed up the work of the liberal economists,
largely English and French, who came before him.

The liberals had demonstrated, at least to their own
satisfaction, the objective harmony of interests among
states. Their rational propositions—that war does not pay,
that peace is in everyone's real interest—confront the irrational practices of states. The problem is: How can the
rational come to prevail over the irrational? But first one
must explain why war, the irrational course for all states,
characterizes relations among them. Why do governments
make war? Because war gives them an excuse for raising
taxes, for expanding the bureaucracy, for increasing their
control over their citizens. These are the constantly iter-
ated accusations of liberals. The ostensible causes of war
are mostly trivial. But the ostensible causes are mere
pretexts, ways of committing the nations to the wars their
governors want for selfish reasons of their own. Bright, in
addressing his constituents at Birmingham in 1858, employed this thesis. It was once England's policy, he told
them, "to keep ourselves free from European complications." But with the Glorious Revolution, a revolution
that enthroned the great territorial families at the same
time that it bridled the king, a new policy was adopted:
"We now began to act upon a system of constant entangle-
ment in the affairs of foreign countries." There were
wars " 'to maintain the liberties of Europe.' There were
wars 'to support the Protestant interest,' and there were
many wars to preserve our old friend 'the balance of
power.' " Since that time, England had been at war "with,
for, and against every considerable nation in Europe."
And to what avail? Would anyone, Bright asks, say that

Europe is better off today for all this fighting? The implication is clear. The English nation lost by these wars; Europe lost; only the "great territorial families" may have gained.[42]

Though the interest of the people is in peace, their governors make war. This they are able to do partly because people have not clearly perceived their true interests, but more importantly because true interests, where perceived, have not found expression in governmental policy. In 1791 Thomas Paine, one of the world's great publicists, described the accomplishments of the French Revolution as follows: "Monarchical sovereignty, the enemy of mankind, and the source of misery, is abolished; and sovereignty itself is restored to its natural and original place, the nation." The consequence of this in international relations Paine indicates in the succeeding sentence. "Were this the case throughout Europe," he asserts, "the cause of war would be taken away." Democracy is preeminently the peaceful form of the state. Control of policy by the people would mean peace.[43]

The faith in democracies as inherently peaceful has two principal bases. The first was developed by Kant who, like Congressman Louis L. Ludlow in the 1930s, would have the future foot soldier decide whether or not to commit the country to war. The premise of both Ludlow and Kant is that giving a direct voice to those who suffer most in war would drastically reduce its incidence. The second was developed by Bentham who, like Woodrow Wilson and Lord Cecil, was convinced that world public opinion is the most effective sanction, and in itself per-

[42] *Ibid.*, pp. 468–69.

[43] Paine, *The Rights of Man*, in *Complete Writings*, ed. Foner, I, 342. In *The Age of Reason*, having found that not all the fruits of the American and French revolutions were sweet, Paine shifts his emphasis from changing governments to changing minds.

haps a sufficient sanction, for peace.[44]   Thus he proposed
a 'common court of judicature, for the decision of differences between the several nations, although such court
were not to be armed with any coercive powers." What
would give meaning to the court's decisions?   Public opinion!   The court's proceedings would be open, and the
court would be charged with publishing its opinions and
circulating them to all states.   Refractory states would be
put under "the ban of Europe," which would be a sanction sufficient to dissuade a state from ignoring the court's
directive.[45]   Interest and opinion combine to ensure a
policy of peace, for if governors are made responsive to
the people's wishes, public opinion can be expected to
operate effectively as a sanction.[46]

Faith in public opinion or, more generally, faith in the
uniformly peaceful proclivities of democracies has proved
utopian.   But the utopianism of the liberals was of a
fairly complex order.   Their proposition is not that at any
moment in time war could have been abolished by acts
of informed will, but rather that progress has brought the
world close to the point where war can be eliminated in
the relations of states.   History approaches the stage where
reason, internationally as well as domestically, can be expected to prevail in human affairs.   Utility is the object
of state, as of individual, action.   For peace, despotism

44 " 'The great weapon we rely upon,' declared Lord Robert Cecil in
the House of Commons on July 21, 1919, 'is public opinion . . . and if we
are wrong about it, then the whole thing is wrong.' " Quoted in Morgenthau, *Politics among Nations*, p. 235.

45 Bentham, "Principles of International Law," in *Works*, ed. Bowring,
II, 552–54. Cf. Cobden, *Speeches*, ed. Bright and Rogers, II, 174: If you
make a treaty binding a country to arbitrate and it refuses to do so when
the occasion arises, then "you will place it in so infamous a position, that
I doubt if any country would enter into war on such bad grounds as
that country must occupy."

46 As James Mill says, "If any man possesses absolute power over the
rest of the community, he is set free from all dependence upon their
sentiments." "Law of Nations," in *Essays*, No. VI, pp. 8–9.

must give way to democracy—so that the utility of the people, and not the utility of minority groups, will be the object sought.   Fortunately, despotism is on the rocks. The faith that remained strong well into the twentieth century, and is not yet dead, was summed up in the early 1790s by Thomas Paine:

> It is not difficult to perceive, from the enlightened state of mankind, that hereditary governments are verging to their decline, and that revolutions on the broad basis of national sovereignty, and government by representation, are making their way in Europe. . . .
> I do not believe that monarchy and aristocracy will continue seven years longer in any of the enlightened countries in Europe.[47]

DIFFICULTIES IN PRACTICE

The nineteenth-century liberals' view of the state was based on an assumption of harmony, often coupled with an assumption of the infinite perfectibility of men, lead ing to a situation where the functions of government would shrivel and most of them blow away.   Their view of international relations was based on an assumption of harmony and of the infinite perfectibility of states, leading to a situation where war would become increasingly unlikely.   To make the liberal ideal of international relations real, states must change.   What are to be the mechanisms of change?   On this question, liberals oscillate between two poles: the optimistic noninterventionism of Kant, Cobden, and Bright on the one hand; the messianic interventionism of Paine, Mazzini, and Woodrow Wilson on the other.   Those clustered at each pole display at once elements of realism and of idealism.

Cobden, as did Kant before him, displayed a deep suspicion of revolution and, conversely, a firm faith in evolution.   Internal reforms should come gradually by education, not suddenly by violence, for only in the former

[47] Paine, *The Rights of Man,* in *Complete Writings,* ed. Foner, I, 344, 352.

case may one expect improvement to last. And as he rejected revolution domestically, so he renounced intervention internationally. "I am against any interference by the government of one country in the affairs of another nation," he wrote in 1858, "even if it be confined to moral suasion." [48] Intervention in the affairs of others Cobden considered futile, for England could not bring liberty to the rest of the world; illogical, for England could not know what was good for the rest of the world; presumptuous, for England had many defects to correct at home without seeking good works to do abroad; unnecessary, for "the honest and just interests of this country . . . are the just and honest interests of the whole world"; [49] and dangerous, for the war to right wrongs in one corner of the world could so easily outrun its original purpose and the conflagration, once ignited, could so quickly spread.

Despite the role of abnegation he prescribed for the greatest and most liberal state of nineteenth-century Europe, Cobden looked with some confidence to the day when peace would prevail among states. In a letter written in 1846 he set forth both the difficulties and the means of overcoming them.

I don't think the nations of the earth will have a chance of advancing morally in their domestic concerns to the degree of excellence which we sigh for, until the international relations of the world are put upon a different footing. The present system corrupts society, exhausts its wealth, raises up false gods for hero-worship, and fixes before the eyes of the rising generation a spurious if glittering standard of glory. It is because I do believe that the principle of Free Trade is calculated to alter the relations of the world for the better, in a moral point of view, that I bless God I have been allowed to take a prominent part in its advocacy. Still, do not let us be too gloomy. If we can keep the world from actual war, and I trust Trade will do that, a great impulse will from this time be given to

---

[48] Quoted in Hobson, *Richard Cobden*, p. 400. Cf. Cobden, *Speeches,* ed. Bright and Rogers, II, 225; Bright, *Speeches,* ed. Rogers, p. 239.

[49] Cobden, *Speeches,* ed. Bright and Rogers, II, 27.

social reforms. The public mind is in a practical mood, and it will now precipitate itself upon Education, Temperance, reform of Criminals, care of Physical Health, etcetera, with greater zeal than ever.[50]

Kant had been, in a sense, still more optimistic. Even wars, he thought, by exhausting a nation that engages in them, and threats of war, by forcing a state to grant its subjects the liberty necessary to make it more powerful, would hasten the advent of republicanism and peace.[51]

The war system has proved more powerful than the instrumentalities of peace described by Cobden, and the waging of wars has often had effects the opposite of those predicted by Kant. Gladstone, who agreed with Cobden on the contribution that free trade would make to the peace of the world, also thought it necessary to keep an eye on the balance of power in Europe. In October of 1853, during the prelude to the Crimean War, he observed that an increase in Russia's power through a defeat of Turkey would endanger the peace of Europe. It was England's duty, at whatever cost, to oppose this.[52] Cobden and Bright, much in contrast to Gladstone, saw a danger to England as the only legitimate cause of her undertaking war and an attempt to invade as constituting the only real danger. Thus Bright, in arguing against war with Russia, took the opportunity to censure Englishmen of another generation for the war waged to determine "that France should not choose its own Government."

[50] Quoted in Morley, *The Life of Richard Cobden*, p. 276.

[51] Kant, "The Principle of Progress Considered in Connection with the Relation of Theory to Practice in International Law," in *Eternal Peace and Other International Essays*, tr. Hastie, p. 63; and "The Natural Principle of the Political Order Considered in Connection with the Idea of a Universal Cosmopolitical History," Eighth Proposition, in *ibid*. For an example of how this might work, see J. S. Mill's comments on the Franco-Prussian War. The loss of Alsace-Lorraine he saw as a relatively painless way of teaching the French people that in the future they must not blindly follow their leaders into wars of aggression but must take an active interest in politics. *Letters*, ed. Elliot, II, 277–78.

[52] Morley, *Gladstone*, I, 476, 483–84.

One need only read the speeches Pitt made at the time
of the French Revolutionary Wars to realize that, for the
head of the government at least, the object of the war
was the safety of England, not restoration of the ancient
constitution of the French state.[53]   A narrow definition
of state safety, however, typifies those who cluster at the
noninterventionist pole of liberalism.   Bryan, for example, took the same position on American participation
in the First World War that Bright had taken earlier.   On
February 2, 1917, he told a gathering of five thousand at
Madison Square Garden that "this country should fight
till the last man was killed, if it were invaded, but that
we should settle all other matters by arbitration."[54]

The position of the noninterventionist liberals is understandable if various assumptions of theirs are borne in
mind.   The good example of the advanced countries, in
freeing trade, reducing arms, and emancipating colonies,
would have a salutary effect on all countries; and public
opinion would force emulation.[55]   The threat of armed
force would then never be posed.   Further, the strength
of a country cannot be equated with its size.   Conquest
in war often leads to weakness.[56]   The argument that considerations of state safety require one country to oppose
the conquests of another is then false.   Finally, a country's
strength is related more to the spirit of the people, which
is higher in free countries, and to the excellence of the
economy than it is to the size of the peacetime military

[53] See Morgenthau and Thompson, *Principles and Problems of International Politics*, where key speeches on the issue of war with France
are conveniently reproduced.

[54] New York *Times*, February 3, 1917, p. 11.

[55] For the survival among socialists of the idea of disarmament by
example, see below, ch. v, pp. 153–54.

[56] Cf. Cobden, *Speeches*, ed. Bright and Rogers, I, 483: "I defy you to
show me any partition where an accession of territory has not been rather
a source of weakness than of strength."   Cf. Bright, *Speeches*, ed. Rogers,
p. 463.

establishment.[57] These assumptions in turn are understandable if one remembers that geography combined with technology to make them plausible for the United States, and to a lesser extent for England, in the nineteenth century. Logically, if Bryan admits that defense is a legitimate concern of the state, he must also admit, and even urge, that his state should watch lest others maneuver into position and build up for an attack. Practically, such worries were remote for the United States until the twentieth century. As for England, the very power she enjoyed obscured for many the extent to which her safety depended upon it.

To build a theory of international relations on accidents of geography and history is dangerous. The non-interventionist liberals were never able to cope with the difficulty Cobden himself posed in the letter previously quoted—how can the nations improve internally while the international relations of the world remain on the old footing? Mazzini saw the problem. As an Italian patriot in the middle of the nineteenth century he could not escape it. The despotic powers, he stated in an address to the Council of the People's International League (1847), "hurl their defiance at us:—'We shall rule, for we have the daring of Evil; we act, you have not the courage to stand up for good.'" "Is it enough," he asks, "to preach peace and nonintervention, and leave Force unchallenged ruler over three-fourths of Europe, to intervene, for its own unhallowed ends, when, where, and how, it thinks

---

[57] Cf. Godwin, *Political Justice*, II, 170–71, 193. Arguments associated with the second image are often used to support preferred domestic arrangements. We find the *Commercial and Financial Chronicle*, for example, editorially calling attention to the threatening world situation, asserting the dependence of military upon economic strength, and concluding that we must "begin forthwith (1) to get our fiscal situation in order, and (2) simultaneously to abolish the New Deal and all its works." "How to Be Strong," *Commercial and Financial Chronicle*, June 5, 1946, sec. ii, p. 1.

fit?" [58]   In sum, what sense does it make to preach laissez faire in international relations when not all states will practice it?   Those who do find themselves at the mercy of those who do not.

This is one problem posed for the noninterventionist liberals.   It raises the more general question: Can one wait with calm confidence for the day when the despotic states that have made wars in the past have been turned, by the social and economic forces of history, into peace-loving democracies?   Are the forces of evolution moving fast enough?   Are they even moving in the right direction?   May not the "good," by doing nothing, make the triumph of "Evil" possible?   There may be the necessity of action.   And even if the means-end relation is correctly described by Kant and Cobden, may men not hasten the processes of evolution by their own efforts?   There may be, if not the necessity, at least the desirability of action.

In internal affairs, liberals begin with the doctrine of the sterile state.   All the good things of life are created by the efforts of individuals; the state exists simply to hold the ring as impartial arbiter among the individual competitors.   They end by urging that the state must not only maintain but in certain instances must create the conditions necessary for the functioning of a liberal society and economy.   Is there a comparable necessity of action in international affairs?   Some liberals proposed nonintervention as a means of allowing the natural harmony of interests among states to take over.   But will the harmony of interests prevail if, to use Carver's phrase, there are "a

---

[58] Mazzini, *Selected Writings*, ed. Gangulee, p. 143.   For the same point more soberly made, see J. S. Mill, "Vindication of the French Revolution of February, 1848; in Reply to Lord Brougham and Others," in *Dissertations and Discussions*, III, 51–52.

few right things" prerequisite to the functioning of the system and if there exists no agency to accomplish them? The means are of an importance comparable to the importance of the end. If the end is peace and if the basis for peace is found in the existence of free states, then some active agency must be substituted for the spontaneously functioning evolutionary forces whenever those forces seem to bog down. With this as their logic, many liberals, in international as in domestic matters, move from proscribing state action to prescribing the kind of action necessary. In international matters, the only agents to which liberals can look are the democratic states that may already exist.

While Cobden and Bright would use force in international relations only where necessary to make their own democracy safe, Paine, Mazzini, and Wilson set out to make the world democratic. Paine, in dedicating the second part of *The Rights of Man* to the Marquis de Lafayette, promises to join him should the unlikely necessity of a spring campaign materialize in order that France may exterminate "German despotism," surround herself with revolutions, and thus be able to live in peace and safety.[59] In 1853 Mazzini, for similar reasons, sought to convince England that her "present duty is war." The war he calls for would not be of the type waged by absolutist states, but—

War, with the scope of solving once for all the ancient problem whether Man is to remain a passive slave trodden underfoot by organized brute-force, or to become a free agent, responsible for his actions before God and his fellow-men. . . . War, in the noble intention of restoring Truth and Justice, and of arresting Tyranny in her inhuman career, of rendering the Nations free and happy, and

[59] Paine, *The Rights of Man*, in *Complete Writings*, ed. Foner, I, 348. He adds, in the manner of many liberals, that France's "taxes, as well as those of Germany, will consequently become less."

causing God to smile upon them benignantly, of crowning political and religious liberty, and making England proud and powerful, having gained the sympathy and gratitude of the nations that she has benefited.[60]

Woodrow Wilson, the third of the interventionists we consider, was quite capable of speaking as though motivated primarily by concern for the safety of the state he led.[61]   This is not unrepresentative of the interventionist liberals.   What is interesting about them is not that they reject balance-of-power politics but that they think it can be superseded.[62]   They would make a leap into the future and take all of us with them.   "Is the present war," Wilson once asked, "a struggle for a just and secure peace, or only for a new balance of power?" [63]   More frequently as the First World War progressed he sounded the call to a war of "the Present against the Past," of "right against wrong," a war to bring an end to the baleful power of autocracies and to establish freedom and justice for the people of the world.   "Nobody has the right," he explained to the foreign correspondents who met with him at the White House in April of 1918, "to get anything out of this war, because we are fighting for peace . . ., for permanent peace.   No injustice furnishes a basis for perma-

60 Mazzini, *Selected Writings*, ed. Gangulee, p. 91.

61 Tumulty, *Woodrow Wilson as I Know Him*, p. 248; and the speech Wilson wrote for Four Minute Speakers, July 4, 1918, in *Woodrow Wilson, Selections for Today*, ed. Tourtellot, pp. 107–8.

62 Cf. J. S. Mill's urging that Gladstone should have used the threat of British intervention to dissuade either France or Germany from attacking the other in 1870. *Letters*, ed. Elliot, II, 274.

63 Wilson's address to the United States Senate, January 22, 1917, in *Woodrow Wilson, Selections for Today*, ed. Tourtellot, p. 131. The same either-or approach is reflected in Wilson's postwar policy. Cf. Secretary Daniel's argument, designed to gather senatorial support for the League: "We have only two courses." Either we must have "a league of nations by which every nation will help preserve the peace of the world without competitive navy building, or we must have incomparably the biggest navy in the world. There is no middle ground." H. and M. Sprout, *Toward a New Order of Sea Power*, p. 71.

nent peace. If you leave a rankling sense of injustice anywhere, it will not only produce a running sore presently which will result in trouble and probably war, but it ought to produce war somewhere." [64]

As a modern English philosopher-historian urged in the face of Hitler's threat to Western civilization, peace is a good cause of war. The existence of a Yahoo-state is itself a danger to the peace-state.[65] It may then be incumbent upon the peace-states to clean up the world, to turn wars from the object of the narrowly defined safety of the state into crusades to establish the conditions under which all states can coexist in perpetual peace. Liberalism, which is preeminently the philosophy of tolerance, of humility, and of doubt, develops a hubris of its own. Thus Michael Straight, a present-day liberal publicist, quotes with approval R. H. Tawney's statement: "Either war is a crusade, or it is a crime. There is no half-way house." [66] Thus Wilson found himself saying, in a variety of ways, "I speak for humanity."

But as there is more than one messiah, so there is more than one mission. In 1880 Dostoievsky proclaimed the Russian's love of his brothers to the West. "Oh, the peoples of Europe have no idea how dear they are to us!" So dear are they that war to redeem them from crass materialism and a selfish ethic becomes the sacred duty of Russia. Dostoievsky had faith in the wisdom and courage of his compatriots: "The future Russians, to the last man," he wrote, "will comprehend that to become a genuine Russian means to seek finally to reconcile all European controversies, to show the solution of European anguish in our all-humanitarian and all-unifying Russian soul, to

---

[64] Reprinted in Tumulty, *Woodrow Wilson as I Know Him*, p. 274. Cf. the address by Wilson cited in the preceding note.

[65] Collingwood, *The New Leviathan*, ch. xxx.

[66] Straight, *Make This the Last War*, p. 1.

embrace in it with brotherly love all our brethren, and finally, perhaps, to utter the ultimate word of great, universal harmony, of the brotherly accord of all nations abiding by the law of Christ's Gospel!" Not conquest, but liberation would be the object of Russian war in the West, and liberation would provide the basis for peace.[67] The aspiration is the same as Mazzini's, but the very symmetry of aspiration increases the probability of conflict. The same is true today. "War, that monster of human fratricide, will inevitably be wiped out by man's social progress and this will come about in the near future. But there is only one way to do it—war against war." These could easily be the words of a Western liberal; instead they are the words of an Eastern communist, Mao Tse-tung.[68] The thesis was later elaborated by Liu Shao-chi, who is often said to rank second in the hierarchy of the Chinese Communist Party. The people of the world, Liu argues, have no alternative but to unite in a struggle to liberate themselves from capitalist oppression. Liberation is an irresistible law of history. Bad states must be demolished so that the good can live in peace.[69] This is precisely the policy of American liberationists. Our mission, to take an academic expression of the doctrine, "is to persuade those still free that they can with its [America's] help profitably and successfully follow its way, and to rescue those who are the victims of tyranny and set them, too, on the right path. . . . it will be our ardent mission not simply to spare the humble but to deliver the oppressed. To that end we shall indeed make war *à outrance*, with no compromise, on the

[67] Dostoievsky, *The Diary of a Writer*, tr. Brasol, II, 666–68, 979–80; cf. I, 476; II, 628–36. The period covered in these parts of the *Diary* is 1876–80.

[68] Mao Tse-tung, *Strategic Problems of China's Revolutionary War*, p. 4. This was written in the fall of 1935.

[69] Liu Shao-chi, *Internationalism and Nationalism*, pp. 24, 31, 41–42, 50–51. This was written in November, 1948.

proud dictators who pervert all principle and debase men whom they have first oppressed." [70]

That two sides should entertain contradictory goals does not in itself prove that either is unworthy. It may indicate that both are impractical. The projected crusades of the liberals, as of Dostoievsky and the Communists, must, if implemented, lead to unlimited war for unlimited ends. They may lead to perpetual war for perpetual peace. This has been pointed out not only by statesmen like George Kennan and scholars like Hans Morgenthau but also by liberals like Cobden and Bright.

The noninterventionist liberals call for no special activities to bring about the widely desired goal of perpetual peace; instead we are to derive all of our hope from their assertion that history is on the side of the angels. This is at once the position of a Dr. Pangloss, as is evident, and the position of a realist, as is perhaps not so evident. What is realistic about the position is this: Reliance on the forces of history to bring about the desired goal may be an admission that man can do little to hasten its coming. Interventionist liberals are, however, not content with a realism that may prolong the era of war forever. Their realism lies in rejecting the assumption of automatic progress in history and in the consequent assertion that men must eliminate the causes of war if they are to enjoy peace. This realism involves them in utopian assumptions that are frightening in their implications. The state that would act on the interventionist theory must set itself up as both judge and executor in the affairs of nations. A good cause may jusify any war, but who can say in a dispute between states whose cause is just? If one state throws around itself the mantle of justice, the opposing state will too. In the words of Emmerich de Vattel, diplomat and writer of the mid-eighteenth century, each will then "arrogate to itself all the rights of war and claim that its enemy has none. . . . The decision of the rights at issue will not be advanced thereby, and the contest will become more cruel, more disastrous in its effects, and more difficult of termination."[71] Wars undertaken on a narrow calculation of state interest are almost certain to be less damaging than wars inspired by a supposedly selfless idealism. Often in history the validity of this logic has been evident. Never has the evidence beer. more succinctly summarized than by A. J. P. Taylor. "Bismarck," he wrote, "fought 'necessary' wars and killed thousands; the idealists of the twentieth century fight 'just' wars and kill millions."[72]

FAILURES IN THEORY

Peace and war are the products, respectively, of good and bad states. Should this be true, what can be done to change states from their present condition to the condition prescribed? This question led to the first criticism of liberal theories of international relations. A second criticism, equally fundamental, is suggested by questioning the original proposition. Bad states may make war. The truth of the statement can be established simply by labeling as "bad" any state that does. But would the existence of numerous states of the type defined as good mean peace? While the first criticism hinged on the practicability of the prescription, the second is concerned with the sufficiency of the analysis that led to it.

Liberals did not look forward to a state of nirvana in which all clashes cease because all conflicts have been eliminated. There would still be disputes among states but not the propensity to settle them by war. With states im-

---

[71] Vattel, *The Law of Nations,* tr. Fenwick, III, 304–5.
[72] Taylor, *Rumours of War,* p. 44.

proving, granting for the moment the assumption that they are, the occasions for war decrease at the same time that the ability of states to compose their differences amicably and rationally increases. Thus T. H. Green, liberal-idealist of the mid-nineteenth century, sees no reason why states, as they become more representative of their people, "should not arrive at a passionless impartiality in dealing with each other." [73] But just what would replace the war system—a system of arbitration, a system of conciliation, a loose system of law in which states voluntarily submit disputes to an international tribunal and voluntarily abide by its decision? On such matters liberals, from Bentham to the present, have disagreed. Until recently, however, most of them have come together on a few fundamentals. There should be a minimum of organization and no use of military force except directly to repulse an invading army. Public opinion would be the great sanction, an equilibrium of interests the underlying guarantee.[74] They would have disputes settled rationally, peacefully, without political manipulation.

This is again the anarchist ideal applied to international relations, but liberals, for the most part, did not see it as such—some because they misconstrued the meaning of politics, others because they applied a logic to international relations different from the logic they had applied within the state. Cobden, for example, seems at times to have misconceived politics. On June 12, 1849, he made

---

[73] Green, *Lectures on the Principles of Political Obligation*, par. 175.

[74] On the idea of equilibrium see, e.g., Bentham, "Principles of International Law," in *Works*, ed. Bowring, II, 538: "From reiterated experience, states ought either to have set themselves to seek out—or at least would have found, their line of least resistance, as individuals of that same society have already found theirs; and this will be the line which represents the greatest and common utility of all nations taken together.

"The point of repose will be that in which all the forces find their equilibrium, from which the greatest difficulty would be found in making them to depart."

an eloquent plea in the House of Commons for a resolution that called upon the British Foreign Office to negotiate treaties of arbitration with other countries. In the course of the speech he described his plan as "simply and solely, that we should resort to that mode of settling disputes in communities, which individuals resort to in private life." [75] William Howard Taft, in the fourth chapter of his book *The United States and Peace,* Senator William Borah in his resolution calling for the outlawing of war, Salmon Levinson and Charles Clayton Morrison in their writings supporting that idea, all reflect the same misunderstanding. Believing that the decisions of the United States Supreme Court are given effect not by the organized power of government but by the spontaneous force of public opinion, they argue that the same methods can achieve comparable results in international relations.[76] Not only does this ignore the difficulties the Supreme Court has at times had—with President Andrew Jackson, for example, or currently with the desegregation decision —but it commits as well the fundamental error of interpreting instances where force is not visible as proof that power is not present. Those who uphold this view would have us settle disputes internationally as they are domestically without first understanding how disputes are settled domestically. In international affairs they would have reason prevail over force, whereas domestically disputes are settled by institutions that *combine* reason with

[75] Cobden, *Speeches,* ed. Bright and Rogers, II, 161.

[76] In the Borah resolution, introduced in the Senate in February, 1923, the argument is summed up as follows: The "judgments [of an international court] shall not be enforced by war under any name or in any form whatever, but shall have the same power for this enforcement as our federal supreme court, namely, the respect of all enlightened nations for judgments resting upon open and fair investigations and impartial decisions, the agreement of the nations to abide and be bound by such judgments, and the compelling power of enlightened public opinion." Reprinted in Madariaga, *Disarmament,* pp. 365–67.

force.[77]   Disputes between individuals are settled not because an elaborate court system has been established but because people can, when necessary, be forced to use it. How many times would the adverse decisions of courts be ignored if it rested upon the defendants to carry them out voluntarily, to march themselves to jail and place their heads meekly in the noose, or to pay voluntarily the very damages they had gone to court in order to avoid?   An international court, without an organized force to back its decisions, is a radically different institution from the courts that exist within every country.   The liberals want the benefits of an effective system of law; they are often unwilling to pay the price for it.

In a limited sense, Wilson marks a turning point.   The majority of earlier liberals had regarded international organization as both unnecessary and dangerous.   Though differences among them remain, the balance has clearly swung the other way.   As many liberals move on questions of domestic policy from a negative to a positive formulation of the policy requirements of a laissez-faire system, so many liberals in international relations have moved from a reliance on education and rational solution of disputes to the advocacy of international organization to perform the inescapable functions of government.   If war is the analogue of government, then to eradicate war provision must be made for performing its functions. Yet the old reasoning persists and, based upon it, the old errors as well.   Wilson foresees a new era in which there will prevail the same moral standards for states as for men. The essential condition, of course, is that states become democratic, a thought that is nowhere more clearly ex-

---

[77] Levinson's view, for example, is diametrically opposed.   To wit: "There are but two ways of compelling settlement of disputes whether intranational or international in character; one is by force and the other is by law." *Outlawry of War*, p. 14.

pressed than in his message to Congress asking for a declaration of war against Germany. "A steadfast concert for peace," he said on that occasion, "can never be maintained except by a partnership of democratic nations. No autocratic government could be trusted to keep faith within it or observe its covenants. . . . Only free peoples can hold their purpose and their honor steady to a common end and prefer the interests of mankind to any narrow interest of their own." [78]

The peace of the world would still rest on force—in Wilson's phrase, "the organized major force of mankind"—but this would be unlike the force displayed in the balance-of-power politics of the past. Not a balance of power but "a community of power" is Wilson's ideal.[79] And with the democratic international community realized, the new force of public opinion would replace the old force of national armies and navies. "What we seek," Wilson once said, "is the reign of law, based upon the consent of the governed and sustained by the organized opinion of mankind." [80] National self-determination is to produce democracy, and democracies are by definition peaceful. Wilson's stipulation that units, if they are to form a community, must share similar values is not irrelevant. We have already referred to the difficulty of achieving similarity, a difficulty that Wilson himself soon experienced. In addition, one must face the question: How much community is necessary before force, conventionally defined, is dispensable in the relations among its units? If states dis-

[78] Wilson's address to Congress, April 2, 1917, in *Woodrow Wilson, Selections for Today,* ed. Tourtellot, pp. 143–44. For the gradual development of Wilson's position and the influence of Secretary Lansing on this development, see Buehrig, *Woodrow Wilson and the Balance of Power,* especially pp. 138–44.

[79] Wilson's address to the United States Senate, January 22, 1917, in *Woodrow Wilson, Selections for Today,* ed. Tourtellot, p. 131.

[80] Wilson's address at Mount Vernon, July 4, 1918, in *ibid.,* p. 54.

played the morality of Englishmen or Americans in their dealings with one another, would that be sufficient? When Wilson called upon states to enter into covenants so that the rights of the small nations might be preserved, he was in effect returning to the optimism of the early laissez-faire liberals who thought that the relations among producers could be satisfactorily governed by contracts among them.[81]

Solutions for the problem of war based upon the pattern of either the first or the second image must assume the possibility of perfection in the conflicting units. Perfection being impossible for states as for men, the liberal system can at most produce an approximation to world peace. With such an approximation can we logically expect one state to rely upon the willingness of others to cooperate? Would a necessarily imperfect equilibrium of interests combined with the force of public opinion end the necessity of each state standing ready to marshal its strength in order to defend its interests? And if the answer is no, then what is to prevent the sorry spectacle of balance-of-power politics from repeating itself once more? The liberal aspiration is hopeless precisely for the reasons that anarchism is an impossible ideal. To maintain order and justice with almost no provision made for reaching and enforcing decisions requires a high order of excellence among the units of the system—be they men or states. To secure the improvements necessary may require more force than would be needed to maintain a modicum of order and justice among subjects much less perfect. And if conflict arises not only from defects in the subjects but also from the quality of the relations among them, it may be that no amount of improvement in the individual subjects would be sufficient to produce harmony in anarchy.

[81] Wilson's address to Congress, February 11, 1918, in *ibid.*, p. 166.

That is, the liberal prescription is impracticable, and the impracticability is directly related to the inadequacy of the liberal analysis. Peace with justice requires an organization with more and more of the qualities of government, just as internal justice was found to require an ever stronger and more active government.

CONCLUSION

The present chapter has presented a patterning of liberal thought, moving internally from laissez-faire liberalism to liberal revisionism, externally from reliance upon improvement within the separate states to acceptance of the need for organization among them. But the type of organization envisioned was insufficiently equipped to accomplish its objectives. At this point, there is painfully in evidence, in international as there often is in domestic affairs, the old inclination of liberals to substitute reason for force. Rigorous application of their own logic would lead them to ask more insistently to what extent organized force must be applied in order to secure the peaceful world they desire. It may be that many who consider themselves liberals will not accept this as the pattern of their thoughts. Indeed the more perspicacious liberal, noticing what we have described as difficulties in practice and failures in theory, may find himself arguing for a genuine world government, or for the unhappy alternative of accepting the necessity of balance-of-power politics, or simply lapsing into despair. In short, he may discover the inadequacy of an analysis of international relations according to the second image.

A world full of democracies would be a world forever at peace, but autocratic governments are warlike. . . . Monarchies are peaceful; democracies are irresponsible and impulsive, and consequently foment war. . . . Not political but economic organization is the key: *capitalist* democracies actively promote war, *socialist* democracies are peaceful. Each of these formulations has claimed numerous adherents, and each adherent has in turn been called to task by critics and by history. Walter Hines Page, ambassador to England during the First World War, commented: "There is no security in any part of the world where people cannot think of a government without a king, and never will be. You cannot conceive of a democracy that will unprovoked set out on a career of conquest." To this the late Dean Inge replied very simply: Ask a Mexican, a Spaniard, a Filipino, or a Japanese! [82] Engels wrote in 1891: "Between a Socialist France and a ditto Germany an Alsace-Lorraine problem has no existence at all." [83] The interests of the two bourgeois governments might clash; the interests of the workers could not. But Tito split with Stalin. One might have predicted, writes Roy Macridis, "that two national Communist countries were bound to show the same incompatibilities that bourgeois nationalist countries have showed in the past." [84] And this is almost exactly what Max Weber, writing some thirty years before the event, did predict.[85]

The optimism of eighteenth-century French rationalists was confounded by the French Revolutionary Wars. The optimism of nineteenth-century liberals was confounded by the First and Second World Wars. For many Frenchmen of the earlier period, enlightened despotism was to provide the guarantee of permanent peace; for most lib-

[82] Inge, *Lay Thoughts of a Dean,* pp. 116–17.
[83] Engels to Bebel, October 24, 1891, in Marx and Engels, *Selected Correspondence,* tr. Torr, p. 491.
[84] Macridis, "Stalinism and the Meaning of Titoism," *World Politics,* IV (1952), 226.
[85] *From Max Weber: Essays in Sociology,* tr. and ed. Gerth and Mills, p. 169.

erals of the later period, republican government was to perform the same function.   Were the optimists confounded because their particular prescriptions were faulty? Is it that democracies spell peace, but we have had wars because there have never been enough democracies of the right kind?   Or that the socialist form of government contains within it the guarantee of peace, but so far there have never been any true socialist governments? [86]   If either question were answered in the affirmative, then one would have to assess the merits of different prescriptions and try to decide just which one, or which combination, contains the elusive secret formula for peace.   The import of our criticism of liberal theories, however, is that no prescription for international relations written entirely in terms of the second image can be valid, that the approach itself is faulty.   Our criticisms of the liberals apply to all theories that would rely on the generalization of one pattern of state and society to bring peace to the world.

Bad states lead to war.   As previously said, there is a large and important sense in which this is true.   The obverse of this statement, that good states mean peace in the world, is an extremely doubtful proposition.   The difficulty, endemic with the second image of international relations, is the same in kind as the difficulty encountered in the first image.   There the statement that men make the societies, including the international society, in which they live was criticized not simply as being wrong but as being incomplete.   One must add that the societies they live in make men.   And it is the same in international relations.   The actions of states, or, more accurately, of men acting for states, make up the substance of international relations.   But the international political environ-

----

[86] Cf. Dedijer, "Albania, Soviet Pawn," *Foreign Affairs*, XXX (1951), 104: Socialism, but not Soviet Union state capitalism, means peace.

ment has much to do with the ways in which states behave. The influence to be assigned to the internal structure of states in attempting to solve the war-peace equation cannot be determined until the significance of the international environment has been reconsidered.   This will be done in Chapters VI and VII.   Meanwhile we shall take a look at a serious attempt to work out in practice a program for peace based on the second image.

CHAPTER V. SOME IMPLICATIONS

OF THE SECOND IMAGE

International Socialism and
the Coming of the First World War

> As soon as one of our industries fails to find a market for its prod-
> ucts a war is necessary to open new outlets. . . . In Third-Zealand
> we have killed two-thirds of the inhabitants in order to compel
> the remainder to buy our umbrellas and braces.
>
> ANATOLE FRANCE, *Penguin Island*

THROUGHOUT the history of man's speculation on political problems have run two partially contradictory thoughts
on the relation between the structure of states and the
types of warfare they wage. *Das Primat der Aussenpoli-
tik*, a view made famous in nineteenth-century Germany
by the number it convinced and the conviction with
which it was held, is a view at least as old as the Greeks.
Aristotle, for example, argued that the political structure
of the state may be greatly affected by its military organization and that the type of military organization necessary
may in turn be determined by such extra-political factors as
geographic location.[1] The opposite opinion, that internal
political structure will determine the organization and
use of military force, is as old and has been considered
equally important. To illustrate, one need mention only
Plato and the example of the French Revolutionary ar-

---

[1] Aristotle, *Politics*, tr. Jowett, 1321a; cf. 1274a, 1304a.

mies.[2] The second image is a more general statement of
the latter opinion: namely, that the internal structure of
states determines not only the form and use of military
force but external behavior generally. Many have believed this, as was indicated in the last chapter. Many
still do. While Woodrow Wilson and Sir Edward Grey
followed the image in explaining why the Central Powers
had started the First World War, the postwar revisionist
historians used it in arguing the comparable culpability
of France, Russia, Britain, and the United States. And in
the 1940s and 1950s the historical revisionists of the Second World War continue to write and speak in the manner of Bentham and Bright. The United States, it is
charged, forsook the policy of keeping itself "free from
European complications," to use Bright's instead of Washington's more familiar language, and plunged into war
where there was no danger to the country and no possible
gain for the people but only power and wealth to be acquired, or kept, by interests in and out of government.
Thus in John Flynn's mind, Franklin D. Roosevelt sought
to use the participation of the United States in the Second
World War as a cover for furthering New Deal domestic
legislation; in Charles Beard's mind, Roosevelt involved
us ever more deeply in world affairs for the opposite reason, to escape from the knotty political problems involved
in securing economic reforms still needed at home.[3]

   Marx and the Marxists represent the fullest development of the second image. On first thought it would seem
that the socialist view of war and peace is nothing more
than this: that capitalist states cause war; that to revolu-

----

[2] Cf. Plato, *Laws*, tr. Jowett, 628: "No one can be a true statesman . . .
who looks only, or first of all, to external warfare; nor will he ever be a
sound legislator who orders peace for the sake of war, and not war for
the sake of peace."

[3] See Flynn, *The Roosevelt Myth, passim;* Beard, *Giddy Minds and
Foreign Quarrels, passim,* and *A Foreign Policy for America,* ch. v.

tionize states, to destroy capitalism and institute socialism, will bring peace. Further, it might appear that the behavior of the various socialist parties during the First World War—not their failure to *prevent* war, but their failure to *oppose* war—is in one way or another an indictment of the socialist parties and the theories on which they were ostensibly based. This simple summary misses most of the interesting points. A more detailed consideration of the past behavior of socialist parties and of socialist theory in relation to war and peace will illustrate the meaning, practical difficulties, and general application of the second image in an especially apt way.

The component parts of the Marxist analysis are so well known that it is necessary only to state them in summary form. (1) The capitalist mode of production gives rise to two antagonistic classes, the bourgeoisie and the proletariat. (2) The capitalist state represents control of the machinery of government in the interest of one of these classes, the bourgeoisie. (3) The capitalist state brings the class struggle under a measure of control without actually ending it. (4) War is the external manifestation of the internal class struggle, which makes the problem of war coeval with the existence of capitalist states.[4] (5) Socialism, on the other hand, will abolish war forever. The fifth point follows with unchallengeable logic from those that precede it. If the state is the domination of one class

---

[4] "The history of all hitherto existing society is the history of class struggles." (Marx and Engels, *Communist Manifesto,* tr. Moore, p. 12.) War and peace among states reflect different phases of these class struggles. This is made clear by Marx and Engels in various comments on history. See, e.g., Marx, *Capital,* tr. Moore and Aveling, Vol. I, ch. xxxi; Engels, *The Origin of the Family, Private Property and the State,* pp. 150–57; Marx and Engels, *Communist Manifesto,* tr. Moore, p. 39. The same view is found among those who, in varying degrees, follow Marx. Cf. Lenin, *The Collapse of the Second International,* tr. Sirnis, p. 22; Laski, "The Economic Foundations of Peace," in Woolf, ed., *The Intelligent Man's Way to Prevent War,* pp. 500–5; Strachey, *A Faith to Fight For,* p. 44.

over another, socialism by destroying all classes thereby abolishes the state. And if war is armed conflict among states, then the abolition of states must be the end of war. The problem of war and peace can no longer exist.[5]

While logically sound, these propositions are ambiguous on a point of primary importance for many later socialists. The ambiguity arises from the failure of socialist theory, in so far as it follows Marx, to declare itself on the question: Is it capitalism or states that must be destroyed in order to get peace, or must both be abolished? Admittedly, there is no ambiguity on this point for those who follow Marx all the way to the socialist millennium. Because in the socialist millennium there are neither states nor capitalism, it makes little difference whether one or the other, or both, were formerly the culprits. And with respect to the period preceding the millennium, the Marxist would argue that although one may pry the various terms apart in order to analyze them, in actuality capitalism is never separate from class struggle, or from states, or from war. For the faithful Marxist, the ambiguity of Marx on war and peace is insignificant. The importance of Marx and Engels in this respect lies not in the thought that the end of states is the end of war but instead lies precisely in the fact that Marxist theory subordinates the problem of war and peace to the triumph of the revolutionary world proletariat, at which point men live no longer in states but are united in a nonpolitical free association.[6] Before the proletarian revolution has enjoyed a universal success, the Marxist in international politics, instead of being concerned with the abolition of war, is concerned with two other problems: the prolongation of peace

[5] In Marxist theory proper, the problem of peace among socialist states can arise only in the period between the revolution and the disappearance of the state, and for that period peace among states was not a problem that occupied the minds of Marx and Engels.

[6] Marx and Engels, *Communist Manifesto,* tr. Moore, pp. 43–44.

so long as peace serves the interests of international socialism, and, where necessary, the tactical use of war to hasten the day of revolution.

Capitalist states cause war, and socialism spells peace. On these points Marx is clear. But would a world of socialist states be a world at peace? From the works of Marx and Engels this question can never be answered; in their theoretical construction, the question, along with the state under socialism, simply "withers away."

THE SOCIALIST PARTIES IN THE PERIOD OF THE FIRST WORLD WAR

What does Marxist theory have to do with the behavior of socialists during the First World War? Simply this: The Second International attempted to translate Marx's assumption of a uniform proletarian interest into a comprehensive program of action to preserve the peace of Europe. The process of translation was difficult indeed, as became increasingly apparent as the fateful year 1914 approached. Each of the numerous conferences of the Second International issued a resolution on peace, and each resolution seemed to say that socialists were united in their opposition to war. They were united in that they agreed that war is bad, yet they differed on how socialists were actually to behave in a war situation. With the support of many French and British socialists, Jean Jaurès and Keir Hardie eloquently urged a positive program of immediate application. Socialists, they said, can force even capitalist states to live at peace. This they can do in a number of ways, culminating in the threat of general strike and insurrection against any government that undertakes war. This view was duly reflected in the resolutions of the Second International.[7] But a different view,

7 Stuttgart, 1907; repeated at Copenhagen, 1910: "In the case of war being imminent, the working classes and their parliamentary representa-

held with equal conviction, was recorded in the same resolutions. Some French and most German socialists argued that capitalist states are by their very nature wedded to the war system; the hope for the peace of the world is then to work for their early demise.[8]

Though the reconciliation of divergent views was only superficial, there nevertheless grew among socialists the conviction that social democracy would serve as an effective instrument against war. It did not. The German party,[9] the largest of all socialist parties, not only failed to oppose the war that began in August of 1914 but on the 4th of that month unanimously supported the granting of war credits to the bourgeois German government, though there had been dissent in the party caucus. The socialist parties in other states that became involved in the war also supported their governments. One may, according to his preconceptions, be surprised either by the breakdown of the International's laboriously constructed peace program or by the durability of a seemingly unstable synthesis. How in the period preceding the war the synthesis could have survived so many disputes has been explained many times. Some have emphasized the artfulness with which Jaurès compromised the various points of view present in each international conclave to give the ap-

tives in the countries concerned shall be bound to do all they can, assisted by the International Bureau, to prevent the war breaking out, using for this purpose the means which appear to them the most efficacious but which must naturally vary according to the acuteness of the class war and of the general political conditions." Quoted in Walling, *The Socialists and the War*, pp. 99–100.

8 Stuttgart: "Wars, therefore, are part and parcel of the nature of capitalism; they will cease only when the capitalist system declines, or when the sacrifices in men and money have become so great as a result of the increased magnitude of armaments that the people will rise in revolt against them and sweep capitalism out of existence." *Ibid.*, p. 38.

Copenhagen: "Wars will cease completely only with the disappearance of the capitalistic mode of production." *Ibid.*, p. 40.

9 The Sozialdemokratische Partei Deutschlands; hereafter referred to as the SPD.

pearance of unity where actually the differences were more important; others, the humanitarian appeal of a peace program, which was itself capable of transcending a good many differences.   More generally one might point out that those in opposition may easily give the appearance of unity even where a number of conflicting views exist. Just as the SPD seemed to be united so long as it was not called upon to act, so the Second International remained one, or nearly one, so long as it was not called upon to implement its antiwar stand.   To illustrate the principle in homely terms: husband and wife may agree that the bedroom is presently painted an unpleasing color, but let them beware if under this surface harmony lies his view that it is now too dark and hers that it is too light.

With the outbreak of war, the superficial harmony achieved in the peace resolutions of the Second International gave way to the conflicts of interest and intention that lay beneath the surface.   The conflict in action among the separate socialist parties could have been explained by reference to the split in socialist ranks on matters of theory as reflected in the debates of the International's conferences.   The argument instead turned on another point. Since it was agreed that socialists could with clear conscience support their own countries in a defensive war, the obsessing question became: For which countries is this war defensive?   In England, France, and Germany the great majority in each party said, clearly and quickly: It is for our country that the war is defensive.   In France, the conviction that the war was defensive, indeed that she, despite her capitalist government, could get into no other kind of war, is reflected in the statement of Jaurès made just before its outbreak:

Our duty as French Socialists is simple; we do not have to impose upon our government a policy of peace, for that is already its policy. Having never hesitated to call down upon myself the hatred of our chauvinists . . . I have the right to say that today the French government desires peace and works to preserve it.[10]

Clearly, in this somewhat partial view of French policy, war could come to France only if forced upon her. But was not the war defensive for Germany just as it was for France? The German socialists thought so, as is indicated by the statement of the SPD in explanation of its war stand:

> . . . we are menaced by the terror of foreign invasion. The problem before us now is not the relative advisability of war or peace, but a consideration of just what steps must be taken for the protection of our country.
>   . . . as far as concerns our people and its independence, much, if not everything, would be endangered by a triumph of Russian despotism, already weltering in the blood of her own noblest sons.
>   It devolves upon us, therefore, to avert this danger, to shelter the civilization and independence of our native land. Therefore, we must to-day justify what we have always said. In its hour of danger Germany may ever rely upon us.
>   We take our stand upon the doctrine basic to the international labor movement, which at all times has recognized the right of every people to national independence and national defense, and at the same time we condemn all war for conquest.[11]

And this despite the fact that, at least until July 31, *Vorwärts*, the semiofficial organ of the SPD, had continued to condemn all wars, specifically including the one that was about to break out, as capitalist inspired and meriting only the opposition of good socialists everywhere. According to the bold declarations published daily in the socialist press of Germany, German workers would not fight for German capitalists even should Russia enter a future war.

Socialists of all the belligerent countries found themselves caught in the web of international politics, as did men of all parties. French socialists feared that in an

[10] Reply to Haase in meeting of the International Socialist Committee, July 28, 1914, at Brussels. Quoted in La Chesnais, *Le Groupe Socialiste du Reichstag et la Déclaration de Guerre*, p. 30.
[11] Reprinted in Walling, *The Socialists and the War*, pp. 143–44.

actual war situation the German socialists would be an ineffective restraint on German militarism.[12] If German socialists could not prevent their government's undertaking war, French socialists would have to help in the defense of France. German socialists, on the other hand, feared that if they were an effective restraint on German militarism the net result would be the conquest of Germany by Russia![13] To prevent this, German socialists would have to cooperate in the defense of Germany. For most Englishmen, socialist and nonsocialist alike, the defensive quality of the war was established by Germany's invasion of Belgium; for most Germans, socialist and non-socialist alike, the invasion of Belgium was an offensive tactic dictated by a defensive strategy.

The prewar peace resolutions had allowed for socialist participation in defensive wars. Now it turned out that the war was defensive for everybody! The difficulty was not unforeseen. To August Bebel's insistence that a disclaimer in favor of defensive war would lead to no ambiguity, Karl Kautsky, in 1907, had replied that even those who were politically most sophisticated might well differ, especially just after the outbreak of a war, on the question of which country had begun it. Kautsky proposed another test, presumably less subjective. Whether or not the proletariat is to participate in a given war should, he urged, be decided according to proletarian

[12] See especially the speech of Jaurès at Amsterdam in 1904, quoted in Lair, *Jaurès et l'Allemagne,* pp. 91–93.

[13] Cf. the statement made by Guesde, a member of the French minority, in the French Socialist Congress held a few weeks before war was declared. "The general strike," he argued, "would be a real danger for the Socialism of the more progressive countries. And how could the International Bureau make the strike simultaneous? And even if it could, would not the difference in the strength of the various labor organizations remain? The more strongly organized country would be crushed. And that is high treason against Socialism." Quoted in Walling, *The Socialists and the War,* p. 60. A similar statement was made by Bebel as early as 1891. See Joll, *The Second International,* p. 73.

interests.[14] Reviewing the controversy in the perspective of the late summer of 1914, Kautsky could come to only one conclusion: Neither the one criterion nor the other provides an obejctive guide. The French and German parties considered both questions—who was responsible for the outbreak of war, and what course best served the interest of the proletariat—and came to opposite conclusions. This would seem to indicate that the international unity of proletarian interests is a fiction, at least in wartime. And this is the conclusion that Kautsky, in proposing a third criterion, accepts.[15] One may, he says, dispute who is the aggressor, and one may differ on whether the proletariat is threatened more by a German victory over France or a Russian victory over Germany; but this much is clear: "Every people, and the proletariat of every people, has a pressing interest in keeping the enemy from crossing the frontier and bringing with it the horror and devastation of war." Since no one can say with authority who is the aggressor or where the international interest of the proletariat lies, each nation must "save its skin as best it can." The third criterion, then, requires that the war be *conducted* as a defensive war. The stipulation that the proletariat can only support a defensive effort requires that the proletariat take part in a war only while the actual defense of a country is at issue.[16] Whether or not this approach provides a more usable criterion is a question that scarcely requires comment. The labored searching for a criterion is comment enough.

As we have pointed out, the resolutions of the Second International did not forbid the proletariat's participation

---

[14] Kautsky's test is better Marxism. Cf. above, pp. 127–28.

[15] Cf. Kautsky, "Die Internationalität und der Krieg," *Die Neue Zeit*, 33d Year, I (November 27, 1914), 248: The International "is not an effective tool in war; it is essentially a peacetime instrument."

[16] Kautsky, "Die Sozialdemokratie im Kriege," *Die Neue Zeit*, 33d Year, I (October 2, 1914), 4, 7–8.

in defensive wars. But there was reflected in these resolutions the conviction that a European war would be a signal for all socialist parties to join in an international movement against war, not for each party to rush to the defense of the homeland. What interest, after all, could socialists have in helping to defend their bourgeois states? Despite the differences that had continually arisen in conference debates, it had seemed clear to many socialists that the answer to this question must be, none.[17] It is then not enough to say that once the war broke out socialists became involved in the still-continuing attempt to distinguish aggressive from defensive war. To explain why the defense of their countries turned out to be important to them, we must consider internal as well as external politics, socialist expectations as well as love of homeland.[18] French security would be jeopardized, perhaps irreparably, by a German-Austrian victory in the East. To make such a victory less likely, France would have to intervene. In so far as French socialists were also French patriots, they, like any bourgeois, had to accept this conclusion. And French socialists, in so far as they followed Jaurès, were French patriots; for Jaurès had advanced the thesis that socialism and national sovereignty, instead of being incompatible, are necessary parts of the happy socialist future. If socialism must develop within the nation, then the nation must be defended. For the German socialists, the question was more difficult if only because their theory had remained, verbally at least, more faithful to Marxist doctrine. On the other hand, the

[17] Cf. Kautsky: "Because we were one in condemning war and because we knew that today war finds its ultimate source in imperialist tendencies, it was easy to assume that we in the International had attained a complete unity on all problems of war." "Die Internationalität und der Krieg," *Die Neue Zeit*, 33d Year, I (November 27, 1914), 240.

[18] On these points see especially Cole, *A History of Socialist Thought*, III, 60, 84, 91-96, 947-48; Schorske, *German Social Democracy*, ch. xi.

German party had grown to the point where, in the election previous to the war, it had captured more than four million votes and had elected almost one third of the Reichstag membership. If Germany should win a quick military victory, an eventuality that in the summer of 1914 seemed more than an idle dream, would not a nonparticipating SPD suffer irreparable damage in domestic politics from the fact that all the credit for victory would go to the bourgeois parties? And if Germany should lose, would not the SPD be accused of having made defeat inevitable by smashing the solidarity of the state in its hour of crisis? In either case, opposition to the war might spell political suicide, and then what would happen to the chances of bringing about socialism in Germany, the industrial giant in the heart of Europe whose future had been regarded as so important for all socialists whether German or non-German? While the German socialists, when faced with the reality of war, took a second look and decided that the defeat of Germany by Russia would be not just a defeat of the capitalist apparatus of the German state but would in fact be a defeat of socialist aspirations in all of Central Europe, so the English socialists decided that without English intervention on behalf of her Entente partners a German victory would be likely—"and the victory of Germany would mean the death of democracy in Europe." [19] Contradictory responses to such pressures were possible even among dedicated socialists. The politics of power, both internal and external, confounded the efforts of socialists to implement the unity they had striven for so diligently in the years preceding the war.

The behavior of the workers in the First World War demonstrated that there was no *international* proletariat, but only *national* socialist parties whose actions would be

---

[19] Declaration signed by 25 Labour M.P.'s; quoted in Humphrey, *International Socialism and the War*, pp. 112–13.

determined by their own definitions of their particular interests. A spontaneous harmony of interests among the various national proletarian parties would then be as difficult to explain as a perceived harmony of interest among the various bourgeois governments! [20] To understand the difficulties standing in the way of spontaneous agreement among national socialist parties, which is what the socialist resolutions had assumed, one need only realize that harmony here requires agreement on tactics as well as on ends. The common aspiration of all socialists, if indeed there was a common aspiration, was no longer a sufficient bond of unity. A merely verbal opposition to the policy of capitalist states was no longer possible; the socialist parties had either to oppose actively or cease to oppose at all. This is precisely where the assumption of a spontaneous harmony broke down—as was inevitable.

If the motives of the various socialist parties in rallying to the support of their governments were conventional ones, such as concern for the defense of the nation and desire to preserve the strength of the party in the competition of domestic politics, what then happens to the Marxist conviction that the interest of the proletariat in the socialist revolution cuts across all other interests and relegates them to the trash heap of outmoded ideas? Kautsky had frankly admitted that the harmony-of-interest doctrine must break down in practice. This is more of a sacrifice of orthodox socialist theory than can be afforded if the socialist goal is to remain as a seemingly practical proposition. Socialist theory, if it is to be salvaged, must

[20] The latter possibility was contemplated by a number of socialists beginning with Marx himself. Kautsky, e.g., sees no reason why farsighted capitalists should not adopt the slogan: "Capitalists of all lands, unite!" "Der Imperialismus," *Die Neue Zeit,* 32d Year, II (September 11, 1914), 920. Hobson also sees the establishment of a capitalist international order as a horrible possibility. *Problems of a New World,* pp. 182–86.

be quickly and cleverly adapted to the new conditions. Lenin took account of them and made the adjustments in theory that he considered appropriate. It is to him that we turn in the next section.

THE ADJUSTMENT OF THEORY TO FACT: LENIN

In the period of the First World War, each socialist party found itself bound to its national state by ties of emotional and material interest; the interests of the workers organized nationally into socialist parties did not in practice coincide perfectly as in theory they were supposed to do. Discovery of this surprised most socialists. Lenin, for example, would not at first believe that Social Democrats had decided to support the war effort of the German government and had thus indicated at least limited approval of the war. When informed of the event, he could explain it only as a plot of the capitalist press. It had, with obvious intent, wrongly reported the stand of the German socialists.

Once Lenin discovered that his first explanation was incorrect, he industriously set about to devise another, as indeed he had to do if socialist theory were to be saved. According to Marx's theory, the proletariat does have a single interest. The failure of national parties to act according to this insight must mean, if the insight were not to be discarded, either that the existing socialist parties could not be equated with the proletariat or that socialist leadership had failed in the interpretation of the true proletarian interest and in the ability and determination to act accordingly—or both of these explanations might be correct. There were other difficulties as well. When dissent prevails where unanimity is supposed to abide, one can always restore unity by excommunicating the dissenters and leaving them to form their own sect. This, however, leads to endless quarrel as to which of the two (or more) bodies faithfully represents the original creed. Lenin could, and did, say that some of the so-called proletarians were not real proletarians at all but had been bought off with a part of the ill-gotten gains of imperialism. This group had set an unholy example for the mass of bona fide proletarians, thus causing them to cling to the small present rewards of capitalism in preference to the future, and thus problematic, promises of socialism.[21] The attempt to reestablish a condition for unanimous agreement by defining the socialist base in more precise terms had the considerable advantage of retaining a strong element of materialist determination. But also, in raising an embarrassing question, it had one big disadvantage. If the proletariat could so easily be seduced, how could they ever work with the solidarity necessary to bring off the socialist revolution? What, in other words, was to prevent the infinite multiplication of sects each claiming to be faithful to the original creed?

For Marx and Engels the problem had existed, but not in such a serious form. They had predicted a clear-cut division of society into two classes, a development that would render the proletariat a monolithic mass, as undifferentiated as it was unhappy. And the objection that divisions might appear within the mass, they answered with the following assertion: "This organization of the proletarians into a class, and consequently into a political party, is continually being upset again by the competition between the workers themselves. *But it ever rises up again, stronger, firmer, mightier.*"[22] Because they were

[21] "Opportunism means the surrender of the *basic* interests of the masses for the *temporary* interests of a small minority of workers, or in other words, it means the union of a portion of the workers with the bourgeoisie in opposition to the mass of the proletariat." Lenin, *The Collapse of the Second International*, tr. Sirnis, p. 47. Cf. especially his *Imperialism, passim.*

[22] Marx and Engels, *Communist Manifesto*, tr. Moore, pp. 24–26. Italics added.

convinced that this is true, they could look upon the proletarian movement as "the self-conscious, independent movement of the immense majority, in the interest of the immense majority." Because the movement is assumed to be both self-conscious and politically aware, there is no gulf between leaders and led; the Communists are simply "the most advanced and resolute section of the working class parties of every country." They express more clearly the interests that the mass already understands, although imperfectly.[23]

Developing economic conditions give rise to a basic harmony of interest among the workers; the function of socialist leadership is to spell out this interest in concrete terms. In theory this sets forth a fairly definite relation of leaders to led, but the theory was difficult to apply. What one's practice should be would depend on the extent to which there was actually a felt harmony of interest among workers. In 1915, three left-wing socialists, Karl Liebknecht, Rosa Luxemburg, and Franz Mehring, recalled with nostalgia the optimistic estimates that socialists had so often made. "Up to this time," they wrote, "we have cherished the belief . . . that the class interests of the proletariat are a harmonious unit, that they are identical, that they cannot possibly come into conflict with one another. That was the basis of our theory and practice, the soul of our agitation." [24] If harmony had prevailed among the proletariat, then the function of socialist leadership would simply have been to educate and encourage. The experience of the First World War exposed the extent to which socialists had deluded themselves. Obviously the interests of the workers, the interests at least that gave impetus to their acts, were not so homogeneous as their theory had led

[23] *Ibid.*, pp. 28–32.
[24] Liebknecht, Luxemburg, and Mehring, *The Crisis in the Social-Democracy*, p. 21.

socialists to expect. This discovery was not in itself fatal to Marxism. One might, for example, argue that the workers had failed to achieve international solidarity because economic conditions had not matured sufficiently to produce a universal interest among them. Greater patience would then be the socialists' answer to the disillusioning experience of the First World War. This answer presupposes that the assigned relation of leaders to led was a correct one.

Lenin was not so sure. In the past he had emphasized the need for strong leadership, but at the same time he had related the functioning of this leadership to the ever-increasing receptivity of the masses. A receptive group of followers; an informed and vigorous leadership: nothing here conflicts with the traditional democratic conception of the political processes.[25] But in the face of the adversities encountered by the socialist revolutionary movement, Lenin tended to emphasize more and more the necessity for a leadership of inflexible will and to castigate the masses for failing to comprehend that their true interests lay in following it—or rather in following those among the Marxist leaders whom Lenin designated as genuine members of the revolutionary vanguard. The power of the party vanguard was to compensate for the failure of the workers to achieve harmony in action. The lesson of the First World War was not that there was no single interest shared by the workers of all lands, but rather that the masses could be brought to act in accordance with their true interest, their revolutionary destiny, only under the pressures of strong leadership. As Lenin put it: "The immediate task that confronts the class conscious vanguard

25 Cf. Lenin, *What Is to Be Done?* p. 52: "The spontaneity of the masses demands a mass of consciousness from us Social-Democrats." This was written in 1902.

of the international labour movement, *i.e.*, the Communist Parties, groups and trends, is to be able to *lead* the broad masses (now, for the most part, slumbering, apathetic, hidebound, inert, and dormant) to their new position." [26]

Lenin's redistribution of emphasis within Marxist theory permits him to return to the original Marxist thesis on war: The proletariat can have no stake in the wars bred by capitalism except to use them to forward the communist revolution. It also permits him to maintain with undiminished ardor that the proletariat everywhere has a single, constant interest. For what Lenin has done is to explain why this one true interest is more difficult to discern than had generally been supposed and then to draw from this explanation the conclusion that the party leadership must possess an iron will in order to impose an iron discipline. In major thesis, Lenin's is the old Marxist vision; in estimate of necessary procedure, it is not. Marx foresaw the necessity of revolution, but not that the socialists would have to adopt Lenin's methods to bring it off. Lenin is in a sense correct. *If* the socialist program requires that substantially all members of the proletariat act as though they had a single and constant interest, then the exercise of great force, even within the working-class movement itself, is the only way in which socialism can be instituted.[27]

THE ADJUSTMENT OF THEORY TO FACT: THE REVISIONISTS

The proletariat seizes the state power, and transforms the means of production in the first instance into state property. But in doing this, it puts an end to itself as the proletariat, it puts an end also to the state as the state. . . . The government of persons is replaced by

[26] Lenin, *"Left-Wing" Communism: An Infantile Disorder*, p. 73.

[27] The "if" is important. It is possible to reject the spontaneous harmony thesis without going to the other extreme of a rigid conformity, which is never attainable without the exercise of great force in some form.

the administration of things and the direction of the processes of production. The state is not "abolished," *it withers away.*[28]

Conventional Marxists had taken Engels's prediction of a change in form literally—out of the proletarian revolution is born the socialist state, which in turn disappears leaving a world of peace amidst plenty. A growing number of "revisionists," beginning late in the nineteenth century, in rejecting other of the Marxist tenets also rejected this. Eduard Bernstein, foremost of the German revisionists, argued against the emphasis on ultimate end and, what had followed from this, the concern over the tactics that could bring it about. Instead he would concentrate on day-to-day improvement of the position of the workers, both economically and politically. For revolution, he would substitute evolution; and the evolution, of course, was the one he saw presently taking place.[29] In France, Jaurès, and in England, the Fabians, gave expression to similar ideas.[30]

The point of present interest is that where the Marxist had emphasized international solidarity at the expense of national independence, the revisionist accepts the state as the embodiment of national unity and the instrument for the progress of the national proletariat. He focuses his attention on the here and now and relegates the "wither-

[28] Engels, *Herr Eugen Dühring's Revolution in Science (Anti-Dühring).* tr. Burns, pp. 306–7.

[29] "To me that which is generally called the ultimate aim of socialism is nothing, but the movement is everything." Bernstein, *Evolutionary Socialism,* tr. Harvey, p. 202; cf. pp. xi–xiii.

[30] German revisionists accepted Marx as the basis of their thought and then claimed to update him. British and French socialists more often took Marx as one of the many sources of their ideas. The term "revisionist" applies, strictly speaking, only to those who follow the former practice. It is convenient here to use the term more broadly to cover a large number of socialists who, often differing in their ideas of suitable domestic policy, found themselves in general agreement on both the causes of war and the means to peace.

ing away of the state" to the category of academic questions. Where the strict Marxist had thought peace coeval with the disappearance of all states, the new socialist looks for the gradual dawn of a peaceful era, and this era is to find its basis in the progressive improvement of the separate states. It is still only socialism that can eliminate war, but socialism no longer means revolution, and certainly it does not mean the disappearance of states. Thus Jaurès, giving his usual vague expression to hopes admittedly sincere, writes that "only socialism . . . will resolve the antagonism of classes and make of each nation, finally at peace internally, a particle of humanity." [31]

Immediately one is struck by a double parallel. On the one hand, the new socialist ideal is related to the historical development that finds its roots specifically in the eighteenth-century nationality doctrine and generally in nineteenth-century liberalism; on the other hand, it is related to the standard socialist aspirations of the prewar period. The first of these two influences, expressed originally in the national-cultural ideals of Herder and others of his period, had found its elaborate political statement in Mazzini. If each nationality were a separate nation, the argument reads, then each nation would be satisfied with its lot and wars would forever cease. The idea of national self-determination as *the* route to peace persisted despite the refutation of events. Indeed it was originally formulated in the face of factual contradiction, for the French state, as soon as it attained a truly national consciousness, had embarked on one of history's most impressive rampages. Conquest and slaughter were then undertaken, in the name of the nationality principle, on a greater scale than had ever been known before. It seems that, to use Alfred Cobban's apt phrase, national self-determination

[31] Lair, *Jaurès et l'Allemagne*, p. 84.

ineluctably gives way to national self-determinism, a thought borne out by the history of almost every nation in the world, not excluding the United States.

Faith in the nationality principle as a basis of peace dies hard. If national self-determination does not bring peace, then nationality plus democracy ought to. Mazzini had assumed that a self-determined state would be a democratic one; Woodrow Wilson explicitly makes the assumption a precondition of world peace. But still the historical credentials of the doctrine are faulty.[32] Should the doctrine therefore be rejected, or will more tampering render it serviceable? The revisionists chose the second alternative. Political democracy had been a front for certain selfish interests, so their reasoning went, and for these selfish interests states went to war *contrary to what the intentions of the people would have been had they been permitted to know the international facts of life.* Socialism will eliminate the influence of "the interests" and for the first time permit the voice of the people to be heard in its pristine purity. This will mean peace.

As the revisionists were related to the mainstream of liberal thought on international political questions, by the same token they were related to the conventionally Marxist thought of the era. Their conviction that socialist states would always see eye to eye on the ultimate question of war and peace is, in a different form, one of the assumptions on which the peace resolutions of the Second International were based. Those who can assume that action according to the perceived interests of any one national socialist party will be in perfect harmony with the similarly motivated action of all other such parties can, by the same mental process, assume that socialist nations will perpetually and automatically be at peace with one another. Before we reach any broad conclusions,

[32] See above, ch. iv.

however, the revisionist position should be examined in more detail.

John Hobson laid the immediate groundwork for the principal views of the school so far as international politics is concerned. His study of the Boer War led him to the conclusion that "a small confederacy of international financiers working through a kept press" had brought about the war. Their objects?—to develop at one stroke a source of cheap labor for the future and an opportunity for quick profits in the present.[33] Hobson soon generalized from the explanation of one war to an explanation for all modern wars, and, in addition, he put alongside this explanation for an unwanted phenomenon a prescription guaranteed to effect its doom. In its explanatory aspect, his argument is so well known that it can be summarized in one sentence: Uncontrolled capitalist production gives rise to industrial surpluses; from the attempt to market these surpluses an international fight for markets ensues; war results, directly or indirectly, from this struggle for markets.

In substantiating his thesis, Hobson first sets forth a profit-and-loss statement for imperialism, which leads him to the conclusion that imperialism does not pay. The costs for any country are higher than the possible returns.[34] Then why should any country ever adopt a policy of imperialism? Hobson finds the answer in the selfish interest of minority groups. For the nation as a whole, imperialism is an especially expensive form of folly; for a minority of financial and industrial interests it is a source of great profit. By this explanation, imperialism, in the phrase Hobson borrows from James Mill, is nothing but "a vast system of outdoor relief for the upper classes." [35]

---

[33] Hobson, *The War in South Africa*, p. 229.
[34] Hobson, *Imperialism*, Part I, ch. ii.
[35] *Ibid.*, p. 51.

Thus, it should be noted, the policy of imperialism is just as irrational for a laissez-faire state as it would be for a socialist state. The crucial difference between the two types is that a socialist state will follow the rational policy whereas a laissez-faire state, under the domination of capitalist interests, will not. The question of merit is settled by the fact, or rather the assumption, that a socialist state has built into it a predisposition toward rationality. The importance of the point merits quoting the relevant passage:

> A completely socialist State which kept good books and presented regular balance-sheets of expenditure and assets would soon discard Imperialism; an intelligent *laissez-faire* democracy which gave duly proportionate weight in its policy to all economic interests alike would do the same. But a State in which certain well-organized business interests are able to outweigh the weak, diffused interest of the community is bound to pursue a policy which accords with the pressure of the former interests.[36]

On this passage all of Hobson and most of revisionism turn so far as the question of war and peace is concerned.

When he labels the foreign policy of capitalist states "folly," Hobson is on strong ground, for there is ever a large admixture of folly in the acts of men and states. But in making imperialism the only folly of importance and in tying the imperialist folly entirely to the aims of a willful and selfish minority, he has traded the materialism of Marx's dialectic for a materialism at once more naïve and less serviceable. This is, in short, single-cause explanation in one of its less impressive forms. The superficial virtue of the single-cause explanation is that it permits a simple, neat solution. Precisely so in this case. Capitalism equals war because it allows minority interest to determine majority will; socialism equals peace because it *is* rule in the interest of the people at large. Under socialism, the archetypes of capitalist villainy will be done

[36] *Ibid.*, pp. 47–48.

away with—special interests, if they exist at all, will no longer be able to corrupt the rational processes of the state.

In Marxism proper, it will be recalled, the state withered away leaving a free and spontaneous association of men. War among states ceased because there were no longer states to fight with each other. For the revisionists the state retains its political characteristic, but the political function becomes less controversial; the interest of the people is put right out in front and that interest is assumed to be clearly and constantly for peace. The socialist state is, to paraphrase Jaurès, truly a particle of humanity at peace with itself and hence at peace with the world. Hobson himself put it this way: "Nationalism is a plain highway to internationalism, and if it manifests divergence we may well suspect a perversion of its nature and its purpose." [37] And the early Laborite, Sir M. E. Grant Duff, subscribed to the same thought when he wrote that England "should aim at living in the community of nations as well-bred people live in society; gracefully acknowledging the rights of others, and confident, if we ever think about the matter at all, that others will soon come to do no less for us." [38] The state itself is not to wither away, but international politics is clearly expected to do so. The revisionists have returned to the liberal ideal—the subordination of external politics to internal development and finally the disappearance of the former entirely.

What effect did the experiences of the First World War have on the optimistic hypotheses of the revisionists? In that war each socialist party had acted on its own interpretation of its interest and not according to an international proletarian interest. This was the great apostasy

[37] *Ibid.*, p. 11.
[38] Quoted in MacDonald, *Labour and the Empire*, p. 15.

the revisionists had to explain. They might have followed Lenin, given up the easy assumption of a spontaneous harmony among socialists organized nationally, and insisted on organizing in the future the power necessary to enforce the harmony that had seemingly proved an illusion. They might, on the other hand, have offered an explanation based on the impossibility of enlightened socialist action within a capitalist framework. They took neither of these courses. By and large, they followed instead a third course—they found a scapegoat. There was, they said, nothing wrong with the revisionist tenets except that the *German* socialist party failed to follow them. That this exception proved the rule was not quite claimed, but still it was never admitted that it provided any disproof. No, the German state was bent on aggression and the German socialists failed in their duty to offer active opposition. Instead of a reflection on the validity of socialist tenets, the failure of the SPD simply gave evidence that long exposure to the perverted political institutions of the autocratic German state had corrupted the SPD, once so widely considered the pillar of strength among national socialist parties. Because the German party had failed in its duty, the other national parties could no longer perform theirs. In fact, their duty to oppose the war was converted by the German defection into a duty to support the war that had thereby become truly defensive. The conviction that Germany, including the German socialists, must bear all the blame for the war only strengthened the revisionists' belief that a change in the internal structure of states is the sovereign remedy for war! [39]

[39] Arthur Henderson's view of the war is one of many examples. "British Labour," he wrote, "is out to strangle and stamp under foot Kaiserism and Militarism and the 'will to world domination'—and to substitute for them goodwill and fraternity." *The Aims of Labour*, p. 50.

External pressure tends to produce internal unity. This simple formula helps to account for the ability of each national socialist party to find, once the war began, that its state was acting defensively (i.e., justly—or at least more justly than the others). From this point of view, it is not difficult to understand how opposition to almost all wars permitted support of the war at hand. It is a little more difficult to understand how the mainstream of revisionist thought could ignore the challenge provided by the various postwar exposés, for after the war there was an *historical* revisionist to point an accusing finger at each of the major states involved, and in every case with some claim to plausibility. But just as Viscount Grey, publishing his memoirs seven years after the war, could ignore the documentary evidence that should have shattered his still firmly held belief in the almost exclusive guilt of the German militarists,[40] so most revisionists could continue to believe that the socialist program had failed to preserve the peace only because German Social Democrats lacked the courage to oppose their own government. At least revisionists were not led to reexamine the fundamentals of their war-and-peace thesis by the disclosures that occurred as national archives were successively opened.

Hobson provides a good example of the pre- to postwar continuity in revisionist thought. In 1909 he believed that a democratic society of nations was rapidly taking shape in which each nation would find its fullest opportunity for development, just as within the democratic state each individual finds his own best life. Practical internationalism, he wrote, is teaching us daily that cooperation "is the distinctive character of national activity." The slogan "from each according to its powers, to each according to its needs" [41] is to be applied to states as well as to individuals; and the condition that, in the former case, is to

---

[40] Grey, *Twenty-five Years*, I, 275–76; II, 22–32, 278.
[41] Hobson, *The Crisis of Liberalism*, p. 260.

make it real is not some change in the structure of the international society but the progressive improvement of each separate state. Under the immediate impact of the war, Hobson did lose some of his faith in the sufficiency of his previous analysis. "Public opinion and a common sense of justice are," he admits, "inadequate safeguards. There must be an executive power enabled to apply an economic boycott, or in the last resort an international force." [42] But the international government to be sought is, by his own specification, not a government properly so called but a concert of powers; and the concert, as one might guess, is to rest on the mutual faith and good will of the participating states. Thus he asserts that the difficulties will diminish "if the League of Nations can once be set upon a fairly stable footing and be given opportunity to assert its inherent virtues. For if the intelligence and faith of nations are strong enough once to establish it, the ambitions, the fears, and the suspicions, which are the spiritual nutriment of special alliances and groups, would wither and decay." [43] As before the war, so during and after the war Hobson continues to look to capitalism as the chief source of the "will to power," [44] to the rapidly approaching socialist organization of states as the effective establishment of the will to international cooperation,[45] and to reason as the keystone of the whole system.[46] Once socialism replaces capitalism, reason will determine the policies of states.

At this point it is possible to summarize Hobson's philosophy of peace and at the same time to reflect the unity of revisionist thought on the subject. The revisionists agree

---

[42] Hobson, *Towards International Government*, p. 6.
[43] *Ibid.*, pp. 23, 82.
[44] Hobson, *Democracy after the War*, p. 7.
[45] To cite a later work, see Hobson's *The Recording Angel*, pp. 121–26.
[46] Hobson, *Problems of a New World*, p. 272; quoted below, pp. 152–53.

that the cause of war is to be found in the existence of capitalist states. The war system can be ended, writes Charles Trevelyan on behalf of the Union of Democratic Control, only "by a direct challenging of the central principles of the system which has ended in the disaster [of the great war]." [47] And what are the central principles of that system? The answer, given unanimously, is that the heart of the matter is "the internal structure of the States concerned." Capitalism and a spurious nationalism: they are the culprits.[48] The cure is no more complicated than the cause, for, it is asserted, "A foreign policy directed to establishing a Cooperative World Commonwealth of Nations is the inevitable corollary to a home policy which looks to the establishment of the Socialist State." [49] And as a basis for the cure, the assurance alike of its sufficiency and its dependability, there stands always the interest of the people in peace. "Open covenants openly arrived at" would be the policy of a Labour Government, and this in itself would be the greatest guarantee of peace. "If Parliament and the country were fully informed on foreign affairs, they would never blindly support a war. Foreknowledge would almost make war an impossibility." [50] Under the new dispensation, the substance of international politics would remain the same, for, as Philip Snowden points out, "A Labour Government would be as jealous of national honour [and] as keenly alive to the great possibilities of Empire Development . . . as any British Government of the past." [51] It is assumed, however, that good will and fraternity will re-

[47] Trevelyan, *The Union of Democratic Control*, p. 9.

[48] "Vigilantes," *Inquest on Peace*, pp. 315–19, 335.

[49] *For Socialism and Peace*, p. 7. Cf. Henderson, *The Aims of Labour*, p. 29: "Freedom at home and domination abroad are incompatible with the ideals of [social] democracy."

[50] Snowden, *If Labour Rules*, p. 51.

[51] *Ibid.*, p. 47.

place militarism and war in proportion as the will of the
people replaces the selfish will of a few, which was thought
to have dominated international politics under a system of
capitalist states.   In the socialist world, states will still exist
and will continue to enjoy their independence, but they
will be much nicer.[52] That is the gist of the matter.

There is a noble optimism here. Is it valid? Nineteenth-century liberals had thought it comparatively easy
to substitute reason for force. They had combined a generally favorable estimate of man's character with the assumption that harmony in social and economic relations would
be realized through free competition among individuals,
in ideas as well as in goods. They were convinced that
protectionism and war are irrationalities imposed upon
the world by the interests of the ruling few. They believed that as states internally approach the forms that
favor the real interests of their citizens, these states will
be increasingly able to regulate relations among themselves by open discussion and voluntarily observed agreements.   Except on the question of domestic economic
arrangements, revisionist thought can seemingly be summarized in similar words.   It may therefore be surprising
to note that Hobson has questioned the easy optimism of
the nineteenth-century liberals, specifically "the feeble-
ness of the safeguards upon which liberal and humane
thinkers had relied," and that he singled out their faith
in "economic internationalism, democracy and the re-
stricted functions of the State" for special criticism. Yet at
the end of the work in which these criticisms appear, he
can assert: "Reason points to economic order, democracy
and internationalism, to a pacific settlement of the con-

[52] Cf. *ibid.*, p. 50: "The internationalism of the Labour Party is not a
sloppy cosmopolitanism. The very term 'internationalism' implies the
existence of nations. The Labour Party's internationalism means the
friendly co-operation of nations for the settlement of common problems."

flicts we see sprouting from the battlefield. The salvation
of the world lies in this assertion of the supremacy of
reason." [53] It appears that Hobson, having criticized the
liberals, in the end adopts their program. The seeming
inconsistency is removed by his economic analysis. Cobden had underestimated the pacific virtues of free trade,
says Hobson, but he had overestimated the ease with
which international free trade could be brought about.[54]
Cobden had assailed imperialism, protectionism, and
militarism; but he had not fully perceived their economic
taproot. First socialism, Hobson is saying, and then the
virtues extolled by the nineteenth-century liberals will
operate effectively to produce a world at peace. Frictions
in trade will no longer inflame the relations of states;
trade will instead bind them together in a mutuality of
interest. Reason will no longer devise new deceits and
new ways to outsmart other countries or, if that fails, to
overpower them; reason will instead be the means by
which the relations of states are adjusted to the mutual
advantage of all of them.

There is more than a trifling logic involved. Wars
have been too horrible and too frequent to give way before some superficial change in the conduct of the present
states, such as might be brought about by urging them to
adopt free trade. The old system has produced war and,
if war is to be abolished, the old system must be radically
changed. So much is incontrovertible. There are, however, two difficulties in the actions and thoughts of the
revisionists. First, there is always within revisionist circles
a tendency to rely on a shock treatment that will in itself
arouse the world to its full sensibilities. Thus Ramsay
MacDonald, prior to the First World War, believed that
"the spell [of militarism, of tariffs, of suspicion, of aggres-

[53] Hobson, *Problems of a New World*, pp. 32, 272.
[54] Hobson, *The New Protectionism*, p. 116.

sive nationalism] is to be broken only by one of the nations boldly walking out from the imprisonment." And England, he thought, was the nation to set the example.[55] Thus Léon Blum, reasoning as had the socialist Louis Garnier-Pagès some sixty years before him, argued that a general disarmament after the First World War could have been brought about by the dramatic example of one great power renouncing its arms. And France, he thought, was the nation to set the example.[56] Thus Hobson hoped that the churches uniting in prayers for "common horse sense" might turn the trick.[57] If only the nations will wake up to the full folly of their behavior—this is at once the hope and the plea of the revisionists. The hope is grounded on an economic analysis that had convinced them of the great peace potentialities of socialist states. The plea is grounded on their great faith in the potency of reason, and so great is the faith that at times they forget the economic-political preconditions that they have themselves specified. They in fact continue the tradition established by the Second International of combining with a belief in the techniques of the bourgeois peace movement—arbitration, disarmament, open diplomacy—the faith that socialists, even though out of power, can exert enough pressure upon national governments to ensure peace.[58]

The first difficulty is incidental, a logical slip under the pressure of a desire for peace in the present rather than a promise of peace in the problematic future. The second, which we now take up, is crucial to the development of our argument. Although revisionists did not always act or talk in ways consistent with their own analysis, they never-

[55] MacDonald, *Labour and the Empire*, p. 109.
[56] Blum, *Les Problèmes de la Paix*, pp. 152–53.
[57] Hobson, *The Recording Angel*, p. 58.
[58] Cf. the Stuttgart and Copenhagen resolutions. The point is well made by Cole, *A History of Socialist Thought*, III, 68–69, 84–85.

theless clearly established the thought that, for peace, the old system must be changed. But *what* in the old system must be changed? The socialist analysis, of both Marx and the revisionists, points to capitalism as the devil; but the socialism that would replace capitalism was for Marx the end of capitalism *and* the end of states. For Marx the international political problem will wither away only as states disappear. For the revisionists the problem will wither away not as states disappear but as the separate states become internally more perfect. Here too the revisionists have forsaken Marx and returned to Kant and the thought of nineteenth-century liberals generally. They had thought that the problem of war would be removed by the internal improvement of the conflicting units, which is exactly the solution of the revisionists. Hobson, like many liberals, had on occasion expressed the conclusion that international agreements unbacked by force are useless.[59] But this conclusion he never applied to the hypothetical case of a number of socialist states existing side by side in a situation where their interests would touch at hundreds of points, some of which would presumably give rise to differences of opinion between two or more of them. Many liberals had expected from the evolution of all states toward the pattern of the ideal republic a double result: decreased incidence of conflict and increased ability to solve conflicts peacefully. Revisionists expect the evolution of all states toward the pattern of the socialist state to produce the same effects. The revisionist recipe differs in its ingredients from the recipe liberals had written in the preceding century. Where they had emphasized political form, the revisionists emphasize economic and social content. The fundamental assumption is, however, the same: Each state because it is

---

[59] See especially Hobson's *Notes on Law and Order, passim.*

internally so perfect becomes in its external policy so enlightened that conflicts can scarcely ever exist and can certainly never lead to violence. For the revisionists, as for liberals, it is not states that disappear but rather the need for an international regulating authority. Establish socialism within the various states, the revisionists say, and then "the ambitions, the fears, and the suspicions, which are the spiritual nutriment of special alliances and groups, would wither and decay." [60]

Kautsky had been willing to admit that there was in wartime no automatic harmony of interest among the proletariat of the various nations. This was accepted by Lenin as well, but Lenin advocated using power to change the fact he found so unpalatable. The revisionists attempted to explain the fact away by fastening all of the blame on one of the national socialist parties, a process that made the future peace of the world depend on winning the then present war and at the same time preserved the fiction of a spontaneous harmony of interest among those truly socialist. The tendency to redefine the category "socialist" as soon as some socialists behave in ways that other socialists do not like raises in different form the question asked in Chapter IV: How excellent must each state be in order to ensure the perpetual peace the revisionists promise? This question must be answered even if the assumption that socialism is the peaceful form of the state is granted.

CONCLUSION

There is no shortage of instances in which the vision of liberals and of socialist revisionists has seemed true. Today, from the Western point of view, it seems almost pain-

[60] Hobson, *Towards International Government*, p. 82. Quoted above, p. 150.

fully true. "If it were not for the Communist threat," says Vice President Richard Nixon, "the free world could live in peace." [61] This recently expressed conviction is an echo of the French, British, and American chant against German militarism early in this century, of the Cobdenite chant against Russia and the Austro-Hungarian Empire in the middle of the last century, and, no doubt, of the chant of the primitive tribes against one another through many ages. If that other state or group were only better, then we would not have these troubles. The revisionists assumed that to remove a scapegoat was tantamount to the introduction of perpetual peace. First defeat militarist Germany, next eliminate the adjective "capitalist" from the phrase "capitalist states," and then there will be no more wars. The immediate malefactor was Germany; in a more general sense the malefactor was capitalism; but in any case to remove that which is bad will solve the problem. Socialist states, they assert, will be peaceful. This may be true, but even so it does not follow automatically that among socialist states there will always be peace. This is what the revisionists did not understand. To say that capitalist states cause war may, in some sense, be true; but the causal analysis cannot simply be reversed, as it is in the assertion that socialist states mean peace, without first making sure that the causal analysis is complete. Is it capitalism, or states, or both that must be abolished? The ambiguity of Marx's analysis, which in the original context disappears with the coming of the socialist millennium, becomes of vital importance in testing the anti-

[61] New York *Times*, November 19, 1953, p. 1. Cf. Harry S. Truman's comment in an article in *ibid.*, April 28, 1957, p. 1. "There are some people—and I regret to say some governments—who have not yet accepted the fact that but for Russian intransigence the world would now be enjoying the pursuits of peace. Mankind today is sick with anxiety and torn by fear of another world war, solely because Russia wants it that way."

millennial revisionist theory.[62] The revisionists themselves apparently never realized this.

The examination of socialist theory and practice provides an example of the continuity and reappearance of thought patterns in international politics and serves as a detailed study of the applicability of the kind of analysis undertaken in this book. It demonstrates that the elaboration and critical comparison of types of thought in international politics can be of use in evaluating analyses and prescriptions widely separated in time and broadly divergent in content. It is at this point not necessary to repeat with reference to the revisionists all of the criticisms raised against liberals. If it is apparent that the same criticisms apply, the purpose of the present chapter is accomplished.

[62] See above, p. 127.

CHAPTER VI. THE THIRD IMAGE

International Conflict and

International Anarchy

For what can be done against force without force?

CICERO, *The Letters to His Friends*

WITH many sovereign states, with no system of law enforceable among them, with each state judging its grievances and ambitions according to the dictates of its own reason or desire—conflict, sometimes leading to war, is bound to occur. To achieve a favorable outcome from such conflict a state has to rely on its own devices, the relative efficiency of which must be its constant concern. This, the idea of the third image, is to be examined in the present chapter. It is not an esoteric idea; it is not a new idea. Thucydides implied it when he wrote that it was "the growth of the Athenian power, which terrified the Lacedaemonians and forced them into war." [1] John Adams implied it when he wrote to the citizens of Petersburg, Virginia, that "a war with France, if just and necessary, might wean us from fond and blind affections, which no Nation ought ever to feel towards another, as our experience in more than one instance abundantly testifies." [2] There is an obvious relation between the concern over

[1] Thucydides, *History of the Peloponnesian War*, tr. Jowett, Book I, par. 23.

[2] Letter of John Adams to the citizens of the town of Petersburg, dated June 6, 1798, and reprinted in the program for the visit of William Howard Taft, Petersburg, Va., May 19, 1909.

relative power position expressed by Thucydides and the admonition of John Adams that love affairs between states are inappropriate and dangerous. This relation is made explicit in Frederick Dunn's statement that "so long as the notion of self-help persists, the aim of maintaining the power position of the nation is paramount to all other considerations." [3]

In anarchy there is no automatic harmony. The three preceding statements reflect this fact. A state will use force to attain its goals if, after assessing the prospects for success, it values those goals more than it values the pleasures of peace. Because each state is the final judge of its own cause, any state may at any time use force to implement its policies. Because any state may at any time use force, all states must constantly be ready either to counter force with force or to pay the cost of weakness. The requirements of state action are, in this view, imposed by the circumstances in which all states exist.

In a manner of speaking, all three images are a part of nature. So fundamental are man, the state, and the state system in any attempt to understand international relations that seldom does an analyst, however wedded to one image, entirely overlook the other two. Still, emphasis on one image may distort one's interpretation of the others. It is, for example, not uncommon to find those inclined to see the world in terms of either the first or the second image countering the oft-made argument that arms breed not war but security, and possibly even peace, by pointing out that the argument is a compound of dishonest myth, to cover the interests of politicians, armament makers, and others, and honest illusion entertained by patriots sincerely interested in the safety of their states. To dispel the illusion, Cobden, to recall one of the many who have

---

[3] Dunn, *Peaceful Change*, p. 13.

argued this way, once pointed out that doubling armaments, if everyone does it, makes no state more secure and, similarly, that none would be endangered if all military establishments were simultaneously reduced by, say, 50 percent.[4] Putting aside the thought that the arithmetic is not necessarily an accurate reflection of what the situation would be, this argument illustrates a supposedly practical application of the first and second images. Whether by educating citizens and leaders of the separate states or by improving the organization of each of them, a condition is sought in which the lesson here adumbrated becomes the basis for the policies of states. The result?—disarmament, and thus economy, together with peace, and thus security, for all states. If some states display a willingness to pare down their military establishments, other states will be able to pursue similar policies. In emphasizing the interdependence of the policies of all states, the argument pays heed to the third image. The optimism is, however, the result of ignoring some inherent difficulties. In this and the following chapter, by developing and examining the third image in detail, we attempt to make clear what these difficulties are.

In preceding chapters we examined the reasoning of a number of men whose thoughts on international relations conform to either the first or second image. In the present chapter, for the sake of varying the treatment and because political philosophy provides insufficiently exploited clues to the understanding of international politics, we shall focus primarily upon the political thought of one man, Jean Jacques Rousseau. For the same pair of reasons, in making comparisons with the first and second images, we shall refer most often to two philosophers who closely followed those patterns—Spinoza for the first image,

---

[4] Cobden, especially his *Speeches on Peace, Financial Reform, Colonial Reform, and Other Subjects Delivered during 1849*, p. 135.

Kant for the second. Though both have been mentioned before, a summary of the reasoning on which they based their views of international relations will make the comparisons more useful.

Spinoza explained violence by reference to human imperfections. Passion displaces reason, and consequently men, who out of self-interest ought to cooperate with one another in perfect harmony, engage endlessly in quarrels and physical violence. The defectiveness of man is the cause of conflict. Logically, if this is the sole cause, the end of conflict must depend on the reform of men. Spinoza nevertheless solved the problem, on the national level only, not by manipulating the supposedly causal factor but by altering the environment in which it operates. This was at once the great inconsistency and the saving grace of his system. Spinoza moved from the individual and the nation to the state among states by adding one to the number of his original assumptions. States, he assumes, are like men; they display both an urge to live and an inability consistently to order their affairs according to the dictates of reason.[5] States, however, can provide against their own oppression, whereas individuals, "overcome daily by sleep, often by disease or mental infirmity, and in the end by old age," cannot. Individuals, to survive, must combine; states, by their very constitution, are not subject to a similar necessity.[6] Wars among states are then as inevitable as are defects in the nature of man.

Kant's analysis, while on some points similar to Spinoza's, is both more complex and more suggestive. Men he de-

[5] Though for Spinoza the unity of the state rests ultimately on the ability of the supreme authority to enforce his will, in explaining the behavior of states he uses both an organismic and a corporate-trust analogy. For the former, see *Political Treatise*, ch. ii, sec. 3; ch. iii, sec. 2. For the latter, see *ibid.*, ch. iii, sec. 14, and *Theologico-Political Treatise*, ch. xvi (I, 208).

[6] Spinoza, *Political Treatise*, ch. iii, sec. 11.

fines as being members of both the world of sense and the world of understanding. If they were wholly of the latter, they would always act according to universally valid, self-imposed maxims. They would follow the categorical imperative. But since they are members of the former as well, impulse and inclination overcome reason, and the categorical imperative is so seldom followed that in the state of nature conflict and violence reign. The civil state appears as a necessary constraint. A number of men acting upon empirical "and therefore merely contingent" knowledge must have a judge among them, and a judge who can enforce his decisions, if violence is to be avoided. After the state is established, men have some chance of behaving morally. Before the state is established, uncertainty and violence make this impossible. Men need the security of law before improvement in their moral lives is possible. The civil state makes possible the ethical life of the individual by protecting the rights that were logically his in the state of nature, though actually he could not enjoy them. The civil state, however, is not enough. Peace among as well as within states is essential to the development of uniquely human capacities. States in the world are like individuals in the state of nature. They are neither perfectly good nor are they controlled by law. Consequently conflict and violence among them are inevitable. But this bit of analysis does not lead Kant to the conclusion that a world state is the answer. Fearing that a world state would become a terrible despotism, stifle liberty, kill initiative, and in the end lapse into anarchy, he must cast about for another solution. The other possibility open to him is that all states so improve that they will act on maxims that can be universalized without conflict. While Kant fears the former solution, he is too cautious and too intelligently critical to hope for the latter. Instead he attempts to combine the two. It

is the aim of his political philosophy to establish the hope
that states may improve enough and learn enough from
the suffering and devastation of war to make possible a rule
of law among them that is not backed by power but is
voluntarily observed.[7] The first factor is the internal improvement of states; the second, the external rule of law.
But the second, being voluntary, is completely dependent
on the perfection with which the first is realized. The
"power" to enforce the law is derived not from external
sanction but from internal perfection.[8] This is a solution according to the second image, that is by the improvement of the separate states, though Kant's own analysis
leads one to question his conclusion. At the level of the
state, an adequate political system permits individuals to
behave ethically; a comparably adequate system is not attainable internationally. Still we are to hope for peace
among states. The inconsistency is apparent, though its
glare is somewhat dimmed by Kant's confession that he has
established not the "inevitability" of perpetual peace but

[7] For the above comments on man and morality, see "Fundamental
Principles of the Metaphysic of Morals," secs. 2 and 3, in *Kant's Critique
of Practical Reason and Other Works on the Theory of Ethics*, tr. Abbott.
On the natural and civil states, see *The Philosopy of Law*, tr. Hastie, secs.
8, 9, 41, 42, 44. On the dependence of morality on a condition of peace
among states, see "The Natural Principle of the Political Order Considered
in Connection with the Idea of a Universal Cosmopolitical History,"
Eighth Proposition, in *Eternal Peace and Other International Essays*, tr.
Hastie. On the characteristics of the international federation, see "The
Principle of Progress Considered in Connection with the Relation of
Theory to Practice in International Law," in *ibid.*, pp. 62–65; "Eternal
Peace," First and Second Definitive Articles, in *ibid.*; and *The Philosophy
of Law*, tr. Hastie, sec. 61.

[8] Each republic, the form of the state that Kant labels good, "unable
to injure any other by violence, must maintain itself by right alone; and
it may hope on real grounds that the others being constituted like itself
will then come, on occasions of need, to its aid." ("The Principle of
Progress Considered in Connection with the Relation of Theory to
Practice in International Law," in *Eternal Peace and Other International
Essays*, tr. Hastie, p. 64.) Republics, Kant must assume, will act in accordance with the categorical imperative.

only that the existence of such a condition is not unthinkable.[9]

In Rousseau's philosophy, considered in this chapter as a theory of international relations, emphasis on the framework of state action makes some of the assumptions of Spinoza and Kant unnecessary; it makes other of their assumptions impossible.

JEAN JACQUES ROUSSEAU

Montesquieu and, like him, Rousseau, upon looking at attempts of other philosophers to understand a real or hypothetical state of nature, were both moved to make the same critical comment. Montesquieu says of Hobbes that he "attributes to mankind before the establishment of society what can happen but in consequence of this establishment." [10] Both Montesquieu and Rousseau maintain that the state of nature of Hobbes—and the same applies to Spinoza—is a fiction constructed by assuming that men in nature possess all of the characteristics and habits they acquire in society but without the constraints imposed by society. Men before the establishment of society have not developed the vices of pride and envy. Indeed they could not, for they see very little of one another. Whenever chance brings them together, consciousness of weakness and impotency dissuades them from attacking one another. Since none knows either pride or envy, thrift or greed, he will attack another only if driven by hunger to do so.[11]

[9] This interpretation, supported by considering Kant's political thought in the context of his moral philosophy, contrasts with that found in Friedrich's book on Kant, *Inevitable Peace*.

[10] Montesquieu, *The Spirit of the Laws*, tr. Nugent, Book I, ch. ii. Cf. Rousseau, *Inequality*, pp. 197, 221–23. Page references are to *The Social Contract and Discourses*, tr. Cole, which contains *The Social Contract, A Discourse on the Arts and Sciences, A Discourse on the Origin of Inequality*, and *A Discourse on Political Economy*.

[11] Montesquieu, *The Spirit of the Laws*, tr. Nugent, Book I, ch. iii; Rousseau, *Inequality*, pp. 227–33.

From one point of view this criticism of Hobbes is mere quibbling. Montesquieu and Rousseau arrive at a different conclusion simply by starting one step further back in their imaginary prehistory than did either Spinoza or Hobbes. In doing so, however, they emphasize an important point. Because of the difficulty of knowing such a thing as a pure human nature,[12] because the human nature we do know reflects both man's nature and the influence of his environment,[13] definitions of human nature such as those of Spinoza and Hobbes are arbitrary and can lead to no valid social or political conclusions. Theoretically at least one can strip away environmentally acquired characteristics and arrive at a view of human nature itself. Rousseau himself has advanced "certain arguments, and risked some conjectures," to this end.[14] The very difficulty of the undertaking and the uncertainty of the result emphasize the error involved in taking the social man as the natural man, as Hobbes and Spinoza have done. And instead of deriving social conclusions directly from assumed human traits, Montesquieu argues that conflict arises from the social situation: "As soon as man enters into a state of society he loses the sense of his weakness; equality ceases, and *then* commences the state of war." [15]

This estimate of the causes of conflict Rousseau takes up and develops.[16] It raises three questions: (1) Why, if the original state of nature was one of relative peace and quiet, did man ever leave it? (2) Why does conflict arise in social situations? (3) How is the control of conflict related to its cause?

[12] Rousseau, *Inequality,* pp. 189–91.

[13] *Les Confessions,* Book IX, in *Oeuvres complètes de J. J. Rousseau,* VIII, 289: "Aucun peuple ne seroit jamais que ce que la nature de son gouvernement le feroit être."

[14] *Inequality,* p. 190.

[15] Montesquieu, *The Spirit of the Laws,* tr. Nugent, Book I, ch. iii. Italics added.

[16] See especially *Inequality,* pp. 234 ff.

For Spinoza and Hobbes, the formation of state and society was an act of will that served as a means of escape from an intolerable situation. Similarly Rousseau at times, in his explanation of the establishment of the state, seems to assume the purely willful employment of art and contrivance.[17] At other times, Rousseau describes the establishment of the state as the culmination of a long historical evolution containing elements of experience, perceived interest, habit, tradition, and necessity. The first line of thought leads to the Social Contract; the second to the explanation found in *A Discourse on the Origin of Inequality*. The seeming contradiction is eliminated by the fact that Rousseau considers the first a philosophical explanation of what happened by historical processes; the second, a hypothetical reconstruction of those processes.[18]

In the early state of nature, men were sufficiently dispersed to make any pattern of cooperation unnecessary. But finally the combination of increased numbers and the usual natural hazards posed, in a variety of situations, the proposition: cooperate or die. Rousseau illustrates the line of reasoning with the simplest example. The example is worth reproducing, for it is the point of departure for the establishment of government and contains the basis for his explanation of conflict in international relations as well. Assume that five men who have acquired a rudimentary ability to speak and to understand each other happen to come together at a time when all of them suffer from hunger. The hunger of each will be satisfied by the fifth part of a stag, so they "agree" to cooperate in a project to trap one. But also the hunger of any one of them will be satisfied by a hare, so, as a hare comes within reach,

---

[17] See, e.g., *Social Contract*, pp. 4, 7 (Book I, chs. i, iv).

[18] In *Inequality*, pp. 190–91, he refers to the state of nature as "a state which no longer exists, perhaps never did exist, and probably never will exist; and of which it is, nevertheless, necessary to have true ideas." Cf. *ibid.*, p. 198.

one of them grabs it. The defector obtains the means of satisfying his hunger but in doing so permits the stag to escape. His immediate interest prevails over consideration for his fellows.[19]

The story is simple; the implications are tremendous. In cooperative action, even where all agree on the goal and have an equal interest in the project, one cannot rely on others. Spinoza linked conflict causally to man's imperfect reason. Montesquieu and Rousseau counter Spinoza's analysis with the proposition that the sources of conflict are not so much in the minds of men as they are in the nature of social activity. The difficulty is to some extent verbal. Rousseau grants that if we knew how to receive the true justice that comes from God, "we should need neither government nor laws." [20] This corresponds to Spinoza's proposition that "men in so far as they live in obedience to reason, necessarily live always in harmony one with another." [21] The idea is a truism. If men were perfect, their perfection would be reflected in all of their calculations and actions. Each could rely on the behavior of others and all decisions would be made on principles that would preserve a true harmony of interests. Spinoza emphasizes not the difficulties inherent in mediating conflicting interests but the defectiveness of man's reason that prevents their consistently making decisions that would be in the interest of each and for the good of all. Rousseau faces the same problem. He imagines how men must have behaved as they began to depend on one another to meet their daily needs. As long as each provided for his own wants, there could be no conflict; whenever the combination of natural obstacles and growth in population made cooperation necessary, conflict arose. Thus in the

[19] *Ibid.*, p. 238.
[20] *Social Contract*, p. 34 (Book II, ch. vi); cf. *Political Economy*, p. 296.
[21] Spinoza, *Ethics*, Part IV, prop. xxxv, proof.

stag-hunt example the tension between one man's immediate interest and the general interest of the group is resolved by the unilateral action of the one man. To the extent that he was motivated by a feeling of hunger, his act is one of passion. Reason would have told him that his long-run interest depends on establishing, through experience, the conviction that cooperative action will benefit all of the participants. But reason also tells him that if he foregoes the hare, the man next to him might leave his post to chase it, leaving the first man with nothing but food for thought on the folly of being loyal.

The problem is now posed in more significant terms. If harmony is to exist in anarchy, not only must I be perfectly rational but I must be able to assume that everyone else is too. Otherwise there is no basis for rational calculation. To allow in my calculation for the irrational acts of others can lead to no determinate solutions, but to attempt to act on a rational calculation without making such an allowance may lead to my own undoing. The latter argument is reflected in Rousseau's comments on the proposition that "a people of true Christians would form the most perfect society imaginable." In the first place he points out that such a society "would not be a society of men." Moreover, he says, "For the state to be peaceable and for harmony to be maintained, *all* the citizens *without exception* would have to be [equally] good Christians; if by ill hap there should be a single self-seeker or hypocrite . . . he would certainly get the better of his pious compatriots." [22]

If we define cooperative action as rational and any deviation from it irrational, we must agree with Spinoza that conflict results from the irrationality of men. But if we

[22] *Social Contract,* pp. 135–36 (Book IV, ch. viii). Italics added. The word "equally" is necessary for an accurate rendering of the French text but does not appear in the translation cited.

examine the requirements of rational action, we find that even in an example as simple as the stag hunt we have to assume that the reason of each leads to an identical definition of interest, that each will draw the same conclusion as to the methods appropriate to meet the original situation, that all will agree instantly on the action required by any chance incidents that raise the question of altering the original plan, and that each can rely completely on the steadfastness of purpose of all the others.   Perfectly rational action requires not only the perception that our welfare is tied up with the welfare of others but also a perfect appraisal of details so that we can answer the question: Just *how* in each situation is it tied up with everyone else's?   Rousseau agrees with Spinoza in refusing to label the act of the rabbit-snatcher either good or bad; unlike Spinoza, he also refuses to label it either rational or irrational.   He has noticed that the difficulty is not only in the actors but also in the situations they face.   While by no means ignoring the part that avarice and ambition play in the birth and growth of conflict,[23] Rousseau's analysis makes clear the extent to which conflict appears inevitably in the social affairs of men.

In short, the proposition that irrationality is the cause of all the world's troubles, in the sense that a world of perfectly rational men would know no disagreements and no conflicts, is, as Rousseau implies, as true as it is irrelevant.   Since the world cannot be defined in terms of perfection, the very real problem of how to achieve an approximation to harmony in cooperative and competitive activity is always with us and, lacking the possibility of perfection, it is a problem that cannot be solved simply by changing men.   Already Rousseau has made it possible to

[23] *A Lasting Peace*, tr. Vaughan, p. 72.   On p. 91 Rousseau refers to men as "unjust, grasping and setting their own interest above all things." This raises the question of the relation of the third image to the first, which will be discussed in ch. viii, below.

dispense with two of the assumptions of Spinoza and Kant. If conflict is the by-product of competition and attempts at cooperation in society, then it is unnecessary to assume self-preservation as man's sole motivation; for conflict results from the seeking of any goal—even if in the seeking one attempts to act according to Kant's categorical imperative.

FROM NATURE TO STATE

In the state of nature, for Rousseau as for Spinoza and Kant, men are governed by "instinct," "physical impulses," and "right of appetite"; and "liberty . . . is bounded only by the strength of the individual." Agreements cannot bind, for "in default of natural sanctions, the laws of justice are ineffective among men." [24] Without the protection of civil law, even agriculture is impossible, for who, Rousseau asks, "would be so absurd as to take the trouble of cultivating a field, which might be stripped of its crop by the first comer?" To be provident is impossible, for without social regulation there can be no obligation to respect the interests, rights, and property of others. But to be provident is desirable, for it makes life easier; or even necessary, for population begins to press on the amount of food available under a given mode of production. Some men unite, set up rules governing cooperative and competitive situations, and organize the means of enforcing them. Others are forced to follow the new pattern, for those outside the organized society, unable to cooperate effectively, cannot stand up against the efficiency of a group united and enjoying the benefits of a social division of labor. [25]

It is clear that in moving from the state of nature to

[24] *Social Contract*, pp. 18–19 (Book I, ch. viii); p. 34 (Book II, ch. vi).
[25] *Inequality*, pp. 212, 249–52. The dialectical development, in which each step toward the social state produces difficulties and near disasters, is especially interesting.

the civil state man gains materially. But there are more than material gains involved. Rousseau makes this clear in a brief chapter of *The Social Contract,* which Kant later followed closely. "The passage from the state of nature to the civil state," Rousseau says, "produces a very remarkable change in man, by substituting justice for instinct in his conduct, and giving his actions the morality they had formerly lacked." Man prior to the establishment of the civil state possesses natural liberty; he has a right to all he can get. This natural liberty he abandons when he enters the civil state. In return he receives "civil liberty and the proprietorship of all he possesses." Natural liberty becomes civil liberty; possession becomes proprietorship. And in addition "man acquires in the civil state, moral liberty, which alone makes him truly master of himself; for the mere impulse of appetite is slavery, while obedience to a law which we prescribe to ourselves is liberty." [26]

THE STATE AMONG STATES

For Rousseau as for Kant the civil state contributes to the possibility of the moral life, though Rousseau conceives of the contribution as a more positive one, somewhat in the manner of Plato and Aristotle. But what of the condition among the civil states themselves? At this point, Spinoza reverted to the analysis he had applied to individuals in the state of nature where, he thought, conflict had resulted from the defective reason of man. Kant too reverted to his analysis of the original conflict among men, but in his case the explanation included both the nature of the conflicting units and their environment. The explanations of Rousseau and Kant are similar, but Rousseau's is the more consistent and complete.

The social contract theorist, be he Spinoza, Hobbes,

[26] *Social Contract,* pp. 18–19 (Book I, ch. viii).

Locke, Rousseau, or Kant, compares the behavior of states in the world to that of men in the state of nature. By defining the state of nature as a condition in which acting units, whether men or states, coexist without an authority above them, the phrase can be applied to states in the modern world just as to men living outside a civil state. Clearly states recognize no common superior, but can they be described as acting units? This question we must examine before considering Rousseau's schematic description of the behavior of the state among states.

Rousseau, like Spinoza, occasionally uses corporate-trust and organismic analogies. The first is implied in his statement that the sovereign cannot do anything derogatory to the continued existence of the state. The end of the state is "the preservation and prosperity of its members." [27] The organismic analogy is reflected in his statement that "the body politic, taken individually, may be considered as an organized, living body, resembling that of man." As a living being, "the most important of its cares is the care of its own preservation." [28] Rousseau, however, cautions that the analogy is loosely used. The identity of individual and state motivation is a possible coincidence, not, as in Spinoza, a necessary assumption. And he defines with considerable care what he means when he describes the state as a unit complete with will and purpose.

In this respect, Rousseau can be considered as distinguishing two cases: states as we find them and states that are constituted as they ought to be. Of the first, he makes clear, there can be no presumption that the interest of the state and the action of the sovereign coincide. Indeed in

[27] *Ibid.*, pp. 16–17 (Book I, ch. vii); p. 83 (Book III, ch. ix).

[28] *Political Economy*, p. 289; *Social Contract*, p. 28 (Book II, ch. iv). Cf. Montesquieu, *The Spirit of the Laws*, tr. Nugent, Book X, ch. ii: "The life of governments is like that of man. The latter has a right to kill in case of natural defense: the former have a right to wage war for their own preservation."

most states it would be strange if they did, for the sovereign, far from caring for the interests of his state, is seldom moved but by personal vanity and greed. Even to such states organismic and corporate analogies have a limited application, for in one way the state is still a unit. The sovereign, so long as he retains sufficient power, carries out his will as though it were the will of the state. This parallels Spinoza, who simply assumes that in international affairs the state must be considered as acting on behalf of all its members. Rousseau adds to this an analysis, which, supplemented and borne out by the subsequent history of nationalism, reveals that the state may become a unit in a deeper sense than the philosophy of Spinoza can comprehend. Rousseau argues that under certain conditions a state will actualize the general will in its decisions, the general will being defined as the decision of the state to do what is "best" for its members considered collectively. The unity of the state is achieved when there exist the conditions necessary for the actualization of the general will.

From this abstract formulation one can scarcely derive an answer to the question that interests Rousseau: Under what conditions will the state achieve the unity that he desires for it? Fortunately it is quite easy to make Rousseau's formulation concrete. Public spirit or patriotism, he says, is the necessary basis of the good state. In the primitive tribe, economic interdependence and pressure from outside produced group solidarity. Amid the greater complexities of the eighteenth century, Rousseau fears that the spirit of solidarity found in the social or political groups of a simpler era has been lost. "There are today," he writes, "no longer Frenchmen, Germans, Spaniards, Englishmen . . .; there are only Europeans." All have the same tastes, passions, and morals because none receives a distinctive shaping of his character from his national institutions.²⁹ Patriotism is, he thinks, in danger of being lost in a welter of counterpassions arising from sub- or transnational interests. How, among so many other interests, can patriotism grow? This is the question Rousseau asks. He answers:

> If children are brought up in common in the bosom of equality; if they are imbued with the laws of the State and the precepts of the general will; if they are taught to respect these above all things; if they are surrounded by examples and objects which constantly remind them of the tender mother who nourishes them, of the love she bears them, of the inestimable benefits they receive from her, and of the return they owe her, we cannot doubt that they will learn to cherish one another mutually as brothers, to will nothing contrary to the will of society, to substitute the actions of men and citizens for the futile and vain babbling of sophists, and to become in time defenders and fathers of the country of which they will have been so long the children.³⁰

In such a state, conflict is eliminated and unity is achieved because, from a negative point of view, equality prevents the development of those partial interests so fatal to the unity of the state; from a positive point of view, the inculcation of public feeling imparts to the citizen a spirit of devotion to the welfare of the whole.³¹ The will of the state is the general will; there is no problem of disunity and conflict.

In studying international politics it is convenient to think of states as the acting units. At the same time, it does violence to one's common sense to speak of the state, which is after all an abstraction and consequently inani-

---

²⁹ *Considérations sur le Gouvernement de Pologne*, in Vaughan, ed., *The Political Writings of Jean Jacques Rousseau*, II, 432. The following, used below, are also cited from this work: *Projet de Constitution pour la Corse* and extracts from *Émile*.

³⁰ *Political Economy*, p. 309.

³¹ On the importance of equality see *Considérations sur le Gouvernement de Pologne*, especially II, 436, 456; *Projet de Constitution pour la Corse*, II, 337–38; and *Political Economy*, p. 306. On the importance of building patriotism see *Considérations sur le Gouvernement de Pologne*, especially II, 437.

mate, as acting.   This is an important point for any theory
of international relations, and especially for the third
image.   How generally applicable are the thoughts of
Rousseau to this problem?

The philologist Eric Partridge has commented on the
widespread tendency of primitive peoples to refer to themselves as *"the* men" or *"the* people," appellations implying
that they are better than, as well as distinct from, other
similar groups.[32]   Herodotus found that the Persians regarded themselves as a greatly superior people who rated
the merit of other peoples according to their geographic
nearness to the Persians.[33]   That the Greeks applied the
same idea to themselves is a commonplace of Hellenic
literature, and the Jews were certain that they were *the*
chosen people of God.   The feeling here expressed is the
sentiment of group or local patriotism.   Prior to the
eighteenth century the sentiment was either confined to a
small part of a population spread over a relatively large
area or it was confined to a larger percentage of those living in a relatively small area.   An example of the first condition is found in the resistance in France to the interference of Pope Boniface VIII in questions that king, no-
bility, and clergy united in regarding as domestic.   An
example of the second is found in the civic feeling in the
Greek city-states and in some of the medieval towns.

The existence of group patriotism has no special meaning for our analysis until, as C. J. H. Hayes says, it becomes fused with the idea of nationality.   Then we have
the immensely important fact of modern nationalism.

---

[32] Partridge, "We Are *The* People," in *Here, There, and Everywhere*,
pp. 16–20. Cf. "War," in Sumner, *War and Other Essays*, ed. Keller,
p. 12: "Perhaps nine-tenths of all the names given by savage tribes to
themselves mean 'Men,' 'The Only Men,' or 'Men of Men'; that is, We
are men, the rest are something else."

[33] *The History of Herodotus*, tr. Rawlinson, I, 71.

Hans Kohn points out that nationalism is impossible without the idea of popular sovereignty; that the growth of nationalism is synonymous with the integration of the masses into a common political form.[34]   Such an integration is the ideal of Rousseau's political writings, but he, like Plato, thought it possible only within a narrowly circumscribed area—the city-state.[35]   With the development of modern technology, especially as applied to the means of transportation and communication, it has become possible for the interests of individuals to be thought of as tightly complementary, even without the use of devices Rousseau thought necessary, over areas larger than Rousseau ever visualized.   The scale of activity has changed; the idea has not.

The idea of nationalism does not imply that allegiance to the nation is the sole allegiance.   It has been increasingly true in recent centuries, however, that most people feel a loyalty to the state that overrides their loyalty to almost any other group.   Men once felt a loyalty to church that made them willing to sacrifice their lives in war for it. The mass of men have, in modern times, felt a similar loyalty to the national state.   Modern nationalism admits of exception, but the exceptions have seldom resulted in numerous denials of the primary claim of the nation on the loyalties of its citizens.

The centripetal force of nationalism may itself explain why states can be thought of as units.   To base one's whole analysis on this point is, however, unnecessary. Rousseau has made it clear that his analysis will apply in

---

[34] Hayes, *Essays on Nationalism,* p. 29; Kohn, *The Idea of Nationalism,* pp. 3–4.

[35] Cf. the advice he gives in *Considérations sur le Gouvernement de Pologne,* II, 442: "Commencez par resserrer vos limites, si vous voulez ré-former votre Gouvernement."

either of two cases: (1) If the state is a unit that can with some appropriateness take the adjective "organismic." This, although Rousseau did not foresee it, has become the case in many states that in most other respects fall far short of his ideal. (2) If the state is a unit only in the sense that some power in the state has so established itself that its decisions are accepted as the decisions of the state.

In any actual state the situation can be described as follows. In the name of the state a policy is formulated and presented to other countries as though it were, to use Rousseau's terminology, the general will of the state. Dissenters within the state are carried along by two considerations: their inability to bring force to bear to change the decision; their conviction, based on perceived interest and customary loyalty, that in the long run it is to their advantage to go along with the national decision and work in the prescribed and accepted ways for its change. The less good the state, by Rousseau's standards, the more important the first consideration, and in the ultimate case the unity of the state is simply the naked power of the *de facto* sovereign. On the other hand, the better the state, or, we can now add, the more nationalistic, the more the second consideration is sufficient; and in the ultimate case the agreement of the citizens with the government's formulation of foreign policy is complete. In either case, the state appears to other states as a unit. Any "state" falling outside the terms of the preceding descriptions could no longer be considered a unit for purposes of international political analysis, but, since it would also cease to be a state, this does not complicate our problem. Some questions become questions of foreign policy; some questions of foreign policy call for single choices; some of these choices must be supported by the state as a whole or the state disappears—and with it the problem of state unity. If we have a state, we have a foreign policy, and in foreign policy the state must on occasion speak with a single voice.

There is a further consideration, which causes the nation to act more consistently as a unit than the preceding analysis suggests. In moments of crisis and especially in the crisis of war, attempts to achieve a nearly unanimous backing for foreign policy are most likely to be successful. The united front is enforced by the feelings of individuals, by their conviction that their own security depends on the security of their state. It is enforced by actions of the state that punish the traitors and reward those who are most effectively or most spectacularly patriotic. It is enforced by pressures from within society: the outrage of the chorus in Aristophanes' *The Acharnians* in reaction to Dicaeopolis' defense of the enemies of Athens is reflected in the wartime experience of every society.

The unity of a nation, in short, is fed not only by indigenous factors but also by the antagonisms that frequently occur in international relations. Such antagonisms become important not when they result in feelings of hatred between individuals in different countries but when the state mobilizes resources, interests, and sentiments behind a war policy. Previously inculcated feelings of enmity may make a war policy more likely and may increase its chances of success. But the war is prosecuted even though the infantryman on the line might rather be anywhere else doing anything other than shooting at the enemy. Individuals participate in war because they are members of states. This is the position of Rousseau who argues that "if war is possible only between such 'moral beings' [states], it follows that the belligerents have no quarrel with individual enemies." One *state* makes war on another *state*. The object of the war is to destroy or alter the opposing state. And if the opposing state "could be dissolved at a single stroke, that instant the war would end." [36]

One need not look far for confirmation of the hypothesis. We fought against Germany in the Second World War because as a whole it followed the lead of Hitler and not because so many people in the United States felt a personal enmity for the people of Germany. The fact that we opposed not individuals but states made possible a rapid realignment of states following the war, which is now spectacularly demonstrated by the cooperation of the United States with the leaders and people of states that were a short time ago our mortal enemies.

We can now return to Rousseau's theory of international relations paying special attention to the points that primarily concern him, namely the political environment and qualities of states. Of the role of the international environment, Rousseau says this:

> It is quite true that it would be much better for all men to remain always at peace. But so long as there is no security for this, everyone, having no guarantee that he can avoid war, is anxious to begin it at the moment which suits his own interest and so forestall a neighbour, who would not fail to forestall the attack in his turn at any moment favourable to himself, so that many wars, even offensive wars, are rather in the nature of unjust precautions for the protection of the assailant's own possessions than a device for seizing those of others. However salutary it may be in theory to obey the dictates of public spirit, it is certain that, politically and even morally, those dictates are liable to prove fatal to the man who persists in observing them with all the world when no one thinks of observing them towards him.[37]

The framework within which nations act makes prudence futile, for to be prudent is useless "when everything is

---

[36] *A Lasting Peace*, tr. Vaughan, p. 123. Cf. *Social Contract*, pp. 9–10 (Book I, ch. iv), and Montesquieu, *The Spirit of the Laws*, tr. Nugent, Book X, ch. iii.

[37] *A Lasting Peace*, tr. Vaughan, pp. 78–79; cf. Montesquieu, *The Spirit of the Laws*, tr. Nugent, Book X, ch. ii.

left to chance." [38] The character of those who act makes the situation more hopeless still. "The whole life of kings," Rousseau says, "is devoted solely to two objects: to extend their rule beyond their frontiers and to make it more absolute within them. Any other purpose they may have is either subservient to one of these aims, or merely a pretext for attaining them." [39] As for their ministers "on whom they shuffle off their duty" whenever possible, they "are in perpetual need of war, as a means of making themselves indispensable to their master, of throwing him into difficulties from which he cannot escape without their aid, of ruining the State, if things come to the worst, as the price of keeping their own office." [40] If in such a world prudence is futile, then sanity is downright dangerous, for "to be sane in a world of madmen is in itself a kind of madness." [41]

Of the relations among states as we find them, Rousseau has said nothing that is not also found in Spinoza and Kant, though in most cases he says it better. But would the existence of a number of good states, whether defined according to the juridical standard of Kant or the more inclusive criteria of Rousseau, add up to a world at peace? To this question Kant answered, yes; Rousseau says, no. The will of the state, which in its perfection is general for each of the citizens, is only a particular will when considered in relation to the rest of the world. Just as the will of an association within the state, while general for itself, may be wrong when considered from the standpoint of the welfare of the state; so the will of a state, though equitable for itself, may be wrong in relation to the world. "Thus it is not impossible," Rousseau says, "that a Republic, though in itself well governed, should

[38] *A Lasting Peace,* tr. Vaughan, p. 88.
[39] *Ibid.,* p. 95.
[40] *Ibid.,* p. 100.
[41] *Ibid.,* p. 91.

enter upon an unjust war." [42]   To achieve a will general for the world, the particularity of the separate states would have to be sublimated, just as Rousseau insists the particularity of private associations must be lost in the state. The nation may proclaim, and mean, that its aspirations are legitimate from the point of view of all states; but, despite the intent, each country's formulation of its goals will be of particular rather than of general validity.[43] Since this is the case, the absence of an authority above states to prevent and adjust the conflicts inevitably arising from particular wills means that war is inevitable.   Rousseau's conclusion, which is also the heart of his theory of international relations, is accurately though somewhat abstractly summarized in the following statement: That among particularities accidents will occur is not accidental but necessary.[44]   And this, in turn, is simply another way of saying that in anarchy there is no automatic harmony.

If anarchy is the problem, then there are only two possible solutions: (1) to impose an effective control on the separate and imperfect states; (2) to remove states from the sphere of the accidental, that is, to define the good state as so perfect that it will no longer be particular. Kant tried to compromise by making states good enough to obey a set of laws to which they have volunteered their assent.   Rousseau, whom on this point Kant failed to follow, emphasizes the particular nature of even the good

[42] *Political Economy*, pp. 290–91.

[43] On the subject of local variations in standards of conduct, of which the above thoughts are an extension, consider *La Nouvelle Héloise*, Part II, Letter xiv, in *Oeuvres complètes de J. J. Rousseau*, IV, 160: "Chaque coterie a ses règles, ses jugemens, ses principes, qui ne sont point admis ailleurs. L'honnête homme d'une maison est un fripon dans la maison voisine. Le bon, le mauvais, le beau, le laid, la vérité, la vertu, n'ont qu'une existence locale et circonscrite."

[44] This parallels Hegel's formulation: "It is to what is by nature accidental that accidents happen, and the fate whereby they happen is thus a necessity." *Philosophy of Right*, tr. Knox, sec. 324.

state and, in so doing, makes apparent the futility of the solution Kant suggests.[45]   He also makes possible a theory of international relations that in general terms explains the behavior of all states, whether good or bad.[46]

In the stag-hunt example, the will of the rabbit-snatcher was rational and predictable from his own point of view. From the point of view of the rest of the group, it was arbitrary and capricious.   So of any individual state, a will perfectly good for itself may provoke the violent resistance of other states.[47]   The application of Rousseau's theory to international politics is stated with eloquence and clarity in his commentaries on Saint-Pierre and in a short work entitled *The State of War*.   His application bears out the preceding analysis.   The states of Europe he writes, "touch each other at so many points that no one of them can move without giving a jar to all the rest; their variances are all the more deadly, as their ties are more closely woven."   They "must inevitably fall into quarrels and dissensions at the first changes that come about." And if we ask why they must "inevitably" clash, Rousseau answers: because their union is "formed and maintained by nothing better than chance."   The nations of Europe are willful units in close juxtaposition with rules neither clear nor enforceable to guide them.   The public law of Europe is but "a mass of contradictory rules which nothing but the right of the stronger can reduce to order: so that in the absence of any sure clue to guide her, reason is bound, in every case of doubt, to obey the promptings of self-interest—which in itself would make war inevitable,

---

[45] Kant is more willing to admit the force of this criticism than is generally realized.   On this point, see above, pp. 164–65.

[46] This is not, of course, to say that no differences in state behavior follow from the different constitutions and situations of states. This point raises the question of the relation of the third image to the second, which will be discussed in ch. viii, below.

[47] *Political Economy*, pp. 290–91.

even if all parties desired to be just." In this condition, it is foolhardy to expect automatic harmony of interest and automatic agreement and acquiescence in rights and duties. In a real sense there is a "union of the nations of Europe," but "the imperfections of this association make the state of those who belong to it worse than it would be if they formed no community at all." [48]

The argument is clear. For individuals the bloodiest stage of history was the period just prior to the establishment of society. At that point they had lost the virtues of the savage without having acquired those of the citizen. The late stage of the state of nature is necessarily a state of war. The nations of Europe are precisely in that stage.[49]

What then is cause: the capricious acts of the separate states or the system within which they exist? Rousseau emphasizes the latter:

Every one can see that what unites any form of society is community of interests, and what disintegrates [it] is their conflict; that either tendency may be changed or modified by a thousand accidents; and therefore that, as soon as a society is founded, some coercive power must be provided to co-ordinate the actions of its members and give to their common interests and mutual obligations that firmness and consistency which they could never acquire of themselves.[50]

But to emphasize the importance of political structure is not to say that the acts that bring about conflict and lead to the use of force are of no importance. It is the specific acts that are the immediate causes of war,[51] the general

[48] *A Lasting Peace,* tr. Vaughan, pp. 46–48, 58–59. Cf. *Inequality,* pp. 252–53, and *Émile,* II, 157–58.

[49] *A Lasting Peace,* tr. Vaughan, pp. 38, 46–47. On p. 121, Rousseau distinguishes between the "state of war," which always exists among states, and war proper, which manifests itself in the settled intention to destroy the enemy state.

[50] *Ibid.,* p. 49.

[51] In *ibid.,* p. 69, Rousseau presents his exhaustive list of such causes. Cf. *Social Contract,* p. 46 (Book II, ch. ix): "There have been known States so constituted that the necessity of making conquests entered into

structure that permits them to exist and wreak their disasters. To eliminate every vestige of selfishness, perversity, and stupidity in nations would serve to establish perpetual peace, but to try directly to eliminate all the immediate causes of war without altering the structure of the "union of Europe" is utopian.

What alteration of structure is required? The idea that a voluntary federation, such as Kant later proposed, could keep peace among states, Rousseau rejects emphatically. Instead, he says, the remedy for war among states "is to be found only in such a form of federal Government as shall unite nations by bonds similar to those which already unite their individual members, and place the one no less than the other under the authority of the Law." [52] Kant made similar statements only to amend them out of existence once he came to consider the reality of such a federation. Rousseau does not modify his principle, as is made clear in the following quotation, every point of which is a contradiction of Kant's program for the pacific federation:

The Federation [that is to replace the "free and voluntary association which now unites the States of Europe"] must embrace all the important Powers in its membership; it must have a Legislative Body, with powers to pass laws and ordinances binding upon all its members; it must have a coercive force capable of compelling every State to obey its common resolves whether in the way of command or of prohibition; finally, it must be strong and firm enough to make it impossible for any member to withdraw at his own pleasure the moment he conceives his private interest to clash with that of the whole body.[53]

It is easy to poke holes in the solution offered by Rousseau. The most vulnerable point is revealed by the ques-

their very constitutions, and that in order to maintain themselves, they were forced to expand ceaselessly." Cf. also *Political Economy*, p. 318; Montesquieu, *The Spirit of the Laws*, tr. Nugent, Book IX, ch. ii.

[52] *A Lasting Peace*, tr. Vaughan, pp. 38–39.

[53] *Ibid.*, pp. 59–60.

tions: How could the federation enforce its law on the states that comprise it without waging war against them, and how likely is it that the effective force will always be on the side of the federation? To answer these questions Rousseau argues that the states of Europe are in a condition of balance sufficiently fine to prevent any one state or combination of states from prevailing over the others. For this reason, the necessary margin of force will always rest with the federation itself. The best critical consideration of the inherent weakness of a federation of states in which the law of the federation has to be enforced on the states who are its members is contained in the *Federalist Papers*. The arguments are convincing, but they need not be reviewed here. The practical weakness of Rousseau's recommended solution does not obscure the merit of his theoretical analysis of war as a consequence of international anarchy.

CONCLUSION

The present chapter provides a basic explanation of the third image of international relations. That there is still important ground to cover is made clear by two points. First, there is no obvious logical relation between the proposition that "in anarchy there is no automatic harmony" and the proposition that "among autonomous states *war* is inevitable," both of which were put forth in this chapter. The next chapter will attempt to make clear their relation to each other and to the third image. Second, although it has by now become apparent that there is a considerable interdependence among the three images, we have not systematically considered the problem of interrelating them. This problem will be considered in Chapter VIII.

CHAPTER VII. SOME IMPLICATIONS

OF THE THIRD IMAGE

Examples from Economics, Politics, and History

So long as there are nations and empires, each prepared callously to exterminate its rival, all alike must be equipped for war.

FREUD, *Civilization, War and Death*

TWO points for consideration are contained in the statement that opens this chapter, one of a positive and one of a negative implication. Positively, to necessitate the arming of peacefully inclined countries some countries must be ready and willing to use force to make their wills prevail. Negatively, there must be lacking the authority that can prevent the unilateral use of such force. If both the positive and negative conditions are present, then the peaceful logically must look to the state of their armaments not because they wish to gain something from war but because they wish both to prevent its occurring and to protect themselves should it occur.

Is force or the threat of force used within or among states because some men or states are evil? Perhaps so, but not only for that reason; even good men and good states resort to force occasionally in their dealings. Is war then brought about by the disagreements that exist among states, be they good or bad? Francis I, when asked what differences accounted for the constant wars between him and his brother-in-law Charles V, supposedly answered:

"None whatever. We agree perfectly. We both want control of Italy!" [1] Goodness and evil, agreement and disagreement, may or may not lead to war. Then what explains war among states? Rousseau's answer is really that war occurs because there is nothing to prevent it. Among states as among men there is no automatic adjustment of interests. In the absence of a supreme authority, there is then constant possibility that conflicts will be settled by force.

What effects does the condition of anarchy among states, a condition in which each state must rely on its own resources and devices to secure its welfare, have upon the policy and behavior of states? This question can be answered on the basis of what is written in Chapter VI. It should be answered more fully and with a sharper pertinence. The present chapter will provide some additional details and raise some further considerations. In the first and second parts, two common but controversial features of international relations, tariffs and the balance of power, will be discussed with an eye open to the explanatory role of the third image. In the last section, the third image will be related to a number of nontheoretical, past and present commentaries on international politics.

NATIONAL TARIFFS AND INTERNATIONAL TRADE

Before applying Rousseau's analysis to problems of international economics, it is worth while to examine a case of conflict within a national economy. The case will illustrate both the origin of conflict and the social control of it.

The interest of workers in any trade is to protect their jobs and to push their wages to the highest possible level. This interest has often led to a stubborn resistance to laborsaving advances in technology on the one hand and

[1] Cited in Schuman, *International Politics*, p. 261.

to the development of conservative apprentice systems on the other. If its restrictive practices are successful, any one group of workers will enjoy a return for its services relatively higher than that of other labor groups, some of which will be in fields less susceptible to such manipulation. Examples are numerous. One of the most fascinating is the series of small-scale wars waged by the teamsters against the first attempts to transport oil by pipeline out of the Pennsylvania oil fields. Counter to the interest of the worker in protecting his present job and wage was the interest of society at large in increasing to the maximum the amount of production per dollar expended. If the interest of one group in society is sufficiently pressing and circumstances make it possible, the group will fight, as it did in Pennsylvania, to preserve the status quo. If the interest of the larger society is sufficiently clear and the society is sufficiently strong, it will bring the dissident group under control. In the example chosen it is clear that the interests of society, present and future, required the teamsters to make what might be a painful adjustment. Since their vested interest prevented their seeing this, guerrilla warfare broke out. A well-organized society will use various means to eliminate such use of force. The existing law may provide penalties, new laws can be made, or aid to those temporarily disadvantaged can be given to coax them into willing adjustment. In most cases the action of those who would seek a solution by force is physically limited by the lack of a territorial base and by a shortage of weapons. Psychologically it may be limited by a customary loyalty to the larger society.

The oil-fields incident is, of course, simplified. Such conflict does not usually occur as group versus society at large but as group versus group. In this case the laws of society backed the employers against the workers. The same thing happening in other cases of conflict between these two groups may run counter to the interest of society as a whole. The important point, however, is not that there is in the state a way of making and enforcing *correct* decisions but that some decision be made and followed. Thus Hans Kelsen has argued that "justice is an irrational ideal. However indispensable it may be for volition and action of men, it is not subject to cognition. Regarded from the point of view of rational cognition, there are only interests, and hence conflicts of interest." One set of interests can be satisfied at the expense of another, or they can be compromised. But one cannot say that one of these ways of dealing with conflict is just, the other unjust.[2] In domestic politics the important arguments over measures that would be a little better or a little worse obscure the greater importance of their being *a* decision. More important, for example, than the merits of the argument over whether strips of tideland should fall under state or federal jurisdiction was the existence of a governmental process to settle the dispute. The settlement was wrong from some points of view, right from others; but a moment's reflection will show that to have an "arbitrary" decision made and enforced is, in most cases, infinitely preferable to having "the rights and wrongs" settled by force. Kant's categorical imperative is in itself no help here. It tells us only that either decision is in accord with the principle of justice and hence acceptable —that we should not fight about it. But fighting is exactly what we may do in the absence of an effective decision-making authority. The authority, not the categorical imperative, is the important factor so far as peace is concerned. Not in all but in a great many cases, an imperfect solution imposed by authority is infinitely preferable to none at all.

On the international level there is most often none at

[2] Kelsen, *General Theory of Law and State*, tr. Wedberg. pp. 13–14.

all. The following example will illustrate the difficulty of achieving one's ends where a system of decisions binding all affected parties is lacking.[3] Assume two countries each trying to maximize the economic welfare of its members—an aim good in itself. The material goods each country will have to divide among its members will be increased through an international division of labor based on a free flow of resources and products between the two countries. We can say, then, that the two countries constitute a "society" in the sense that their citizens share a common aim. But given a quite common elasticity of demand on the part of country A for country B's products, country B can increase its national welfare by imposing a tariff.[4] Then country A, if it is clever, will counter the tariff of B with a tariff of its own. At each step the welfare of the two countries taken together will decrease, but after each increase by B, A recoups some of its recent loss by further increasing its own tariff. This can continue to a determinate point, which will probably be reached before all trade is eliminated, after which there is no longer even a relative advantage to be gained from further tariff increases. The important point is that originally each of the two countries sought only to increase its welfare. Unilateral actions in "rational" pursuance of a legitimate goal led to a net decrease in the welfare of both countries.

Should not both countries have foreseen the outcome from the beginning and have refrained from a competition in foolishness? Having pursued the game to its unsatisfactory conclusion, will they not agree between themselves to go back to the original situation and stay there? Both

---

[3] Based on Scitovszky, "A Reconsideration of the Theory of Tariffs," in *Readings in the Theory of International Trade;* Robbins, *The Economic Basis of Class Conflict and Other Essays in Political Economy,* especially pp. 108–17; and Robbins, *Economic Planning and International Order,* especially pp. 311–16.

[4] B improves its terms of trade.

questions are good ones if we continue to assume but two countries. With many countries in the picture, however, any one of them may think that it can neglect the danger of retaliation. The trouble is that once the competition in protectionism starts, the immediate interest of each country causes it to follow along. In Rousseau's stag-hunt allegory, one man seizes the hare even though his doing so means that the rest will lose the stag. In the present example each country is trying to snatch the hare (an advantage over its neighbors) *without* losing the stag (the advantages of an international division of labor). Is it correct then to have said that the result follows from each country *rationally* pursuing its economic interest? Scitovszky answers: "To call the raising of tariffs on these assumptions irrational, would be similar to calling competitive behavior irrational." [5]

On the basis of a similar analysis, Lionel Robbins does call protectionism irrational.[6] It is apparent that logically he then has to call the efforts of any individual or group to attain a monopolistic or monopsonistic position irrational and must consequently call the effort to maximize profits irrational—which he clearly does not intend. That Scitovszky and Robbins agree in their analyses and evaluations and yet differ in assigning a descriptive term to the type of action that leads to protectionism is explained by the fact that "rational" is here used in two distinct senses, as is often done. (1) An act is rational if it turns out well in the long run. Restriction in international trade would be a rational policy, for example, if its goal were to increase the economic welfare of the country and it in fact succeeded in doing so. (2) An act that is based on a calculation of factors, including the actions of others, is rational.

[5] Scitovszky, "A Reconsideration of the Theory of Tariffs," in *Readings in the Theory of International Trade*, pp. 375–76.

[6] Robbins, *The Economic Basis of Class Conflict*, p. 122.

In this sense, rational refers to a mental process. An act may in fact be *wrong* (not correctly calculated to achieve its end) without thereby being *irrational*. Given a certain legal structure, action by individuals to maximize profit is rational in the first sense: the results of such action are generally considered good. Given a legal structure different in kind, the efforts of each state to "maximize profits" lead to results that are hard to imagine as having come from rational behavior. Reason should have told all countries to stay out of the "competition in foolishness." But once one country starts, other countries are sorely tempted to follow. The point is that the pursuit of profit, which can be controlled in such a way as to lead to desirable results domestically, produces clearly undesirable results in international relations, where activities are not similarly controlled. We can call the activities rational on a domestic level and irrational on the international level if we choose, but to do so obscures the fact that we are dealing with similar problems in dissimilar settings, that in both situations the policy makers may well be trying to calculate correctly.[7] Overlooking the different environments of action leads us to explain by human agency where explanation by social-political structure is both more accurate and more helpful.

And, it should be added, in a sense the national and international problems merge. Suppose that the steel indus-

---

[7] Robbins realizes this. For example, he says: "If there be an 'invisible hand' in a non-collectivist order, it only operates in a framework of deliberately contrived law and order." Further, he makes the point that conflict may be the product of *objective* disharmonies: "When the conditions of supply and demand are such as either to confront buyers and sellers with monopolistic organizations or to permit buyers or sellers themselves to act as groups, then the objective conditions of conflict are present." (*The Economic Basis of Class Conflict*, pp. 6, 14.) It is obvious, then, that in the context of his analysis Robbins's use of the word "irrational" is not significant. In discussing the meaning of the words "rational" and "irrational" we intended not to criticize Robbins but rather to clarify some of the problems underlying situations of conflict.

try achieves a domestic monopoly. In the absence of altruistic motives, the quantity of steel produced will be lowered [8] to the point where the now increased price multiplied by the decreased quantity will maximize the profits of the industry. The owning interests gain by the amount of the net increase in profit. Now suppose the same thing happens in more and more industries. It is not difficult to visualize a progressive constriction of the economy that will result in a generally lowered standard of living and will leave everyone in a position absolutely worse than that of the premonopolistic state. This extreme hypothetical situation can result from the perfectly normal and, under certain conditions, admirable drive of every entrepreneur to maximize profits. There is nothing irrational about the individual's pursuit of profit, but there may well result from it a condition which, similar to that in international trade, is difficult to conceive as having resulted from a number of separate "rational" calculations. The end result is bad, but even though this is recognized, there may be no movement away from the system of monopolies. Why? Although most industries will benefit if all of them abandon monopolistic practices, any single industry will lose by abandoning its monopolistic position while others refrain from doing so. In the absence of spontaneous and nearly unanimous agreement, governmental action is required.

In absolute terms, private monopoly in domestic trade is as undesirable to everyone as is protectionism in international trade. Yet for any one or a small number of entrepreneurs to refrain from efforts to maximize profits—efforts that involve drives for monopolistic position—would work directly to their own disadvantage. On this point the testimony that Harlow Curtice, then president of General Motors, offered before the Senate Committee on

[8] From what it would be under conditions of competition.

Banking and Currency, is as instructive as it is incontrovertible.

> The only way that a company like General Motors can even stay where it is competitively is to work as aggressively as possible to better its position. To relax for a moment would be only to lose position. For a period of 4 years in the early 1920's, one company sold between 55 and 60 percent of all automobiles in the American market. It offered the lowest-priced car in the industry, yet could not withstand the competitive drive of other companies. This could happen again. Therefore, there can be no compromise between full, aggressive competition and loss of competitive position through any tendency to rest on one's laurels.
>
> General Motors has no assured markets. We have no protection against competition. Nor do we have any guaranteed rate of return on our capital.[9]

A given firm can limit its strivings only if others do too. To expect all firms to do so is utopian. In domestic economic affairs this is generally recognized. If the forces of competition fail to regulate individual activities, law is substituted. And if this fails, the individual entrepreneur should not be blamed for having followed his "economic instincts." Adam Smith once remarked that he had "never known much good done by those who affected to trade for the public good." [10] There are, however, always some people who believe in the administration of economic policy by exhortation. Thus, businessmen are from time to time urged to hold prices down voluntarily, this presumably being in the interest of the national economy and hence in the real interest of every entrepreneur.[11]

---

[9] *Stock Market Study.* Hearings before the Committee on Banking and Currency, U. S. Senate, 84th Congress, 1st session (March 18, 1955), pp. 821–22. With Curtice compare Catherine the Great who, under conditions roughly comparable, remarked that "he who wins nothing, loses." Cited in Martin, *The Rise of French Liberal Thought*, p. 262.

[10] Smith, *The Wealth of Nations*, p. 399 (Book IV, ch. ii).

[11] Cf. President Eisenhower's statement to the press on February 6, 1957: "Now, when I said business and labor must exercise their, must discharge their responsibilities, and exercise their authority in conformity with the needs of the United States, I wasn't merely asking them to be

But, given a number of entrepreneurs, the logic of the appeal is destroyed, for the cooperation of the majority would serve to enrich the noncooperating minority. Individual wisdom may represent collective insanity, but under the conditions described it is difficult to see what the individual can do about it.

In international affairs it is less frequently understood that to expect each country to formulate an economic policy that happens to work to the advantage of all countries is utopian.[12] Each state's failure to do so is to the disadvantage of all states, including itself; yet even were this noted the "right" policies would not be spontaneously and universally adopted. Individual calculations rationally arrived at from the point of view of each of the calculators considered separately do not, in a condition of anarchy, automatically result in social harmony. Whether or not an approximation to harmony results depends on the framework of action as well as on the action itself.

The tariff example, like the oil-fields example, was simplified. However, to add in the more common impulses toward restrictionism only strengthens the argument. The reasoning just applied somewhat artificially to states applies with equal logic and less artificiality to the groups within states on whose behalf tariffs or quotas are instituted. The woolgrowers of Wyoming and Oregon have gained from the protective tariff on wool; the United States as a whole has lost. But groups that expect to benefit directly from protection cannot be expected to refrain from demanding it any more than the automobile in-

---

altruistic by any manner of means. Their own long-term good is involved, and I am asking them merely to act as enlightened Americans." New York *Times*, February 7, 1957, p. 12. Former President Truman made a similar point in an article in *ibid.*, May 28, 1957, p. 1.

12 Strausz-Hupé, for example, treats free trade simply as something that ought to be. *The Balance of Tomorrow*, p. 226.

dustry can be expected to lose interest in making money. Reasons other than those included in Scitovszky's model, such as the pressure from domestic industries that are unable to compete with relatively more efficient foreign producers, more frequently account for an upward spiral of restrictionist devices. This should not be allowed to obscure the importance of his analysis. He assumes that the interest of each country, and not the interest of sub-national groups, is the goal of state policy and then asks what may happen. In doing so he puts the problem in its least difficult form and makes clear the minimum of imperfection that will suffice to bring about the undesired result. If one country inaugurates a policy of protection, other countries are tempted to follow. That one country will adopt a policy of protection is fairly well assured by the desire to maximize economic welfare. That the long-run futility of this policy will be overlooked is fairly well assured by the finite quality of human reason and, more significantly, by the requirements of rational action imposed by a condition of anarchy.

There are, of course, some plausible arguments for restriction, many of them more popular now among economists than at any time since Adam Smith. Hardly anyone of technical competence, however, would argue that the present set of restrictions is in the interest of any one country. If there must be controls in the interest, say, of domestic planning,[13] it is generally agreed that those controls should be at a level that will permit an expanded volume of trade throughout the world. The problem is how to expand trade in the world at large so long as each country is jockeying for national advantage. How is

13 See, e.g., Webb, "The Future of International Trade," *World Politics*, V (1953), especially pp. 430, 435–37; Keynes, "National Self-Sufficiency," *Yale Review*, XXII (1933), especially pp. 761–63.

country A, in any downward revision of restrictions, to make sure that B doesn't get the better of it? Both countries will gain, but B may gain a little more. This worry, even were there not many other factors operating, would be quite likely to bring into play the considerations embodied in Scitovszky's model—not just because each country is selfish but because competition in foreign trade is so keen.

Here certainly is a case where an imperfect solution would be better than none at all. A decision to reduce the barriers to trade among states would benefit some countries more than others, but in the long run and in absolute terms it would benefit all countries. In a condition of anarchy, however, relative gain is more important than absolute gain! This is a proposition that will become clearer when, in the next section, considerations of political power are added to purely economic concerns.

THE BALANCE OF POWER IN INTERNATIONAL POLITICS

The whole notion of balance of power, said John Bright one hundred years ago, is "a mischievous delusion which has come down to us from past times." The balance of power is an impossible thing like perpetual motion, a will-o'-the-wisp in pursuit of which Britain has expended thousands of millions of pounds.[14] Not a will-o'-the-wisp, not a delusion, but a fact of political life, a descriptive, scientific law said Hume nearly one hundred years earlier and Morgenthau nearly one hundred years later.[15]

If the balance of power is a delusion, it is, as Bright says, one of long standing. In the fifth century B.C., Thucydides explained the policy of Tissaphernes, King of the Persians,

---

[14] Bright, *Speeches,* ed. Rogers, pp. 233, 460–61, 468–69.
[15] Hume, "Of the Balance of Power," in *Essays Moral, Political, and Literary,* I, 348–56; and Morgenthau, *In Defense of the National Interest,* pp. 32–33.

as one of holding "the balance evenly between the two contending powers," Athens and Lacedaemon.[16] In the second century B.C., Polybius, in his explanation of the policies of Hiero,[17] makes brilliantly clear the effect of balance-of-power worries on the thinking of a statesman. When the Roman legions first arrived in Sicily to aid the Mamertines, Hiero, perceiving the relative strength of the Romans and concluding that their prospects were better than those of the Carthaginians, made proposals of peace and alliance to the Romans, which they accepted. Some years later, though still an ally of Rome, Hiero became alarmed at the extent of the Romans' success and sent assistance to Carthage. He was convinced, as Polybius explains it, that

it was in his own interest for securing both his Sicilian dominions and his friendship with the Romans, that Carthage should be preserved, and that the stronger power should not be able to attain its ultimate object entirely without effort. In this he reasoned very wisely and sensibly, for such matters should never be neglected, and we should never contribute to the attainment by one state of a power so preponderant, that none dare dispute with it even for their acknowledged rights.[18]

Yet "balance of power" is sometimes a frightening, sometimes a bewildering, phrase. People differ on whether it is good or bad, on who has approved it and who has not, and even on whether or not it exists. William Graham Sumner, for example, lines himself up with the Founding Fathers—he is against the balance of power.[19]

[16] Thucydides, *History of the Peloponnesian War,* tr. Jowett, Book VIII, par. 57; cf. par. 87.

[17] King of Syracuse, 270–216 B.C.

[18] Polybius, *The Histories,* tr. Paton, I, 41, 225 (Book I, secs. 16, 83). The Hiero example is one used by Hume.

[19] According to the Founding Fathers, he says, "There was to be no balance of power and no 'reason of state' to cost the life and happiness of citizens." Sumner, "The Conquest of the United States by Spain," in *War and Other Essays,* p. 333.

But Hamilton, who has always been considered one of the Founding Fathers, perceived and stated, in his usual clear style, that United States security if not dependent upon was certainly enhanced by the involvement of the European powers with each other.[20]   Somewhat like Sumner, Frank Tannenbaum emphatically rejects balance-of-power doctrine and attributes the past successes of American foreign policy to the fact that we have, in our acts, renounced the balance of power in favor of the policies of the coordinate state.   Balance-of-power policy is, in his opinion, so against all the traditions and institutions of the United States that our adopting it is inconceivable.[21] Alfred Vagts has concluded, however, after careful study of European and American diplomatic and military history, that the survival and well-being of the United States have always been closely tied to the functioning of a system of balance in Europe.[22]

Is the balance of power illusion or reality? Is it something pursued by the vicious and stupid, rejected by the pure and wise? Did the United States throughout its history extricate itself from dependence on the external politics of balance, or in saying now that it did are we behaving like the rich man who proclaims that money means nothing to him? These questions can be answered only by looking more closely at the logic of the balance of power, a logic that is intimately connected with the third image of international relations.

A man attacked by would-be thieves on Main Street may fairly hope that the police will either thwart the

[20] Hamilton, "Americanus II," in *Works,* ed. Lodge, V, 88–94. Cf. *The Federalist,* Nos. 4–5 (Jay), 6–8 (Hamilton).

[21] Tannenbaum, "The American Tradition in Foreign Relations," *Foreign Affairs,* XXX (1951), 31–50; and "The Balance of Power versus the Co-ordinate State," *Political Science Quarterly,* LXVII (1952), 173–97.

[22] Vagts, "The United States and the Balance of Power," *Journal of Politics,* III (1941), 401–49.

attackers or recover the loot. The chances of getting away with the crime are sufficiently small to reduce such incidents well below the point at which the ordinary citizen begins to carry arms. States, however, do not enjoy even an imperfect guarantee of their security unless they set out to provide it for themselves. If security is something the state wants, then this desire, together with the conditions in which all states exist, imposes certain requirements on a foreign policy that pretends to be rational. The requirements are *imposed* by an automatic sanction: Departure from the rational model imperils the survival of the state.[23] The clue to the limitations of policy imposed by the condition of anarchy among states is contained in the maxim: "Everybody's strategy depends on everybody else's," a statement that appears in John McDonald's popularization of the game theory of John von Neumann and Oskar Morgenstern.[24] One who wants to win a simple card game, in fact any game with two or more players, must follow a strategy that takes into consideration the strategies of the other player(s). And if there are three or more

[23] For a variety of reasons the pressure to adopt the "correct" strategy may be resisted. Tacitus, speaking of the wars among the Germans, said: "May the nations retain and perpetuate, if not an affection for us, at least an animosity against each other! since, while the fate of the empire is thus urgent, fortune can bestow no higher benefit upon us, than the discord of our enemies." (*A Treatise on the Situation, Manners, and Inhabitants of Germany*, par. 33, in *Works*, Oxford tr., revised, Vol. II.) In the terms used here, the German tribes were not sufficiently interested in winning the game of power competition with Rome to give up the games they were playing with each other.

[24] McDonald, *Strategy in Poker, Business and War*, p. 52. The reference to game theory does not imply that there is available a technique by which international politics can be approached mathematically. Balance-of-power politics, however, can profitably be described using the concepts of von Neumann and Morgenstern—what can be explained without reference to their speculations can perhaps be made clearer by qualified comparisons between the behavior of players of games and participants in international politics. For references to some of the unsolved difficulties in game theory, see below, n. 28. For an impressive attempt to apply game theory to strategy in international politics see Kaplan, *System and Process in International Politics*, Part IV.

players, he will, on occasion, have to form a coalition even though this may mean cooperating with his recent "enemy," one who still remains a potential enemy. Such a necessity arises most obviously where one man will win shortly unless his opponents help each other. There is, of course nothing automatic about the forming of the coalition. It may not be formed at all: because the two men we would expect to help each other are inveterate noncooperators, because they dislike each other too much to cooperate even for mutual advantage, because they are not intelligent enough to do so, or because the game is one in which it is difficult to perceive the proper moment for cooperation. But what would we say of one who under these conditions denounced the mere thought of coalition? Simply that he has either missed the point of the game or has decided that other things, contrary feelings or moral principles, are worth more than winning it.

Can the actions of states in international politics be considered in terms of this roughly sketched model? A considerable elaboration, requiring us to go beyond John McDonald's popularization to the original theory of von Neumann and Morgenstern, is necessary. A card game, such as poker, is a zero-sum game: my winnings plus your winnings are exactly equal to the losses of our opponent or opponents. In a zero-sum game, the problem is entirely one of distribution, not at all one of production. But the activities in which men and states are engaged seldom correspond to the zero-sum model. The problem may be one of production as well as distribution. The game, in the terminology of von Neumann and Morgenstern, becomes a general game. In a general game, "the advantage of one group of players need not be synonymous with the disadvantage of the others. In such a game moves—or rather changes in strategy—may exist which are advantageous to both groups. In other words, there may exist an oppor-

tunity for genuine increases of productivity, simultaneously in all sectors of society." [25] This is a situation in
which we have not just a pie to divide but the problem
of how much pie to make as well. Under these conditions
the game can tend toward either of two extremes. (1) It
may become a simple problem in maximization: all the
players may cooperate to make the largest possible pie.[26]
In international politics this corresponds to the hypothetical case in which all states band together with nature as
their adversary. (2) All the players may be so intent on
the question of how the pie already in existence should be
divided that they forget about the possibility of increasing
the amount each will have by working together to make
more of it. Instead of a simple maximum problem, the
game then reverts to a zero-sum or constant-sum game.[27]
In international politics this corresponds roughly to the
situation now prevailing, in which two sides have formed
and the gain of one side is often considered to be the loss
of the other. There is another possibility. It may be that
nobody likes pie, or that everybody likes something else
better. In this case the game is not played at all.

To what extent do states have a choice among these
three alternatives? A game must have an object. In poker
the object of each player is to win the largest possible
amount of money. States have many objects. Some states
may aim at the conquest of the world, other states may aim
at a local hegemony, other states may aim at no hegemony
at all but desire simply to be left alone. Common to the
desires of all states is the wish for survival. Even the
state that wants to conquer the world wants also, as a
minimum, to continue its present existence. If all states

[25] Von Neumann and Morgenstern, *Theory of Games and Economic Behavior*, p. 540.
[26] *Ibid.*, p. 517.
[27] Strategically these are equivalents. *Ibid.*, p. 348.

wanted simply to survive, then none would need to maintain military forces for use in either defensive or offensive action. But whenever some states give the impression that survival does not exhaust their political ambitions, others are forced, logically, to look to their defenses. Many states may prefer to play a game in which all states cooperate in the attempt to solve problems of maximization. Others may prefer to play no game at all. The implication of game theory, which is also the implication of the third image, is, however, that the freedom of choice of any one state is limited by the actions of all others. And this limitation applies as much to the process of deciding which game to play as it does to the actual playing of the game!

Given a sufficient number of players engaged in a competitive game, von Neumann and Morgenstern demonstrate with convincing mathematical rigor the possible advantages of combinations among them.[28] The clever player will be on the watch for a chance to increase his gains or cut his losses by cooperating with another. Similarly in international politics, so long as the participants do not consider themselves players of a game in which all concentrate on production and none worries about distribution, states will ever be tempted to form coalitions for the simple reason that those who combine acquire an advantage over those who do not. If some states seek an advantage over others, they combine; if other states want to counteract this advantage, they in turn combine. If the advantage sought is measured in

[28] The minimum numbers required are two or more for a general game, three or more for a zero-sum game. Game theory, however, cannot specify the distribution of gains or losses among the coalition partners. For comments on this and other limitations of game theory, see McKinsey, *Introduction to the Theory of Games*, especially chs. 15–18; Williams, *The Compleat Strategyst*, pp. 20–24, 30–34, 213–14.

terms of power to destroy or damage another state, then the threatened state refrains from the effort to increase its strength only at the risk of its survival. Pursuing a balance-of-power policy is still a matter of choice, but the alternatives are those of probable suicide on the one hand and the active playing of the power-politics game on the other. The factors that distinguish international politics from other games are: (1) that the stakes of the game are considered to be of unusual importance and (2) that in international politics the use of force is not excluded as a means of influencing the outcome. The cardinal rule of the game is often taken to be: Do whatever you must in order to win it. If some states act on this rule, or are expected to act on it, other states must adjust their strategies accordingly. The opportunity and at times the necessity of using force distinguishes the balance of power in international politics from the balances of power that form inside the state. In both cases we can define power, following Hobbes, as the capacity to produce an intended effect. In domestic politics one of the possible capacities —the use of physical force—is ordinarily monopolized by the state. In international politics there is no authority effectively able to prohibit the use of force. The balance of power among states becomes a balance of all the capacities, including physical force, that states choose to use in pursuing their goals.

If there is an advantage in forming coalitions, then logically the players will pursue the advantage until all of them are divided into two blocs. Yet the game of power politics does not often eventuate in two blocs unalterably opposed and using whatever means come to hand in order to weaken each other. This is explained, still in terms of game theory, by the fact that all states are playing more than one game. The aim of game theory is "a set of rules for each participant which tell him how to behave in every situation which may conceivably arise." [29]   But no set of rules can specify how important the game should be considered!   If, for example, survival were the only goal of the United States it would be irrational for us to neglect any means of strengthening ourselves vis-à-vis possible attackers.   If adopting a Spartan regimen would make us stronger, then clearly we should adopt it.   However, at the same time that we play the game of power politics, a game that we are forced to play so long as survival remains a goal, we pursue a number of other goals—in a sense we play other games—such as the maximization of economic welfare or, in the most general terms, the maintenance of a way of life.   The ideal strategy in international politics may, in terms of the other games the state is playing, cost too much.   To say, then, that international politics is a game the general rules of which are disregarded at the peril of the player's very existence does not necessarily mean that every state must bend all its efforts toward securing its own survival.   Clausewitz, for example, pointed out that he who uses force ruthlessly will gain an advantage if his opponent does not do likewise, but he noted as well that social institutions may moderate the extent and the savagery of the competition for power.[30] States may cooperate as well as compete, and even when competition becomes more important than cooperation their domestic aims may mitigate the external competition among them.   Nevertheless, if survival is one of the ends of the state, the state that would ignore balance-of-power considerations while others do not is analogous to the player of games who refrains from joining a coalition—for what is a balance of power but a series of coalitions in

[29] Von Neumann and Morgenstern, *Theory of Games and Economic Behavior*, p. 31.
[30] Clausewitz, *On War*, tr. Jolles, p. 4.

which the momentarily disadvantaged combine and re-combine to prevent the ascendancy (the winning of the game) of the opposing country or coalition?

The preceding analysis indicates that the balance of power among states has a firm basis in reality, that it is much more than a "delusion." The analysis also puts into perspective the frequent allegations that statesmen in pursuing balance-of-power policies often behave immorally. To most people there is nothing immoral about a game of cards, but there is definitely something immoral about cheating at cards. In cards, the code of morals is established by custom and enforced by the fact that anyone who cares to stop playing may do so. In international politics there are some rules of law to guide states both in peace and in war, but if it is found that some states break them, the others cannot simply quit playing the game. A state may then have to consider whether it would prefer to violate its code of behavior or abide by the code and risk its survival. Or, more accurately, the leaders of the state may have to choose between behaving *immorally* in international politics in order to preserve the state, on the one hand, and, on the other, abandoning their *moral* obligation to ensure their state's survival in order to follow preferred ways of acting in international politics. The conclusion? Moral behavior is one thing in a system that provides predictable amounts and types of security; another thing where such security is lacking. Kant, a philosopher never called immoral, recognized this as well as did Machiavelli, a philosopher often so described.[31] Those who call "power politicians" immoral simply because they play the game of power politics have trans-

---

[31] Notice Kant's justification of preventive war: "Lesion of a less powerful country may be involved merely in the condition of a more powerful neighbor *prior* to any action at all; and in the State of Nature an attack under such circumstances would be warrantable." *The Philosophy of Law,* tr. Hastie, sec. 56; cf. sec. 60.

ferred a definition of immorality from one social setting to another, and in the other it is not applicable without serious qualification.

Is the balance of power inevitable? Obviously not. But if it depends on a wish for state survival in a condition of anarchy among states, then it will disappear in its present form only when the wish or the condition disappears. The most ardent desire cannot bring about its abolition unless one or both of these factors are first modified.

A balance of power may exist because some countries consciously make it the end of their policies, or it may exist because of the quasi-automatic reactions of some states to the drive for ascendancy of other states. Even if the anti-balance-of-power people are in control of a state's policy, they will tend to act in ways that perpetuate or establish a balance. This need affect neither their verbal disavowal of balance-of-power politics nor the honesty of those disavowals. The last statement is well illustrated by the conclusion of one of the Tannenbaum articles previously cited.[32] Is the Atlantic Security Pact a power-substitute for a United Nations that has failed, he asks? No, he replies, for it is temporary, defensive, and "has nothing to do with the balance of power idea and less to do with dividing the world into spheres of interest between Russia and ourselves." In accordance with our traditions, the United States will organize as much of the world as possible on the basis of the coordinate state. We will not do this for the sake of the balance of power but in order to build a system of collective security for all who wish to join without having to sacrifice their independence or dignity. Then, if we have to fight, at least we will be fighting for what we believe worth defending. To pursue

[32] Tannenbaum, "The Balance of Power versus the Co-ordinate State," *Political Science Quarterly*, LXVII (1952), 195–97.

a balance-of-power settlement would, on the other hand, alienate others and destroy the only hope for an association of coordinate states organized to resist Russian efforts to dominate the world.

The lofty tone of Tannenbaum's description of our policy does not obscure the fact that the Western Defense Community was, in large part at least, motivated by fear of Soviet power and intentions and is intended to deter the Soviet Union from using that power in wars of aggression. For possible opponents to act with the possibility of a future war in mind is, in the light of history, no more difficult to understand than is baseball's yearly spring training. If Tannenbaum chooses to call this something other than balance-of-power politics, that is, of course, his privilege. It becomes apparent, however, that he objects more to the "realists'" terminology than to the foreign policies they recommend. If Tannenbaum were Secretary of State his foreign policy would apparently differ little from Morgenthau's or Kennan's, the two men he considers his principal intellectual opponents.

In summary, then, it can be said that the balance of power is not so much imposed by statesmen on events as it is imposed by events on statesmen. It is not to be eliminated by declamation but, if it is to be eliminated at all, by altering the circumstances that produce it. The circumstances are simply the existence of a number of independent states that wish to remain independent. Freedom is implied in the word "independence" but so is the necessity of self-reliance. Competition takes a number of forms, but the units in all systems of competition tend to drive for favored positions. If the drive of some units appears to promise success, it is blocked by other units whose similar motives cause them in turn to counter and thrust. Where an effective law-enforcing authority exists, balance is measured in terms other than force.[33] Where there is nothing to prevent the use of force as a means of altering the forms and the results of competition, the capacity to use force tends to become the index by which the balance of power is measured. No system of balance functions automatically. A drive for hegemony by any one state may be successful despite the resistance of other states, or for some reason the other states may not resist; but under certain conditions, conditions that have often existed in international politics, systems of balance do develop. If a condition of balance becomes the conscious goal of states, then one would expect the balancing process to be one of greater precision and subtlety. In the midst of a large number of roughly equal states, competition is intense and the balancing process intricate. Thus among the Greek and Italian city-states and among the European nation-states, any state threatening to outstrip the others in power could expect that an attempt would be made to check it. And this was the case not because they enjoyed the process of checking each other, but because for each state its power in relation to other states is ultimately the key to its survival.

HISTORICAL REFLECTIONS OF THE THIRD IMAGE

The logical construction of the third image, attempted in Chapter VI, gains cogency from the study of history. Though examples can be taken from many places and times, we shall content ourselves with a quick look at the three just mentioned. In his *History of the Peloponnesian War*, Thucydides argues many of the policy considerations that lead to and follow from our construction. It is his opinion that "among neighbors antagonism is ever a

[33] But a balancing process there will be nevertheless. That Tannenbaum realizes this makes his more recent articles on the balance of power all the more surprising. See his "The Balance of Power in Society," *Political Science Quarterly*, LXI (1946), 481–504.

condition of independence." [34] The opinion takes on substance in the statements he puts into the mouths of various participants in the politics and wars of the period. A brief sampling, with the names of speakers omitted, indicates that implicit in his historical writings is a view of international politics closely related to Rousseau's and to the third image. The following are summaries of and excerpts from some of the speeches he records: For our interests we go to war, and when our interests seem to require, we sue for peace. For we all know "that into the discussion of human affairs the question of justice only enters where there is equal power to enforce it." [35] Since states "are not at law" with each other, they cannot consider what is just —their object cannot be to reward the righteous and punish the guilty. Of a country that has wronged us "the question for us rightly considered is not, what are their crimes? but, what is for our interest?" [36] It is folly to make alliances unless they are rooted in the interest of all members. Indeed, "mutual fear is the only solid basis of alliance." [37] Since each state acts on its own interpretation of its requirements for security and well-being, one state has to forecast the intentions of other states. Thus "to remain at peace when you should be going to war may be often very dangerous." [38] "For mankind do not await the attack of a superior power, they anticipate it." [39] The policy of a state, in short, is determined by its goals and by its relation to other states.

Machiavelli takes the theme of Thucydides and plays a

[34] Thucydides, *History of the Peloponnesian War*, tr. Jowett, Book IV, par. 92. Cf. Rousseau, *A Lasting Peace*, tr. Vaughan, pp. 47, 122.

[35] Thucydides, *History of the Peloponnesian War*, tr. Jowett, Book V, par. 89.

[36] *Ibid.*, Book III, par. 44.

[37] *Ibid.*, Book III, par. 11; cf. Book I, pars. 32–35; Book V, par. 106.

[38] *Ibid.*, Book I, par. 124.

[39] *Ibid.*, Book VI, par. 18. Cf. Rousseau, *A Lasting Peace*, tr. Vaughan. pp. 78–79; Montesquieu, *The Spirit of the Laws*, tr. Nugent, Book X, ch. ii.

number of intricate if not beautiful variations upon it.
That *The Prince* must be read in the context of *The Discourses* and both in the context of conditions in Italy at
the time is often said but less often done. That Machiavelli was the theorist of *Realpolitik* makes it easy to assume that to have a general understanding of *Realpolitik*
is to have an adequate understanding of Machiavelli himself. The great political philosophers demand being read
and read again, and one finds that each rereading brings
an enlarged and deepened understanding. With Machiavelli, the least philosophical of the political philosophers,
one is inclined to forego recurring consideration of the
whole of his thought and instead to dip into his political
writings and extract maxims, which may enlighten, horrify
—or even amuse, for Rousseau once referred to *The Prince*
as a satire.

"The end justifies the means." This statement is often
taken, with some injustice, as an epigrammatic summary
of Machiavelli's political thought. The injustice arises
from the failure to mention the double qualification that
Machiavelli attaches, in *The Prince* as in *The Discourses*.
These ends justify the means, he is saying, and the means
appropriate depend upon the conditions under which the
ends are sought. If you want to preserve your power in
the state and your state among others, then you may be
justified in doing things often termed unscrupulous.[40]
Not all, but some, ends justify the means. "For he is to be
reprehended who commits violence for the purpose of
destroying, and not he who employs it for beneficent purposes."[41]   Given constructive ends, whether or not one is

40 And similarly if one seeks an increase in power.
41 *The Discourses*, Book I, ch. ix; cf. Book II, ch. xiii; Book III, ch. xli.
Cf. also *The Prince*, chs. xix, xxvi. Reference throughout is to Ricci's
translation of *The Prince*, as revised by Vincent, and to Detmold's translation of *The Discourses*.

justified in using unsavory means will depend, further, upon "the necessity of the case." Men are successful so long as their ways "conform to circumstances." The prince, according to Machiavelli, "must have a mind disposed to adapt itself according to the wind, and as the variations of fortune dictate, and . . . not deviate from what is good, if possible, but be able to do evil if constrained." [42]

But does this double qualification help to meet the two criticisms most often brought against him? The first is conveyed by the question: Did Machiavelli's recommended methods contain the possibility of success—could they, if followed, conceivably have brought about the regeneration of Italy, or were they in effect a codification of the very behavior that had made of Italy an arena of violent contention among principalities and thus a prey to foreign powers? The second and closely related criticism is conveyed by the question: Does not one who acts on the precept that an end justifies its means find in practice that the means he adopts determine the end? Establishing the validity of the propositions implied in these questions, which I think can be done, does not establish their relevance. Answering them in ways that seem to cut the ground from under Machiavelli does not in fact do so, for such answers do not demonstrate the existence of alternate modes of behavior, promising success, which a single prince could follow. Willingness to use the means Machiavelli thought necessary may have given but slight possibility of success, but how wide was the range of choice? The supposedly Machiavellian quality of his recommendations to the prince is lessened if we bear in mind the almost tragic quality of his insight. "A man who wishes to make a profession of goodness in every-

[42] *The Prince,* chs. xv, xxv, xviii. Cf. *The Discourses,* Book III, ch. ix.

thing," he writes, "must necessarily come to grief among so many who are not good." [43] This may not make unscrupulous behavior attractive, but to argue that on occasion one must behave unscrupulously because others may do so does strip the adverb of its unsavory meaning and thus render it inappropriate. Men employ law; beasts use force. The prince must have recourse to the latter not because it is more admirable but because the former is often insufficient.[44]

The thought that the chicanery of one may itself prompt the deceit of another does not escape Machiavelli, but he refuses to blink the dilemma by arguing, as Roosevelt and Stimson were both fond of doing, that the way to make a man trustworthy is to trust him. Such a belief was difficult to entertain in the Italy of Machiavelli's day. Men were "constrained" to do evil, for the well mannered and moral came to grief with demonstrable frequency. And yet so did the vicious and mean. To understand fully the depth of Machiavelli's understanding of the necessities of politics one must add, as he did, a third qualification. What the prince must do to increase his chances of success depends upon the goal he entertains, the conditions under which he seeks it, *and* upon the qualities of the prince himself. In reading Machiavelli, the third factor is most easily overlooked. Where greatness has disappeared, as Machiavelli believed it had, one must give advice that the small-minded can follow. But he makes sufficiently clear

---

[43] *The Prince,* ch. xv. "Even Machiavelli himself," Garrett Mattingly points out, "was not in practice Machiavellian." *Renaissance Diplomacy,* p. 40. And J. S. Mill, committing to his diary thoughts on the age of Machiavelli, finds it understandable that under the circumstances then prevailing "even good men reserved their conscientiousness for the choice of ends. . . . Macchiavelli [*sic*] was a man of real patriotism, a lover of liberty, and eager for the good of his country. But he saw no reason for fighting with foils against those who fight with poniards." *Letters,* ed. Elliot, II, 367.

[44] *The Prince,* ch. xviii.

that in his estimate either of two types may succeed: the person who is consistently able to act the beast *or* the one who is truly a man. Doubtless the ways of Philip of Macedon, he writes, "are cruel and destructive of all civilized life, and neither Christian nor even human, and should be avoided by every one. In fact, the life of a private citizen would be preferable to that of a king at the expense of the ruin of so many human beings. Nevertheless, whoever is unwilling to adopt the first and humane course must, if he wishes to maintain his power, follow the latter evil course." [45] The content of Machiavelli's advice to the prince is accounted for not only by the fact that in this world even the good men do not often succeed, for neither do the evil ones, but also by the fact that there are so few saints among us. To whom could Machiavelli address his appeal? He nevertheless opposes neither the one type nor the other; his severest judgments are reserved for those who attempt to follow a middle way.[46]

And yet why should the success of the prince in establishing internal order and contriving a defense against external enemies be taken as the criterion by which any act can be justified? Why define success in terms of princely or state interest instead of, say, in terms of living a moral life? This question raises a fundamental point but not a difficult one. To Machiavelli, as to Rousseau and Kant later, internal order and external security are necessary before there is even the possibility of men living lives of some freedom and decency. The study of politics then becomes the most important of all studies and the political art, the most meritorious. Thus Machiavelli describes Italy as "a country without dykes or banks of any kind" to protect her against foreign incursion, adding that had she been "protected by proper measures, like Ger-

---

[45] *The Discourses*, Book I, ch. xxvi; cf. Book III, ch. xxii.
[46] See especially *The Discourses*, Book III, ch. xxii.

many, Spain, and France, this inundation would not have caused the great changes that it has, or would not have happened at all." [47]   If by cruelty the dykes and banks are built and kept in good repair, then cruelty is the greatest mercy.   If by practicing virtue they are torn down again, then virtue is the greatest vice.

Realpolitik is a loosely defined method, which is described as being necessary when a given purpose is sought under a specified condition.   The purpose is the security of the separate states and the condition, anarchy among them.   Most often the word brings to mind as well a balance-of-power model.   Machiavelli stands forth so clearly as the exponent of *Realpolitik* that one easily slips into the assumption that he develops an idea of the balance of power as well.   Yet the concept is more clearly foreshadowed in the *History* of Thucydides than in *The Prince* and *The Discourses*. While *Realpolitik* is a method, the politics of balance forms its content and conditions its operation.   Today as earlier the relevance of *Realpolitik* and of the balance of power in international relations is often questioned.   Frank Tannenbaum can be taken as an example of the many who think that balance-of-power politics is passé and accuse present-day realists of arriving at their erroneous conclusions by assuming that the exceptional experience of modern Europe represents normal state behavior.[48]   In the era of hydrogen bombs, with a world fragmented by two colossi eyeing each other often with hatred and fear, always with suspicion, the relevance of lessons seemingly drawn from observing a number of states in periodic conflict may well seem questionable.   To stem the doubts and make concrete the lessons abstractly deduced from the preceding discussion of game theory,

---

[47] *The Prince,* ch. xxv; with reference to domestic order, see ch. xvii.
[48] "The Balance of Power versus the Co-ordinate State," *Political Science Quarterly,* LXVII (1952), 175.

the promised discussion of past European experience will be tied to a consideration of the present configuration of international relations. In the eighteenth century and through most of the nineteenth, there were balance-of-power systems, involving the ability and willingness of states to shift their allegiance from one grouping to another. Today, as before the First World War, shifts of major consequence are less easily possible, but because balancing according to the classical model can no longer take place, one cannot say that a balance of power does not exist. Where adjustment by international moves is less possible, internal development of industry and armaments becomes more important. And the more intense the competition becomes, the more difference small moves can make. In any event, the following discussion is not intended to suggest how a balance-of-power analysis now must differ from such an analysis applied to the nineteenth or eighteenth centuries, but rather to suggest the fundamental points on which there is continuity despite the many and important changes induced by shifts in the distribution of power and transformations in technology.[49]

In May of 1891, French and Russian soldiers, leading the way to military convention and alliance, met for discussions in Paris. Their conclusions were presented to the Tsar by the Deputy Chief of the French General Staff, Boisdeffre. Among them were "that mobilization was the declaration of war; that to mobilize was to force one's neighbor to do the same; . . . that to allow a million men to be mobilized along one's frontiers without doing as much oneself at the same time meant denying oneself all possibility of moving later and placing oneself in a situation of an individual who, with a pistol in his pocket,

---

[49] For different ways in which the term "balance of power" has been used, see Haas, "The Balance of Power: Prescription, Concept, or Propaganda?" *World Politics*, V (1953), 442–77.

would allow his neighbor to put a loaded gun against his forehead without drawing his own." With these propositions, Alexander III agreed.[50] The alliance system, inaugurated by Bismarck in 1879, had, after 1890, rapidly become a two-bloc system. The forming of its second side made it all but inevitable that mobilization, once begun, would become general and that general mobilization would mean war.[51] Clearly in the appraisal of the participants everyone's strategy depended upon everyone else's—a confirmation of the third image. One may object that the third image alone, because unable to explain why any country should mobilize in the first place, cannot explain the coming of the war. The objection is valid. To understand the coming of the First World War one must look to the vulnerabilities and strengths, the ambitions and fears, of all the states involved. Any explanation of these factors must focus upon the first and second images. What kinds of people were in control of state policy? What scope were they permitted by the economic and demographic, the social and political, underpinning of their states? Under what internal pressures and restraints did they labor? These factors are crucial in any historical analysis. Their possible effects, however, cannot be estimated without constant attention to the external pressures to which all the states of Europe were subject. Austria and Germany looked east and saw a Russian economy still backward but advancing rapidly in many sectors, a population increasing nearly twice as fast as their own, a tsar sitting uneasily on his throne and thus unlikely to be able always to follow a policy of moderation in crises that might arise. France too looked east. She saw a country

---

[50] Quoted in Vagts, *Defense and Diplomacy*, p. 398.

[51] Cf., for example, von Moltke's estimate of future possibilities in his correspondence with Conrad von Hötzendorf in January, 1891, and Lloyd George's statement in his *War Memoirs:* "In 1914, mobilization made for war—it meant war." In Vagts, *Defense and Diplomacy*, pp. 97, 399.

militarist in organization, a kaiser impetuous in action, and a population and economy that had long since outstripped hers and were still advancing by leaps and bounds. England looked to the continent and saw a German navy preparing to question British supremacy in local waters and under the leadership of von Tirpitz already referring to the North Sea as a German lake, a German economy that challenged where it did not surpass British industrial and commercial leadership, a German foreign policy that threatened to overturn the balance of Europe upon which British security traditionally rested.

The alliance system was proclaimed by some to be a system of security.[52] It was. Each step in its formation, from the Dual Alliance to the British-Russian Entente, has to be explained largely in terms of the attempts of the participants to get out from under a feeling of danger to themselves. The states of Europe combined and recombined, Italy being the greatest recombiner, until they stood face to face with lines drawing tighter in each moment of crisis.

This was a security system—but only until someone jiggled. The game of European power politics had become, with rough equivalence, a two-person, zero-sum game. A gain for any one state became a gain for its side, and simultaneously a loss for the other. A single move then had a double effect, and, with the two sides roughly balanced, neither could permit the other the gain that would be its own loss as well. Believing that mobilization meant war may have helped to make it so, but there were other factors as well, among them the closeness of the balance, that made the area of maneuver narrower than is sometimes

---

[52] Note, e.g., the assurance given to Premier Freycinet in May of 1890 by one of the Russian grand dukes that, if he had any say in the matter, "our two armies will form one in time of war. And that fact, once well known, will avert war. For no one would care to face France and Russia arm in arm." In *ibid.*, p. 105.

thought. In June of 1914, the seemingly small matter of
Serbia involved not only the prestige but also the security of both sides. Because Russia could not afford to
let Austria have her own way with Serbia, she reacted;
because Germany could not afford to let Austria back
down, she reacted; and so on around the vicious and tragic
circle. Some would call it a meaningless circle as well.
One may, however, recall from Chapter VI the paraphrase
of Hegel—"that among particularities accidents will occur
is not accidental but necessary." Given imperfect states in
a condition of anarchy, crises will arise, a fact that in the
third image is assumed rather than explained. With this
as a starting point, it is possible to describe almost abstractly the kinds of calculations that as a logical minimum
each state, under the pressure of its security interests, must
make. The above and, in a different way, the next example as well make clear how difficult it can be to keep
international politics from tending toward a zero-sum
game.

Fools learn by experience, Bismarck once said, wise men
learn by other people's experience. Neville Chamberlain,
in the late 1930s, behaved as though he had taken Bismarck's aphorism to heart. In the alliance system preceding the First World War, the states of Europe had seemingly traded a momentary feeling of security for the near
certainty of eventual war. England, Chamberlain thought,
should profit by the mistakes of her previous generation.
France and Russia, without the assured support of Britain,
would not have felt strong enough to challenge the Central Powers; they in turn, not feeling threatened, would
have behaved in more gentlemanly fashion. Britain then
would not have become involved in a world war over a
narrow patch of territory in the faraway southeast of
Europe. Chamberlain's proclaimed policy of appeasement, the willingness to grant concessions in order to settle
disputes peacefully, would remove at once the need for

alliances and the assumed causes of war. Thus in March of 1938, with the Czechoslovakian crisis rapidly developing, Chamberlain turned down the Soviet suggestion for a conference to be attended by a limited number of states, with the comment that it envisioned "less a consultation with a view to settlement than a concerting of action against an eventuality that has not yet arisen." And he added "that the indirect, but none-the-less inevitable, consequence of such action as is proposed by the Soviet Government would be to aggravate the tendency towards the establishment of exclusive groups of nations, which must, in the view of His Majesty's Government, be inimical to the prospects of European peace." [53] With an eye on the Europe of 1914, Chamberlain sought to avoid giving Germany cause to feel that she was being encircled. Intent upon applying what he had learned from the First World War, he failed to consider that appeasement may increase the relative strength of the favored state and, if its goals are not strictly limited, this strength may in the future be turned against the appeaser.

Balance-of-power politics is risky; trying to ignore it is riskier still. Clausewitz once sounded a warning that is relevant here.

If bloody slaughter is a horrible spectacle, then it should only be a reason for treating war with more respect, but not for making the sword we bear blunter and blunter by degrees from feelings of humanity, until once again someone steps in with a sword that is sharp and hews away the arms from our body. [54]

It is not only that a state, becoming too fond of peace, may thereby perish; but also that the seeming somnolence of one state may invite a war of aggression that a more aggressive pose by the peace-loving state might have avoided altogether. This lesson, learned by the United States in two world wars, has now become an official part of State De-

[53] Chamberlain, *In Search of Peace*, pp. 85–86.
[54] Clausewitz, *On War*, tr. Jolles, p. 210.

partment doctrine. "Peace," Secretary John Foster Dulles has said, "requires anticipating what it is that tempts an aggressor and letting him know in advance that, if he does not exercise self-control, he may face a hard fight, perhaps a losing fight." [55]

But, as Chamberlain learned to England's sorrow, equally implied in the third image is the warning that any lesson learned may be incorrectly applied. Like generals laying their plans in a way that would have won the previous war, statesmen strive to prevent it. On March 5, 1946, Churchill urged that states seeking safety cannot work on the narrow margins of the balance of power.[56] Preponderance, not balance, must be their goal. As has been said above, however, a balance of power may result either because most states seek it or because some states react to the drive for preponderance of others. Where a balance of power does exist, it behooves the state that desires peace as well as safety to become neither too strong nor too weak. One must add to the dictum of the preceding paragraph that the seeming aggressiveness of one state may invite a war of prevention that a more pacific pose might have avoided altogether. There is in international politics no simple rule to prescribe just how belligerent, or how peaceful, any given state should strive to appear in order to maximize its chances of living at peace with neighboring states. One cannot say in the abstract that for peace a country must arm, or disarm, or compromise, or stand firm. One can only say that the possible effects of all such policies must be considered. The third image makes this clear. The peace strategy of any one country must depend on the peace or war strategies of all other countries. As

[55] Dulles, address to the American Legion Convention, St. Louis. Text in New York *Times*, September 3, 1953, p. 4.

[56] Churchill, speech at Fulton, Missouri, in Morgenthau and Thompson, *Principles and Problems of International Politics*, p. 416.

competition in international politics becomes more intense, a process that none of the arch competitors acting alone can prevent, the peace-loving state faces the necessity of balancing between too little and too much strength, between too many failures that strengthen the potential enemy and too many successes that scare him unduly. Partly because the United States has become so well acquainted with the pitfalls of appeasement, the danger that the prehistory of the Third World War, if it comes, will read like the first rather than the fourth decade of this century is increased. There is conceivably a danger of one side lowering its guard and thus tempting the other to aggression. But with the lessons of the Second World War fresh in our minds, this danger is less than the danger that one side by using its strength unwisely will cause the other to react with force. The tragedy of Dulles's proclaimed liberation policy is then not that it is impossible but rather that its "successful" implementation would carry the world over the brink of war, a thought well though painfully illustrated by Dulles's own reactions to the Hungarian revolt in the fall of 1956. As was true when the Triple Alliance faced the Triple Entente, neither of the major protagonists can safely tolerate a major success scored by its potential opponent.

If this seems complicated to the point of frustration to some, to others it is what makes international politics a fascinating "game." That it is a game, with no frivolity intended, will be clear if the comments just made are compared with those based on the equally frustrating and fascinating mathematical speculations of von Neumann and Morgenstern. The third image in general and balance-of-power analysis in particular are relevant in the present as they have been in the past histories of multistate systems.

CHAPTER VIII.   CONCLUSION

THROUGHOUT the first half of the present century, Norman Angell has argued with persistence, eloquence, and clarity the proposition that war does not pay. Increasingly, under the influence of "the balance of terror," one finds men speaking as though the argument Angell first popularized fifty years ago has been made true by recent advances in the technology of warfare. But, in the sense Angell intended, it has always been true. Angell was a rationalist and individualist in the nineteenth-century mold, much less concerned with the relative gains and losses of this or that nation than with the unchallengeable fact that war at best takes men away from the work that produces the necessities and comforts of life, at worst destroys what they have already produced. War may achieve a redistribution of resources, but labor, not war, creates wealth. Perhaps not from the perspective of a nation or a tribe but from the perspective of mankind, war has never "paid."

Yet war recurs. The beast in man may glory in the carnage; the reason in man rebels. War and the threat of war stimulate speculation upon the conditions of peace. Seemingly critical thought may, however, embody uncritical reactions to the immediately impressive aspects of the situation faced. Peace programs, whether they would rely for their efficacy upon irenic diplomacy, armed crusade, moral exhortation, or psychic-cultural readjustment, are based at least implicitly on the ideas of the causes of war we entertain. As was argued in the introductory chapter, our estimates of the causes of war are determined by our presuppositions as much as by the events of the world about us. A systematic study of the assumed causes of war then becomes a direct way of estimating the conditions of peace. Our primary concern has not been with building models from which policies promoting peace can be derived but with examining the presuppositions upon which such models are based. This puts the problem in academic terms. Its relevance is much broader, for the policies of statesmen as well as the interests and procedures of scholars are the product of a conjunction of temper, experience, reason, and event. The practice of politics is greatly influenced by the images the politicians entertain.

When Ranke argued that the external relations of states determine their internal conditions, his argument had considerable cogency. So great was the importance of diplomacy in nineteenth-century Europe and so many were the statesmen trained in its ways that even internal governance at times corresponded in method to the techniques by which affairs among states were conducted. One need mention only Metternich and Bismarck. Diplomacy then, as it often has, took on many of the qualities of a game of chess. Perhaps the last illustration of this on the grand scale is provided by Bismarck's manipulations in the Balkan crises of 1885–87. But already by the dawn of the nineteenth century, factors internal to states were becoming more important in international relations. And with their greater importance, one finds a growing tendency to explain relations among states in terms of their internal condition. Most notably among English liberals, the practice of Metternich as well as the dictum of Ranke was reversed. Attempts were made to apply the supposed methods and sanctions of internal governance— judicial settlement, public opinion—to affairs among states.

The vogue of an image varies with time and place, but no single image is ever adequate. Thus Bismarck's skepticism about a possible alliance with Russia was based in part on fear of her internal instability. One who would play a game of chess has to consider the weight of the different pieces as well as the possible moves, and in international politics the weights change with time. Thus John Stuart Mill, writing to an Italian correspondent in June of 1859, expressed England's sympathy for the cause of Italian national freedom but justified England's inaction by pointing out that Austria was the only ally on which England could count should she have to fight for her liberty against France and Russia united.[1] Mill's thoughts and Bismarck's policies can often be adequately described in terms of the second and third images, respectively, but especially when considering the possibilities of state policy the calculations of each comprehended elements from more than one image. This is generally the case. Yet the firmness with which a person is wedded to one image colors his interpretation of the others. Bismarck was inclined more than Mill to keep his eye on the map of Europe, the chessboard; Mill more than Bismarck to focus upon the qualities of peoples and their governments, the chessmen.

In contrast to Metternich and Bismarck, who were diplomatists in domestic as well as international affairs, statesmen of the twentieth century more frequently transfer the methods of the party politician to external politics. Woodrow Wilson, to cite an example used earlier, saw clearly one of the essential elements of a third-image analysis, that everyone's policy depends upon everyone else's. With many authoritarian states in the world, he realized that even the nonauthoritarian state must on occasion be prepared to use force in order to defend its interests. But, convinced that democratic states are peaceful because their governments reflect the aspirations of

[1] J. S. Mill, *Letters*, ed. Elliot, I, 222.

the people, he foresaw a day when the internal condition of all states would mean not the constant possibility of war but rather the assurance of perpetual peace. Wilson's emphasis upon the second image led him to particular interpretations of the first and third, rather than to a complete ignoring of them.

According to the third image, there is a constant possibility of war in a world in which there are two or more states each seeking to promote a set of interests and having no agency above them upon which they can rely for protection. But many liberals and socialist revisionists deny, or at least minimize, the possibility that wars would occur in a world of political or social democracies. An understanding of the third image makes it clear that the expectation would be justified only if the minimum interest of states in preserving themselves became the maximum interest of all of them—and each could rely fully upon the steadfast adherence to this definition by all of the others. Stating the condition makes apparent the utopian quality of liberal and socialist expectations. The criticism could be extended by questioning as well their interpretations of the first image. But the point as it applies here—that emphasizing one image frequently distorts, though it seldom excludes, the other two—is perhaps sufficiently clear. It may profit us more to shift our attention briefly to similar effects that may follow from concentration upon the third image.

While from the sociologist's perspective government is simply one of many social institutions, it is at the same time a precondition of society. The first perspective without the second is misleading, as was illustrated in one way in Chapter III, in another way in Chapter VI. The state of nature among men is a monstrous impossibility. Anarchy breeds war among them; government establishes the conditions for peace. The state of nature that continues to prevail among states often produces monstrous behavior but so far has not made life itself impossible. The ahistorical analyses of Spinoza, Rousseau, and Kant lay bare the logic of civil society and at the same time make clear why the logic does not carry men past the establishment of separate states to the founding of a world state. Yet in the international as in the domestic sphere, if anarchy is the cause, the obvious conclusion is that government is the cure; and this is true even though the disease in the former case is not fatal. The problem, however, becomes a practical one. The amount of force needed to hold a society together varies with the heterogeneity of the elements composing it. World federalists write as though the alternatives before us were unity or death. "World government is necessary and therefore possible," Robert Maynard Hutchins avers.[2]   But demonstrating the need for an institution does not bring it into existence. And were world government attempted, we might find ourselves dying in the attempt to unite, or uniting and living a life worse than death.

The third image, like the first two, leads directly to a utopian prescription.   In each image a cause is identified in terms of which all others are to be understood.   The force of the logical relation between the third image and the world-government prescription is great enough to cause some to argue not only the merits of world government but also the ease with which it can be realized.[3]   It is of course true that with world government there would no longer be international wars, though with an ineffective world government there would no doubt be civil wars. It is likewise true, reverting to the first two images, that

[2] Hutchins, "The Constitutional Foundations for World Order," in *Foundations for World Order*, p. 105.

[3] Cf. Popper, *The Open Society and Its Enemies*, pp. 158–59, 574–79; Esslinger, *Politics and Science, passim.*

without the imperfections of the separate states there would not be wars, just as it is true that a society of perfectly rational beings, or of perfect Christians, would never know violent conflict. These statements are, unfortunately, as trivial as they are true. They have the unchallengeable quality of airtight tautologies: perfectly good states or men will not do bad things; within an effective organization highly damaging deviant behavior is not permitted. The near perfection required by concentration upon a single cause accounts for a number of otherwise puzzling facts: the pessimism of St. Augustine, the failure of the behavioral scientists as prescribers for peace, the reliance of many liberals on the forces of history to produce a result not conceivably to be produced by the consciously directed efforts of men, the tendency of socialists to identify a corrupting element every time harmony in socialist action fails to appear. It also helps to explain the often rapid alternation of hope and despair among those who most fully adopt a single-cause approach to this or to almost any other problem. The belief that to make the world better requires changing the factors that operate within a precisely defined realm leads to despair whenever it becomes apparent that changes there, if possible at all, will come slowly and with insufficient force. One is constantly defeated by the double problem of demonstrating how the "necessary changes" can be produced and of substantiating the assertion that the changes described as necessary would be sufficient to accomplish the object in view.

The contrary assertion, that all causes may be interrelated, is an argument against assuming that there is a single cause that can be isolated by analysis and eliminated or controlled by wisely constructed policy. It is also an argument against working with one or several hypotheses without bearing in mind the interrelation of all causes.

The prescriptions directly derived from a single image are incomplete because they are based upon partial analyses. The partial quality of each image sets up a tension that drives one toward inclusion of the others. With the first image the direction of change, representing Locke's perspective as against Plato's, is from men to societies and states. The second image catches up both elements. Men make states, *and* states make men; but this is still a limited view. One is led to a search for the more inclusive nexus of causes, for states are shaped by the international environment as are men by both the national and international environments. Most of those whom we have considered in preceding chapters have not written entirely in terms of one image. That we have thus far been dealing with the consequences arising from differing degrees of emphasis accounts for the complexity of preceding chapters but now makes somewhat easier the task of suggesting how the images can be interrelated without distorting any one of them.

THE FIRST AND SECOND IMAGES IN RELATION TO THE THIRD

It may be true that the Soviet Union poses the greatest threat of war at the present time. It is not true that were the Soviet Union to disappear the remaining states could easily live at peace. We have known wars for centuries; the Soviet Union has existed only for decades. But some states, and perhaps some forms of the state, are more peacefully inclined than others. Would not the multiplication of peacefully inclined states at least warrant the hope that the period between major wars might be extended? By emphasizing the relevance of the framework of action, the third image makes clear the misleading quality of such partial analyses and of the hopes that are often based upon them. The act that by individual moral standards would be applauded may, when performed by a state, be an invitation to the war we seek to avoid. The third image, taken not as a theory of world government but as a theory of the conditioning effects of the state system itself, alerts us to the fact that so far as increasing the chances of peace is concerned there is no such thing as an act good in itself. The pacification of the Hukbalahaps was a clear and direct contribution to the peace and order of the Philippine state. In international politics a partial "solution," such as one major country becoming pacifistic, might be a real contribution to world peace; but it might as easily hasten the coming of another major war.

The third image, as reflected in the writings of Rousseau, is based on an analysis of the consequences arising from the framework of state action. Rousseau's explanation of the origin of war among states is, in broad outline, the final one so long as we operate within a nation-state system. It is a final explanation because it does not hinge on accidental causes—irrationalities in men, defects in states—but upon his theory of the framework within which *any* accident can bring about a war. That state A wants certain things that it can get only by war does not explain war. Such a desire may or may not lead to war. My wanting a million dollars does not cause me to rob a bank, but if it were easier to rob banks, such desires would lead to much more bank robbing. This does not alter the fact that some people will and some will not attempt to rob banks no matter what the law enforcement situation is. We still have to look to motivation and circumstance in order to explain individual acts. Nevertheless one can predict that, other things being equal, a weakening of law enforcement agencies will lead to an increase in crime. From this point of view it is social structure—institutionalized restraints and institutionalized methods of altering and adjusting interests—that counts. And it counts in a way different from the ways usually associated with the word "cause." What causes a man to rob a bank are such things as the desire for money, a disrespect for social proprieties, a certain boldness. But if obstacles to the operation of these causes are built sufficiently high, nine out of ten would-be bank robbers will live their lives peacefully plying their legitimate trades. If the framework is to be called cause at all, it had best be specified that it is a permissive or underlying cause of war.

Applied to international politics this becomes, in words previously used to summarize Rousseau, the proposition that wars occur because there is nothing to prevent them. Rousseau's analysis explains the recurrence of war without explaining any given war. He tells us that war may at any moment occur, and he tells us why this is so. But the structure of the state system does not directly cause state A to attack state B. Whether or not that attack occurs will depend on a number of special circumstances—location, size, power, interest, type of government, past history and tradition—each of which will influence the actions of both states. If they fight against each other it will be for reasons especially defined for the occasion by each of them. These special reasons become the immediate, or efficient, causes of war. These immediate causes of war are contained in the first and second images. States are motivated to attack each other and to defend themselves by the reason and/or passion of the comparatively few who make policies for states and of the many more who influence the few. Some states, by virtue of their internal conditions, are both more proficient in war and more inclined to put their proficiency to the test. Variations in the factors included in the first and second images are important, indeed crucial, in the making and breaking of periods of peace— the immediate causes of every war must be either the acts of individuals or the acts of states.

If every war is preceded by acts that we can identify (or at least try to identify) as cause, then why can we not eliminate wars by modifying individual or state behavior? This is the line of thinking followed by those who say: To end war, improve men; or: To end war, improve states. But in such prescriptions the role of the international environment is easily distorted. How can some of the acting units improve while others continue to follow their old and often predatory ways? The simplistic assumption of many liberals, that history moves relentlessly toward the millennium, is refuted if the international environment makes it difficult almost to the point of impossibility for states to behave in ways that are progressively more moral. Two points are omitted from the prescriptions we considered under the first and second images: (1) If an effect is produced by two or more causes, the effect is not permanently eliminated by removing one of them. If wars occur because men are less than perfectly rational and because states are less than perfectly formed, to improve only states may do little to decrease the number and intensity of wars. The error here is in identifying one cause where two or more may operate. (2) An endeavor launched against one cause to the neglect of others may make the situation worse instead of better. Thus, as the Western democracies became more inclined to peace, Hitler became more belligerent. The increased propensity to peace of some participants in international politics may increase, rather than decrease, the likelihood of war. This illustrates the role of the permissive cause, the international environment. If there were but two loci of cause involved, men and states, we could be sure that the appearance of more peacefully inclined states would, at worst, not damage the cause of world peace. Whether or not a remedy proposed is truly a remedy or actually worse than none at all depends, however, on the content and timing of the acts of all states. This is made clear in the third image.

War may result because state A has something that state B wants. The efficient cause of the war is the desire of state B; the permissive cause is the fact that there is nothing to prevent state B from undertaking the risks of war. In a different circumstance, the interrelation of efficient and permissive causes becomes still closer. State A may fear that if it does not cut state B down a peg now, it may be unable to do so ten years from now. State A becomes the aggressor in the present because it fears what state B may be able to do in the future. The efficient cause of such a war is derived from the cause that we have labeled permissive. In the first case, conflicts arise from disputes born of specific issues. In an age of hydrogen bombs, no single issue may be worth the risk of full-scale war. Settlement, even on bad grounds, is preferable to self-destruction. The use of reason would seem to require the adoption of a doctrine of "non-recourse to force." One whose reason leads him down this path is following the trail blazed by Cobden when in 1849 he pointed out "that it is almost impossible, on looking back for the last hundred years, to tell precisely what any war was about," and thus implied that Englishmen should never have become involved in them.[4] He is falling into the trap that ensnared A. A. Milne when he explained the First World War as a war in which ten million men died because Austria-Hungary sought, unsuccessfully, to avenge the death of one archduke.[5] He is succumbing to the illusion of Sir Edward Grey who, in the memoirs he wrote some thirty years ago, hoped that the horrors of the First World War would make it possible for nations "to find at least one

---

[4] Cobden, *Speeches*, ed. Bright and Rogers, II, 165.
[5] Milne, *Peace with Honour*, p. 11.

common ground on which they should come together in confident understanding: an agreement that, in the disputes between them, war must be ruled out as a means of settlement that entails ruin." [6]

It is true that the immediate causes of many wars are trivial. If we focus upon them, the failure to agree to settlement without force appears to be the ultimate folly. But it is not often true that the immediate causes provide sufficient explanation for the wars that have occurred. And if it is not simply particular disputes that produce wars, rational settlement of them cannot eliminate war. For, as Winston Churchill has written, "small matters are only the symptoms of the dangerous disease, and are only important for that reason. Behind them lie the interests, the passions and the destiny of mighty races of men; and long antagonisms express themselves in trifles." [7] Nevertheless Churchill may be justified in hoping that the fear induced by a "balance of terror" will produce a temporary truce. Advancing technology makes war more horrible and presumably increases the desire for peace; the very rapidity of the advance makes for uncertainty in everyone's military planning and destroys the possibility of an accurate estimate of the likely opposing forces. Fear and permanent peace are more difficult to equate. Each major advance in the technology of war has found its prophet ready to proclaim that war is no longer possible: Alfred Nobel and dynamite, for example, or Benjamin Franklin and the lighter-than-air balloon. There may well have been a prophet to proclaim the end of tribal warfare when the spear was invented and another to make a similar prediction when poison was first added to its tip. Unfortunately, these prophets have all been false. The development of atomic and hydrogen weapons may nurture

6 Grey, *Twenty-five Years*, II, 285.
7 Churchill, *The World Crisis, 1911–1914*, I, 52.

the peace wish of some, the war sentiment of others. In the United States and elsewhere after the Second World War, a muted theme of foreign-policy debate was the necessity of preventive war—drop the bomb quickly before the likely opponent in a future war has time to make one of his own. Even with two or more states equipped with similar weapon systems, a momentary shift in the balance of terror, giving a decisive military advantage temporarily to one state, may tempt it to seize the moment in order to escape from fear. And the temptation would be proportionate to the fear itself. Finally, mutual fear of big weapons may produce, instead of peace, a spate of smaller wars.

The fear of modern weapons, of the danger of destroying the civilizations of the world, is not sufficient to establish the conditions of peace identified in our discussions of the three images of international relations. One can equate fear with world peace only if the peace wish exists in all states and is uniformly expressed in their policies. But peace is the primary goal of few men or states. If it were the primary goal of even a single state, that state could have peace at any time—simply by surrendering. But, as John Foster Dulles so often warns, "Peace can be a cover whereby evil men perpetrate diabolical wrongs." [8] The issue in a given dispute may not be: Who shall gain from it? It may instead be: Who shall dominate the world? In such circumstances, the best course of even reasonable men is difficult to define; their ability always to contrive solutions without force, impossible to assume. If solutions in terms of none of the three images is presently—if ever—possible, then reason can work only within the framework that is suggested by viewing the first and second images in the perspective of the third, a

[8] "Excerpts from Dulles Address on Peace" (Washington, April 11, 1955), in New York *Times*, April 12, 1955, p. 6.

perspective well and simply set forth in the *Federalist Papers,* especially in those written by Hamilton and Jay.

What would happen, Jay asks, if the thirteen states, instead of combining as one state, should form themselves into several confederations? He answers:

Instead of their being "joined in affection" and free from all apprehension of different "interests," envy and jealousy would soon extinguish confidence and affection, and the partial interests of each confederation, instead of the general interests of all America, would be the only objects of their policy and pursuits. Hence, like most *bordering* nations, they would always be either involved in disputes and war, or live in the constant apprehension of them.[9]

International anarchy, Jay is here saying, is the explanation for international war. But not international anarchy alone. Hamilton adds that to presume a lack of hostile motives among states is to forget that men are "ambitious, vindictive, and rapacious." A monarchical state may go to war because the vanity of its king leads him to seek glory in military victory; a republic may go to war because of the folly of its assembly or because of its commercial interests. That the king may be vain, the assembly foolish, or the commercial interests irreconcilable: none of these is inevitable. However, so many and so varied are the causes of war among states that "to look for a continuation of harmony between a number of independent, unconnected sovereigns in the same neighborhood, would be to disregard the uniform course of human events, and to set at defiance the accumulated experience of the ages." [10]

Jay and Hamilton found in the history of the Western state system confirmation for the conclusion that among separate sovereign states there is constant possibility of war. The third image, as constructed in Chapter VI, gives a theoretical basis for the same conclusion. It reveals why,

[9] *The Federalist,* pp. 23–24 (No. 5).
[10] *Ibid.,* pp. 27–28 (No. 6); cf. p. 18 (No. 4, Jay), and pp. 34–40 (No. 7, Hamilton).

in the absence of tremendous changes in the factors included in the first and second images, war will be perpetually associated with the existence of separate sovereign states. The obvious conclusion of a third-image analysis is that world government is the remedy for world war. The remedy, though it may be unassailable in logic, is unattainable in practice. The third image may provide a utopian approach to world politics. It may also provide a realistic approach, and one that avoids the tendency of some realists to attribute the necessary amorality, or even immorality, of world politics to the inherently bad character of man. If everyone's strategy depends upon everyone else's, then the Hitlers determine in part the action, or better, reaction, of those whose ends are worthy and whose means are fastidious. No matter how good their intentions, policy makers must bear in mind the implications of the third image, which can be stated in summary form as follows: Each state pursues its own interests, however defined, in ways it judges best. Force is a means of achieving the external ends of states because there exists no consistent, reliable process of reconciling the conflicts of interest that inevitably arise among similar units in a condition of anarchy. A foreign policy based on this image of international relations is neither moral nor immoral, but embodies merely a reasoned response to the world about us. The third image describes the framework of world politics, but without the first and second images there can be no knowledge of the forces that determine policy; the first and second images describe the forces in world politics, but without the third image it is impossible to assess their importance or predict their results.

BIBLIOGRAPHY

Adams, Henry. The Education of Henry Adams. New York: The Book League of America, 1928.

Adams, Walter, and Horace M. Gray. Monopoly in America. New York: The Macmillan Co., 1955.

Almond, Gabriel A. The American People and Foreign Policy. New York: Harcourt, Brace and Co., 1950.

—— "Anthropology, Political Behavior, and International Relations," World Politics, II (1950), 277–84.

Angell, Norman. The Great Illusion. London: William Heinemann, 1914.

Approaches to World Peace. Fourth Symposium of the Conference on Science, Philosophy, and Religion. New York: Distributed by Harper & Brothers, 1944.

Aristotle. Politics. Translated by B. Jowett. New York: The Modern Library, 1943.

Aron, Raymond, and August Heckscher. Diversity of Worlds. New York: Reynal & Co., 1957.

Augustine, Saint. The City of God. Translated by Marcus Dods. 2 vols. New York: Hafner Publishing Co., 1948.

Bailey, Stephen K., et al. Research Frontiers in Politics and Government. Washington: The Brookings Institution, 1955.

Beard, Charles A. A Foreign Policy for America. New York: Alfred A. Knopf, 1940.

—— Giddy Minds and Foreign Quarrels. New York: The Macmillan Co., 1939.

Benedict, Ruth. Patterns of Culture. New York: Penguin Books, 1946.

Bentham, Jeremy. Deontology. Edited by John Bowring. 2 vols. London: Longman, Rees, Orme, Browne, Green, and Longman, 1834.

—— The Works of Jeremy Bentham. Edited by John Bowring. 11 vols. Edinburgh: William Tait, 1843. Vols. II, III, and IV.

Berlin, Isaiah. "Political Ideas in the Twentieth Century," Foreign Affairs, XXVIII (1950), 351–85.

Bernard, L. L. War and Its Causes. New York: Henry Holt and Co., 1944.

Bernstein, Eduard. Evolutionary Socialism. Translated by Edith C. Harvey. New York: B. W. Huebsch, 1909.

Blum, Léon. Les Problèmes de la Paix. Paris: Librairie Stock, 1931.

Bodin, Jean. Six Books of the Commonwealth. Abridged and translated by M. J. Tooley. Oxford: Basil Blackwell, n.d.

Borberg, William. "On Active Service for Peace," *Bulletin of the World Federation for Mental Health,* II (1950), 6–9.

Bright, John. Speeches. Edited by James E. Thorold Rogers. London: Macmillan & Co., 1869.

Buehrig, Edward H. Woodrow Wilson and the Balance of Power. Bloomington: Indiana University Press, 1955.

Callis, Helmut. "The Sociology of International Relations," *American Sociological Review,* XII (1947), 323–34.

Cantril, Hadley, ed. Tensions That Cause Wars. Urbana: University of Illinois Press, 1950.

Carver, Thomas Nixon. Essays in Social Justice. Cambridge, Mass.: Harvard University Press, 1915.

Casserley, J. V. Langmead. Morals and Man in the Social Sciences. London: Longmans, Green and Co., 1951.

Chamberlain, Neville. In Search of Peace. New York: G. P. Putnam's Sons, 1939.

Churchill, Winston S. The World Crisis, 1911–1914. 4 vols. New York: Charles Scribner's Sons, 1923–29. Vol. I.

Clausewitz, Karl von. On War. Translated by O. J. Matthijs Jolles. Washington: Infantry Journal Press, 1950.

Cobban, Alfred. National Self-Determination. Rev. ed. Chicago: University of Chicago Press, 1948.

Cobden, Richard. Speeches on Peace, Financial Reform, Colonial Reform and Other Subjects Delivered during 1849. London: James Gilbert, n.d.

—— Speeches on Questions of Public Policy. 2 vols. Edited by John Bright and James E. Thorold Rogers. London: Macmillan & Co., 1870.

Cole, G. D. H. A History of Socialist Thought. 3 vols. London: Macmillan & Co., 1953–56. Vol. III.

Collingwood, R. G. The New Leviathan. Oxford: Clarendon Press, 1942.

Commager, Henry Steele, ed. Documents of American History. 3d ed. New York: F. S. Crofts & Co., 1946.

Cook, Thomas I., and Malcolm Moos. Power through Purpose: The Realism of Idealism as a Basis for Foreign Policy. Baltimore: The John Hopkins Press, 1954.

Cottrell, W. Fred. "Research to Establish the Conditions for Peace," *Journal of Social Issues,* XI (1955), 13–20.

Dedijer, Vladimir. "Albania, Soviet Pawn," *Foreign Affairs,* XXX (1951), 103–11.

Dennis, Wayne, *et al.* Current Trends in Social Psychology. Pittsburgh: University of Pittsburgh Press, 1948.

Deutsch, Karl. "The Growth of Nations: Some Recurrent Patterns of Political and Social Integration," *World Politics*, V (1953), 168–95.

Dewey, John. Reconstruction in Philosophy. New York: The New American Library, 1950.

Dickinson, G. Lowes. The European Anarchy. New York: The Macmillan Co., 1917.

Diderot, Denis. Oeuvres complètes de Diderot. Edited by J. Assézat. 20 vols. Paris: Garnier Frères, 1875–77. Vol. XIV.

Dollard, John, *et al.* Frustration and Aggression. New Haven: Yale University Press, 1939.

Dostoievsky, F. M. The Diary of a Writer. Translated by Boris Brasol. 2 vols. New York: Charles Scribner's Sons, 1949.

Dunn, Frederick S. Peaceful Change. New York: Council on Foreign Relations, 1937.

—— War and the Minds of Men. New York: Council on Foreign Relations, 1950.

Durbin, E. F. M., and John Bowlby. Personal Aggressiveness and War. New York: Columbia University Press, 1939.

Durkheim, Emile. The Rules of Sociological Method. Translation of 8th edition by Sarah Solovay and John Mueller. Glencoe, Ill.: The Free Press, 1938.

Dymond, Jonathan. An Inquiry into the Accordancy of War with the Principles of Christianity, and an Examination of the Philosophical Reasoning by Which It Is Defended. 3d ed. Philadelphia, 1834.

Engels, Friedrich. Herr Eugen Dühring's Revolution in Science (Anti-Dühring). Translated by Emile Burns. New York: International Publishers, 1939.

—— The Origin of the Family, Private Property and the State. New York: International Publishers, 1942.

—— *See also* Marx, Karl.

Esslinger, William. Politics and Science. New York: The Philosophical Library, 1955.

Flynn, John T. The Roosevelt Myth. New York: The Devin-Adair Co., 1948.

For Socialism and Peace. London: Transport House, 1934.

Foundations for World Order. Denver: University of Denver Press, 1949.

Frank, Lawrence. Society as the Patient. New Brunswick: Rutgers University Press, 1949.

Freud, Sigmund. Civilization, War and Death. Edited by John Rickman. London: The Hogarth Press and the Institute of Psychoanalysis, 1953.

Friedrich, Carl J. Inevitable Peace. Cambridge, Mass.: Harvard University Press, 1948.

Galilei, Galileo. Dialogues concerning Two New Sciences. Translated by Henry Crew and Alfonso de Salvio. New York: The Macmillan Co., 1914.

Godwin, William. Enquiry concerning Political Justice. 3d ed., 2 vols. London, 1798.

Goldhamer, Herbert. "The Psychological Analysis of War," *Sociological Review* (London), XXVI (1934), 249–67.

Green, Thomas Hill. Lectures on the Principles of Political Obligation. London: Longmans, Green and Co., n.d.

Gregg, Richard B. The Power of Non-Violence. Philadelphia: J. B. Lippincott Co., 1934.

Grey, Edward. Twenty-five Years. 2 vols. New York: Frederick A. Stokes Co., 1925.

Haas, Ernest B. "The Balance of Power: Prescription, Concept, or Propaganda?" *World Politics*, V (1953), 442–77.

Hamilton, Alexander. The Works of Alexander Hamilton. Edited by Henry Cabot Lodge. 12 vols. New York: G. P. Putnam's Sons, 1904. Vol. V.

Hamilton, Alexander, John Jay, and James Madison. The Federalist. New York: The Modern Library, 1941.

Hayes, C. J. H. Essays on Nationalism. New York: The Macmillan Co., 1928.

—— The Historical Evolution of Modern Nationalism. New York: The Macmillan Co., 1950.

Hegel, G. W. F. Philosophy of Right. Translated by T. M. Knox. Oxford: Clarendon Press, 1942.

Helvétius, Claude Adrien. A Treatise on Man: His Intellectual Faculties and His Education. Translated by W. Hooper. 2 vols. London, 1810. Vol. II.

Henderson, Arthur. The Aims of Labour. London: Headley Bros., 1918.

Herodotus. The History of Herodotus. Translated by George Rawlinson. 2 vols. Everyman's Library Edition. London: J. M. Dent & Sons, Ltd., 1949.

Herz, John. Political Realism and Political Idealism. Chicago: University of Chicago Press, 1951.

Herzfeld, Hans. "Bismarck und die Skobelewepisode," *Historische Zeitschrift*, CXLII (1930), 279–302.

Hirst, Margaret E. The Quakers in Peace and War. London: The Swarthmore Press, 1923.

Hobson, John. The Crisis of Liberalism. London: P. S. King & Son, 1909.

—— Democracy after the War. London: George Allen & Unwin, 1917.

—— Imperialism. 3d ed. London: George Allen & Unwin, 1938.

—— The New Protectionism. London: T. Fisher Unwin, 1916.

—— Notes on Law and Order. London: The Hogarth Press, 1926.

—— Problems of a New World. London: George Allen & Unwin, 1921.

—— The Recording Angel. London: George Allen & Unwin, 1921.

—— Richard Cobden, the International Man. London: T. Fisher Unwin, 1919.

—— Towards International Government. London: George Allen & Unwin, 1915.

—— The War in South Africa. New York: The Macmillan Co., 1900.

Homo, Leon. Roman Political Institutions. Translated by M. R. Dobie. London: Kegan Paul, Trench, Trubner & Co., 1929.

Hume, David. Essays Moral, Political, and Literary. Edited by T. H. Green and T. H. Grose. 2 vols. London: Longmans, Green and Co., 1875. Vol. I.

Humphrey, A. W. International Socialism and the War. London: F. S. King & Co., 1915.

Hutchison, T. W. A Review of Economic Doctrines, 1870–1929. Oxford: Clarendon Press, 1953.

Hutt, W. H. "Pressure Groups and *Laissez-Faire,*" *South African Journal of Economics,* VI (1938), 1–23.

Inge, William R. Lay Thoughts of a Dean. New York: Garden City Publishing Co., 1926.

James, William. Memories and Studies. New York: Longmans, Green and Co., 1912.

Joll, James. The Second International. London: Weidenfeld and Nicolson, 1955.

Kant, Immanuel. Critique of Practical Reason and Other Works on the Theory of Ethics. Translated by T. K. Abbott. London: Longmans, Green and Co., 1909.

—— Eternal Peace and Other International Essays. Translated by W. Hastie. Boston: The World Peace Foundation, 1914.

—— The Philosophy of Law. Translated by W. Hastie. Edinburgh: T. & T. Clark, 1887.

Kaplan, Morton A. System and Process in International Politics. New York: John Wiley & Sons, 1957.

Kautsky, Karl. "Der Imperialismus," *Die Neue Zeit,* 32d Year, II (1914), 908–22.

—— "Die Internationalität und der Krieg," *Die Neue Zeit,* 33d Year, I (1914), 225–50.

Kautsky, Karl (*Continued*)
—— "Die Sozialdemocratie im Kriege," *Die Neue Zeit,* 33d Year, I (1914), 1–8.

Kegley, Charles W., and Robert W. Bretall, eds. Reinhold Niebuhr, His Religious, Social, and Political Thought. New York: The Macmillan Co., 1956.

Kelsen, Hans. General Theory of Law and State. Translated by Anders Wedberg. Cambridge, Mass.: Harvard University Press, 1946.

Kennan, George F. Realities of American Foreign Policy. Princeton: Princeton University Press, 1954.

Keynes, John Maynard. "National Self-Sufficiency," *Yale Review,* XXII (1933), 755–69.

Kirk, Grayson. "In Search of the National Interest," *World Politics,* V (1952), 110–15.

Kisker, George, ed. World Tension. New York: Prentice-Hall, 1951.

Klineberg, Otto. Tensions Affecting International Understanding. New York: Social Science Research Council, 1950.

Kluckhohn, Clyde. Mirror for Man. New York: McGraw-Hill Book Co., 1949.

Kohn, Hans. The Idea of Nationalism. New York: The Macmillan Co., 1944.

La Bruyère, Jean de. Oeuvres complètes. Edited by Julien Benda. (Bibliothèque de la Pléiade, Vol. 23.) Paris: Librairie Gallimard, 1951.

La Chesnais, P. G. Le Groupe Socialiste du Reichstag et la Déclaration de Guerre. Paris: Librairie Armand Colin, 1915.

Lair, Maurice. Jaurès et l'Allemagne. Paris: Librairie Académique Perrin, 1935.

Lasswell, Harold. Psychopathology and Politics. Chicago: University of Chicago Press, 1930.

—— World Politics and Personal Insecurity. New York: McGraw-Hill Book Co., 1935.

Leighton, Alexander H. "Dynamic Forces in International Relations," *Mental Hygiene,* XXXIII (1949), 17–24.

—— Human Relations in a Changing World. New York: E. P. Dutton & Co., 1949.

Leiserson, Avery. "Problems of Methodology in Political Research," *Political Science Quarterly,* LXVII (1953), 558–84.

Lenin, Vladimir Ilyich. The Collapse of the Second International. Translated by A. Sirnis. Glasgow: The Socialist Labour Press, n.d.

—— Imperialism. New York: International Publishers, 1939.

—— "Left-Wing" Communism: An Infantile Disorder. New York: International Publishers, 1934.

—— What Is to Be Done? New York: International Publishers, 1929.

Lerner, Daniel, and Harold Lasswell, eds. The Policy Sciences. Stanford: Stanford University Press, 1951.

Levinson, Salmon. Outlawry of War. Chicago: American Committee for the Outlawry of War, 1921.

Lewin, Kurt. Resolving Social Conflicts. New York: Harper & Brothers, 1948.

Liebknecht, Karl, Rosa Luxemburg, and Franz Mehring. The Crisis in the Social-Democracy. New York: The Co-operative Press, n.d.

Link, Arthur S. Woodrow Wilson and the Progressive Era, 1910–1917. New York: Harper & Brothers, 1954.

Linton, Ralph, ed. The Science of Man in the World Crisis. New York: Columbia University Press, 1945.

Liu Shao-chi. Internationalism and Nationalism. Peking: Foreign Language Press, n.d.

MacCurdy, J. T. The Psychology of War. Boston: John W. Luce and Co., n.d.

MacDonald, J. Ramsay. Labour and the Empire. London: George Allen, 1907.

McDonald, John. Strategy in Poker, Business and War. New York: W. W. Norton & Co., 1950.

Machiavelli, Niccolò. The Prince and The Discourses. Translated by Luigi Ricci and Christian E. Detmold. New York: The Modern Library, n.d.

McKinsey, J. C. C. Introduction to the Theory of Games. New York: McGraw-Hill Book Co., 1952.

Macridis, Roy. "Stalinism and the Meaning of Titoism," *World Politics,* IV (1952), 219–38.

Madariaga, Salvador de. Disarmament. New York: Coward-McCann, 1929.

Malthus, Thomas. An Essay on the Principle of Population. Parallel Chapters from the First and Second Editions. New York: Macmillan & Co., 1895.

Mandeville, Bernard. The Fable of the Bees. London, 1806.

Mao Tse-tung. Strategic Problems of China's Revolutionary War. Bombay: People's Publishing House, 1951.

Martin, Kingsley. The Rise of French Liberal Thought. Boston: Little, Brown and Co., 1929.

Martineau, Harriet. Illustrations of Political Economy. 9 vols. London: Charles Fox, 1834. Vol. III.

Marx, Karl. Capital. Translated by Samuel Moore and Edward Aveling. 3 vols. Chicago: Charles H. Kerr & Co., 1909–10. Vol. I.

Marx, Karl, and Friedrich Engels. Communist Manifesto. Translated by Samuel Moore. Chicago: Charles H. Kerr & Co., 1946.

—— The German Ideology. Translated by R. Pascal. New York: International Publishers, 1939.

—— Selected Correspondence, 1846–1895. Translated by Dona Torr. New York: International Publishers, 1942.

Mattingly, Garrett. Renaissance Diplomacy. Boston: Houghton Mifflin Co., 1955.

May, Mark. A Social Psychology of War and Peace. New Haven: Yale University Press, 1943.

Mazzini, Giuseppe. Selected Writings. Edited by N. Gangulee. London: Lindsay Drummond, 1945.

Mead, Margaret. And Keep Your Powder Dry. New York: Wm. Morrow & Co., 1942.

—— Coming of Age in Samoa. New York: The New American Library, 1949.

—— "Warfare Is Only an Invention—Not a Biological Necessity," *Asia*, XL (1940), 402–5.

Mill, James. Essays on Government, Jurisprudence, Liberty of the Press, Prisons and Prison Discipline, Colonies, Law of Nations, Education. Reprinted, by Permission, from the Supplement to the Encyclopaedia Britannica. London, n.d.

Mill, John Stuart. Dissertations and Discussions. 5 vols. New York: Henry Holt and Co., 1874–82. Vols. III and V.

—— The Letters of John Stuart Mill. Edited by Hugh S. R. Elliot. 2 vols. London: Longmans, Green and Co., 1910.

—— On Liberty, Representative Government, The Subjection of Women. Oxford: The World's Classics, No. 170. London: Oxford University Press, 1946.

—— Principles of Political Economy. Edited by J. W. Ashley, from 7th edition of 1871. London: Longmans, Green and Co., 1909.

—— Socialism. Edited by W. D. P. Bliss. New York: The Humboldt Publishing Co., 1891.

Milne, A. A. Peace with Honor. New York: E. P. Dutton & Co., 1934.

Milton, John. The Prose Works of John Milton. 5 vols. London: Henry G. Bohn, 1848–81. Vol. III.

Montesquieu, Charles Louis de Secondat, Baron de la Brède et de. The Spirit of the Laws. Translated by Thomas Nugent. New York: Hafner Publishing Co., 1949.

Morellet, André. Lettres de l'abbé Morellet a Lord Shelburne, 1772–1803. Paris: Librairie Plon, 1898.

Morgenthau, Hans J. "Another 'Great Debate': The National Interest of the United States," *American Political Science Review,* XLVI (1952), 961–88.

—— In Defense of the National Interest. New York: Alfred A. Knopf, 1951.

—— Politics among Nations. 2d ed. New York: Alfred A. Knopf, 1954.

—— Scientific Man vs. Power Politics. Chicago: University of Chicago Press, 1946.

Morgenthau, Hans J., and Kenneth W. Thompson. Principles and Problems of International Politics, Selected Readings. New York: Alfred A. Knopf, 1952.

Morley, John. The Life of Richard Cobden. Boston: Roberts Brothers, 1881.

—— The Life of William Ewart Gladstone. 3 vols. New York: The Macmillan Co., 1903.

Morrison, Charles Clayton. The Outlawry of War. Chicago: Willett, Clark & Colby, 1927.

Neumann, John von, and Oskar Morgenstern. Theory of Games and Economic Behavior. Princeton: Princeton University Press, 1944.

Newcomb, Theodore M., and Eugene L. Hartley, eds. Readings in Social Psychology. New York: Henry Holt & Co., 1947.

Nichols, Beverly. Cry Havoc! New York: Doubleday, Doran & Co., 1933.

Niebuhr, Reinhold. Beyond Tragedy. New York: Charles Scribner's Sons, 1938.

—— The Children of Light and the Children of Darkness. New York: Charles Scribner's Sons, 1945.

—— Christianity and Power Politics. New York: Charles Scribner's Sons, 1940.

—— Christian Realism and Political Problems. New York: Charles Scribner's Sons, 1953.

—— Discerning the Signs of the Times. New York: Charles Scribner's Sons, 1946.

—— Does Civilization Need Religion? New York: The Macmillan Co., 1928.

—— Faith and History. New York: Charles Scribner's Sons, 1949.

—— An Interpretation of Christian Ethics. New York: Harper & Brothers, 1935.

—— The Irony of American History. New York: Charles Scribner's Sons, 1952.

—— "Is Social Conflict Inevitable?" *Scribner's Magazine,* XCVIII (1935), 166–69.

Niebuhr, Reinhold (*Continued*)
—— Leaves from the Notebook of a Tamed Cynic. Hamden, Conn.: The Shoe String Press, 1956. Original copyright 1929.
—— Moral Man and Immoral Society. New York: Charles Scribner's Sons, 1941.
—— The Nature and Destiny of Man. 2 vols. New York: Charles Scribner's Sons, 1951.
—— Reflections on the End of an Era. New York: Charles Scribner's Sons, 1934.
—— The Self and the Dramas of History. New York: Charles Scribner's Sons, 1955.
Niebuhr, Reinhold, and Sherwood Eddy. Doom and Dawn. New York: Eddy and Page, 1936.
Oliver, F. S. The Endless Adventure. 3 vols. London: Macmillan & Co., 1930–35. Vol. III.
Paine, Thomas. The Complete Writings of Thomas Paine. Edited by Philip Foner. 2 vols. New York: The Citadel Press, 1945.
Partridge, Eric. Here, There, and Everywhere. 2d ed. London: Hamish Hamilton, 1950.
Pear, T. H., ed. Psychological Factors of Peace and War. New York: The Philosophical Library, 1950.
Plato. The Dialogues of Plato. Translated by B. Jowett. 3d ed., 5 vols. London: Oxford University Press, 1892. Vol. V.
Polybius. The Histories. Translated by W. R. Paton. 6 vols. London: William Heinemann, 1922–27. Vol. I.
Popper, Karl. The Open Society and Its Enemies. Princeton: Princeton University Press, 1950.
Readings in the Theory of International Trade. Selected by a Committee of the American Economic Association. Philadelphia: The Blakiston Co., 1949.
Robbins, Lionel. The Economic Basis of Class Conflict and Other Essays in Political Economy. London: Macmillan & Co., 1939.
—— Economic Planning and International Order. London: Macmillan & Co., 1937.
Röpke, Wilhelm. Civitas Humana. Translated by Cyril Spencer Fox. London: William Hodge and Co., 1948.
—— The Social Crisis of Our Time. Translated by Annette and Peter Schiffer Jacobson. Chicago: University of Chicago Press, 1950.
Rousseau, Jean Jacques. A Lasting Peace through the Federation of Europe and The State of War. Translated by C. E. Vaughan. London: Constable and Co., 1917.
—— Oeuvres complètes de J. J. Rousseau. 13 vols. Paris: Librairie Hachette, 1871–77. Vols. IV and VIII.

—— The Political Writings of Jean Jacques Rousseau. Edited by C. E. Vaughan. 2 vols. Cambridge: University Press, 1915.

—— The Social Contract and Discourses. Translated by G. D. H. Cole. Everyman's Library Edition. New York: E. P. Dutton and Co., 1950.

Russell, Bertrand. Political Ideals. New York: The Century Co., 1917.

Schorske, Carl E. German Social Democracy, 1905–1917. Cambridge, Mass.: Harvard University Press, 1955.

Schuman, Frederick L. International Politics. 5th ed. New York: McGraw-Hill Book Co., 1953.

Sherwood, Robert E. Roosevelt and Hopkins. New York: Harper & Brothers, 1948.

Shotwell, James. War as an Instrument of National Policy. New York: Harcourt, Brace and Co., 1921.

Simonds, Frank H., and Brooks Emeny. The Great Powers in World Politics. New York: American Book Co., 1939.

Smith, Adam. Adam Smith's Moral and Political Philosophy. Edited by Herbert W. Schneider. New York: Hafner Publishing Co., 1948.

Snowden, Philip. If Labour Rules. London: The Labour Publishing Co., 1923.

Spencer, Herbert. Social Statics, abridged and revised; together with The Man versus the State. New York: D. Appleton and Co., 1897.

Spinoza, Benedict de. The Chief Works of Benedict de Spinoza. Translated by R. H. M. Elwes. 2 vols. New York: Dover Publications, 1951.

Sprout, Harold, and Margaret Sprout. Toward a New Order of Sea Power. Princeton: Princeton University Press, 1940.

Stephen, Leslie. The English Utilitarians. 3 vols. London: Duckworth and Co., 1900. Vol. III.

Stock Market Study. Hearings before the Committee on Banking and Currency, United States Senate, Eighty-Fourth Congress, First Session, on Factors Affecting the Buying and Selling of Equity Securities. March, 1955. Washington: United States Government Printing Office, 1955.

Stourzh, Gerald. Benjamin Franklin and American Foreign Policy. Chicago: University of Chicago Press, 1954.

Strachey, John. A Faith to Fight For. London: Victor Gollancz, 1941.

Straight, Michael. Make This the Last War. New York: Harcourt, Brace and Co., 1943.

Strausz-Hupé, Robert. The Balance of Tomorrow. New York: G. P. Putnam's Sons, 1945.

Sumner, William Graham. War and Other Essays. Edited by Albert G. Keller. New Haven: Yale University Press, 1911.

Swanton, John. Are Wars Inevitable? Washington: Smithsonian Institute War Background Studies, No. 12, 1943.

Tacitus. The Works of Tacitus. Oxford translation, revised. 2 vols. New York: Harper & Brothers, 1858. Vol. II.

Taft, Robert A. A Foreign Policy for Americans. New York: Doubleday & Co., 1951.

Taft, William Howard. The United States and Peace. New York: Charles Scribner's Sons, 1914.

Tannenbaum, Frank. "The American Tradition in Foreign Relations," *Foreign Affairs*, XXX (1951), 31–50.

―― "The Balance of Power in Society," *Political Science Quarterly*, LXI (1946), 481–504.

―― "The Balance of Power versus the Co-ordinate State," *Political Science Quarterly*, LXVII (1952), 173–97.

Taylor, A. J. P. Rumours of War. London: Hamish Hamilton, 1952.

Thompson, Kenneth W. "Beyond National Interest: A Critical Evaluation of Reinhold Niebuhr's Theory of International Politics," *Review of Politics*, XVIII (1955), 167–88.

Thompson, W. S. Danger Spots in World Population. New York: Alfred A. Knopf, 1930.

Thucydides. History of the Peloponnesian War. Translated by B. Jowett. 2d ed. London: Oxford University Press, 1900.

Tolman, Edward. Drives toward War. New York: D. Appleton-Century Co., 1942.

Treitschke, Heinrich von. Politics. Translated by Blanche Dugdale and Torben de Bille. 2 vols. London: Constable and Co., 1916.

Trevelyan, Charles. The Union of Democratic Control: Its History and Its Policy. London: Simson & Co., 1919.

Tumulty, Joseph. Woodrow Wilson as I Knew Him. Printed Exclusively for the *Literary Digest*, 1921.

Vagts, Alfred. Defense and Diplomacy. New York: King's Crown Press, 1956.

―― "The United States and the Balance of Power," *Journal of Politics*, III (1941), 401–49.

Vattel, E. de. The Law of Nations. 3 vols. The 3d volume is a translation of the 1758 edition by Charles G. Fenwick. Washington: The Carnegie Institution, 1916. Vol. III.

"Vigilantes," Inquest on Peace. London: Victor Gollancz, 1935.

Von Laue, Theodore H. Leopold Ranke, the Formative Years. Princeton: Princeton University Press, 1950.

Walling, William E. The Socialists and the War. New York: Henry Holt and Co., 1915.

Webb, Leicester. "The Future of International Trade," *World Politics*, V (1953), 423–41.

Weber, Max. From Max Weber: Essays in Sociology. Edited and translated by H. H. Gerth and C. Wright Mills. London: Kegan Paul, Trench, Trubner & Co., 1947.

Williams, J. D. The Compleat Strategyst. New York: McGraw-Hill Book Co., 1954.

Wilson, Woodrow. Woodrow Wilson, Selections for Today. Edited by Arthur Bernon Tourtellot. New York: Duell, Sloan and Pearce, 1945.

Wolfers, Arnold, and Laurence W. Martin, eds. The Anglo-American Tradition in Foreign Affairs. New Haven: Yale University Press, 1956.

Woolf, Leonard, ed. The Intelligent Man's Way to Prevent War. London: Victor Gollancz, 1933.

Wright, Quincy. "Realism and Idealism in International Politics," *World Politics*, V (1952), 116–28.

INDEX